ON PURPOSE

COLLECTED PAPERS

of

HAROLD H. MOSAK, Ph.D.

Y10 5

ALFRED ADLER INSTITUTE
OF CHICAGO

Library of Congress Catalog Card Number: 76-42942
ISBN No. 0-918560-19-5

Printed in the
United States of America

TABLE OF CONTENTS

PREFACE

For those of us who have known Harold Mosak as a clinician and teacher, for those of us who hunger for a fuller understanding of Adlerian theory and technique, the collection and publication of ˚these papers is embraced with a rush of enthusiasm and a shout of "finally!" In previous years we had to ransack the libraries, plead for reprints, or take laborious notes from borrowed copies. At last we will have a single source—to relish and devour.

Even a cursory examination of the titles here will give an indication of the range and depth of Mosak's work: from psychological research to interpretation and testing, from theoretical explication to practical application—the full gamut of concerns that reside in the realm of clinical psychology. What these titles do not indicate is the *importance* of these papers, both for the field of psychology as a whole, and for Adlerian psychology in particular. Moreover, since this volume contains only a portion of Mosak's work, it seems essential to comment at least briefly on some of the significant omissions.

To begin with the latter, it is interesting to note that Mosak's work, from the very beginning, was that of an *innovator*. Starting with his doctoral dissertation, *Evaluation in Psychotherapy*, completed in 1950 at the University of Chicago, and the later summary of this work, published as a chapter in Wolff and Precker's (1952) *Success in Psychotherapy*, Mosak was not only helping to initiate a field of research that he would continue in later studies, but was adding impetus to a discipline that would soon become a major focal point for clinical research. Prior to this, the effectiveness of psychotherapy was largely ignored, taken for granted, or set aside as an inscrutable, nonmeasurable dimension. Mosak was one of the few clinicians who not only took the problem seriously, but also—in typical Adlerian fashion—considered it a challenge to be met in open combat. As a consequence, his early struggles were both significant in content—helping to delineate some clinical tools that have been used frequently in subsequent research—and helped to open a crack that has today been widened to a mine-shaft.

Mosak's role as an innovator is apparent in at least four additional areas, all of which are fortunately represented in this collection. Furthermore, his work in two of these areas can be considered *classic*—in the sense that it is commonly included as "required reading" for advanced university courses on personality theory and psychotherapy, and because it has become the foundation for numerous research studies.

The first of these classic works—known with special fondness to most Adlerians—is his paper on "Early Recollections As A Projective Technique" (1958): a paper that summarizes the multiple strands of contemporary research, distinguishes between early recollections and "reports," clarifies the dimensions of importance to Adlerians, indicates some of the clues used by clinicians in the interpretation of recollections, gives vivid examples of their use in clinical context, and concludes with a comparison of Adlerian and Freudian approaches to the interpretation of recollections, revealing the multi-dimensional quality of ER's their openness to a variety of orientations. It is difficult to imagine a time when this paper will no longer be read with the excitement of discovery; for it illuminated in bright strokes a territory that for most of us, without this paper, would still be shrouded in mystery and inaccessibility. It is also gratifying to know that Mosak has continued his work in this area, not only by writing several subsequent papers—on the use of ER's for clinical prediction (1965) and reviewing some of the recent research in this area (1969)—but also through service as a consultant for numerous dissertations and research studies.

Mosak's second classic work has been in the field of time-limited psychotherapy. In 1960, with the assistance of R. Dreikurs and J. Shlien, Mosak undertook an in-depth study of the effectiveness of time-limited psychotherapy. This project was doing what many clinicians had talked about, but few had attempted: it was breaking ground in two new areas—in the comparison of psychotherapy from different schools of thought (Adlerian and client-centered), and the examination of consequences of deliberately specifying a "time limit" at the start of therapy. The results, needless to say, were not only impressive at the time—confirming the efficacy of such limits—but have subsequently been validated by other studies designed along similar lines. Here again was a pace-setting innovative study, an early opening for a whole new approach to clinical practice.

In two other areas, Mosak has also been on the forefront of new developments, but in these cases the field of psychotherapy still lags behind: perhaps at some time in the future, when other clinicians "catch up" with him, his work in these areas will be given the recognition it deserves. In the first case, his papers on multiple-psychotherapy, written with R. Dreikurs and B. Shulman (1952), described the many advantages of this procedure, for both the therapist and the client. Mosak and his colleagues have used this technique with great success for many years; but in spite of its obvious benefits—one of which is frequently a much desired acceleration of the therapeutic process—it has not become an accepted practice in the field.

In the second case, recognition of Mosak's innovative approaches to the training of psychotherapists has also been delayed. Here, as described in his article on "A Full-Time Internship In Private Practice" (1970), Mosak has not only continued Adler's tradition of public demonstrations—both for Family Education Centers and for students of psychotherapy—but in 1969 he accepted into his private practice the first clinical psychology intern, (dramatically) moving away from the traditional procedure of training interns almost exclusively in in-patient institutional facilities. His intern was still exposed to in-patient work—for Mosak was not only a member of the staff of St. Joseph's Hospital, but was also serving as a consultant at several Veterans Administration Hospitals—but the majority of the intern's experience was with an out-patient population, the kind of population most clinical psychologists ultimately treat. The opportunities for intensive supervision were multiplied tenfold—especially since Mosak was a consistent practitioner of the multiple-therapy model. Instead of having an intern ramble at loose ends among a group of in-patients, occasionally meeting with his supervisors for scheduled interviews, Mosak's intern was a virtual live-in, elbow-to-elbow apprentice; he observed his supervisors' individual psychotherapy sessions, participated in multiple psychotherapy, worked intensively with his own caseload of clients, participated in regular seminars, discussed problems during lunch and coffee breaks, exchanged progress notes while riding on trains and buses—in short, it was a kind of therapeutic marriage, where the flow of information and learning was practically osmotic. While this approach, like that of multiple-psychotherapy, has not been widely accepted, there are many reasons to hope that it soon will be—not only for the sake of individuals in search of quality clinical training, but for the benefit of the public that will ultimately gain or suffer from the relative expertise of the available clinicians.

The remainder of Mosak's work, while perhaps not as interesting to clinicians of differing orientations, contains several major contributions to the field of Individual Psychology, and therefore should be of special interest to all Adlerians. Most of these papers are succinct, beautifully illustrated elaborations of special topics that are mentioned only briefly or non-systematically in the writings of Adler. In this category, one will find Mosak's papers on lifestyle, the getting personality, the interrelationship of the neuroses, the life tasks, the various purposes of symptoms, and thoughts on the topics of aggression and normality. In addition, there are a whole series of papers on psychological interpretation from the Adlerian perspective—both in the context of psychological testing, and in the process of psychotherapy. Finally, he has written a series of very practical papers on therapeutic technique—for use in both individual psychotherapy, and in work with families and schools.

Taken as a unit, these papers accomplish several important aims. First, they explicate and broaden the mainstream of Adlerian *theory*. Mosak's recent chapter in *Current Psychotherapies* (1973) is a significant omission in this regard: for while it covers some familiar territory that is available in other sources, it introduces some new material and emphases, as well as the excellent clinical illustrations that are so characteristic of Mosak's work in general. What his individual papers contribute is a sharper focus and more detail—a kind of loving thoroughness which, parenthetically, is also present, under different guise, in yet another significant omission from this collection: the massive *Bibliography for Adlerian Psychology*, completed in 1975, after years of dedicated, painstaking labor, by Harold and his courageous wife, Birdie. It is difficult to overstate the importance of this contribution, for even if this present volume were never completed, this one work would be of inestimable benefit—not only for allowing us to locate all of the papers in this collection, but placing us in contact with the whole range of Adlerian thinking, both national and international. It is work like this that transforms an interest into a discipline, graduating an adolescent to full adulthood. It is work like this that qualifies Harold and Birdie among the true "founding parents" of Adlerian psychology.

Secondly, these papers enlarge the domain of Adlerian *practice*—in the areas of multiple-therapy, individual therapy, counseling with parents and children, group work with teachers and school systems. The one lament, from those of us who have had the privilege of working closely with Mosak in a clinical context—if anything this outrageous is even remotely permissible in light of such extensive and significant contributions—is that *more* of his clinical insights are not included in this collection: for in this regard, Mosak has *lived* his ideas, in his day to day practice, and only a small portion of his vast repertoire of practical techniques has been committed to paper. Those of us who have rubbed shoulders with him have grown enormously—by osmosis and imitation—and can only regret that others are not yet able to garner the benefits of his knowledge from the leaves of a library.

Finally, these papers constantly reveal the *connectedness* of Adlerian thinking to other schools of thought—sometimes by contrast, but more frequently by corroboration: noting the consensus of all socially-interested, future-oriented, purposive, wholistic models of man—despite their superficial differences, disparate terminologies, or varying emphases. In the long run, these papers solidify Adlerian thinking, in the broad sense, in the heartland of humanistic thinking about the nature of man and the ways to wholeness.

R. S. Gushurst
Mary Washington College
January, 1976

Performance on the Harrower-Erickson Multiple Choice Test of Patients with Spinal Cord Injuries*

One of the most amazing medical feats after the recent war was achieved by medical officers of the armed forces and the Veterans Administration in keeping alive servicemen who had incurred spinal cord injuries which resulted in a paralysis of the lower portion of the body. Approximately three hundred of these paraplegic patients were being treated at Hines VA Hospital when this study was initiated in 1947. The very nature of the injury made psychological problems inevitable. Voluntary control of the portion of the body below the level of the transection of the spinal cord was impossible, the sexual functions were lost, and incontinence of the bowel and bladder created additional problems. Frustration, anxiety, and depression ruled supreme. Beyond the overt behavorial manifestations, little knowledge was possessed of the patient's attitudes toward his condition, toward himself, and toward other people. It was with these conditions in mind that the writer performed the following experiment to investigate in what ways their outlook upon life differed from that of nonparaplegic veterans.

EXPERIMENTAL PROCEDURES

The Harrower-Erickson Multiple Choice Test of three hundred choices was administered to 25 paraplegic and 25 nonparaplegic veterans. The latter group, composed of volunteers from the American Veterans Committee, hereafter referred to as the AVC group, [1] was of nearly the same average age and

[1]The writer wishes to express his gratitude to those paraplegic patients who served as subjects, as well as to those members of Thomas Jefferson Chapter #243, American Veterans Committee, who so kindly volunteered to serve as the control group.

*Reprinted by permission from the JOURNAL OF CONSULTING PSYCHOLOGY, 1951, 15(4), 346-349. Copyright 1951 by the AMERICAN PSYCHOLOGICAL ASSN., INC.

socioeconomic status as the patient group. The hospital group, also a volunteer group, was small because the physical condition of many precluded their being tested. No quadriplegic patients (patients with injuries to the cervical region of the spinal cord preventing the use of both arms and legs) were included in the experimental group. The ten Rorschach blots were projected upon a screen and exposed for three minutes, during which time the subjects indicated three responses for each blot. Secondary responses were not permitted, so that the total number of responses was kept constant at 30 for each subject. Each response was scored numerically in the manner suggested by Harrower-Erickson (3), responses scored 1 through 5 constituting so-called "good" responses and including movement, good form, animal, good form-color, small detail, and space percepts. Responses scored 6 through 10 included poor form, vague percepts, pure color, card description, and card rejections. In addition to the numerical scoring, each response was scored in terms of determinants and content according to the system advanced by Beck (1). With the exception of Dd responses it was impossible to judge the "location" of these percepts, for the subject did not indicate whether he saw the suggested percept as a whole or as a detail. This was especially true of such responses as "cloud," "smoke," and "animal skin." It remained possible, therefore, to score for M, CF, FC, Y, YF, FY, FV, $F+$, $F-$, Dd, Sex, Blood, Dirt, A, H, An, P, S, Card Description, and Card Rejection.

TABLE 1
**MEAN NUMBER OF RESPONSES FOR RORSCHACH
LOCATION AND DETERMINANT CATEGORIES**

Response	$M_{paraplegic}$	M_{AVC}	t
Dd	1.12	1.52	1.21
M	2.24	3.84	3.02
C	0.68	0.12	2.55
CF	2.88	1.44	3.43
FC	1.44	1.44	——
ΣC	4.62	2.34	3.74
Y	1.16	0.40	2.53
YF	0.84	0.56	1.08
FY	2.92	2.40	1.33
FV	0.12	0.16	0.29
$F+$	11.92	15.12	2.81
$F-$	3.16	1.64	2.41

RESULTS

When scored on a numerical basis, it immediately becomes apparent that the paraplegic group designated a larger number of "bad" responses. The mean for this group was 11.6 "bad" responses as against 6.6 for the AVC group, a difference significant at the 1 per cent level. Further scrutiny of the responses in terms of location, determinants, and content unearthed some of the factors responsible for this difference. Table 1 gives the t's for location and determinant scorings of the test. We note that the differences for M, CF, and $F+$ are significant at the 1 per cent level; C, Y, and F— at the 2 per cent level; and ΣC at the .1 per cent level of significance. The remaining differences were not statistically significant.

TABLE 2
MEAN NUMBER OF RESPONSES FOR MISCELLANEOUS RORSCHACH SCORING CATEGORIES

Response	$M_{paraplegic}$	M_{AVC}	t
A	10.24	11.28	0.78
H	3.64	6.48	3.19
An	4.28	2.28	2.04
Bl	0.56	0.12	2.20
Dirt	0.76	0.08	3.09
Fi	0.96	0.32	2.29
Sex	0.12	0.32	1.43
P	10.80	13.00	1.96
S	0.16	0.52	1.50
Card Des.	0.96	0.12	2.15
Card Rej.	1.52	2.12	0.94

Table 2 presents the t's for content and miscellaneous scorings. Of these, six were statistically significant—Bl, Fi, An, and Card Description at the 5 per cent level, and Dirt and H at the 1 per cent level of significance.

3

DISCUSSION

What do these differences tell us qualitatively about the personality of the paraplegic veterans? Let us first examine the means for the movement responses and attempt to formulate a possible explanation for this difference. According to Table 1 the mean number of M responses for the patients was 2.24, while that for the AVC group was 3.84. The difference between means was at the 1 per cent level of significance. The movement responses, according to Beck (1) "are representatives of very deep wishes, innermost psychic activity." These responses, he continues, are "kinaesthetically determined." If we accept this hypothesis, then it is altogether reasonable to assume that a reduction in kinaesthetic stimulation, as occurs in paraplegia, would result in the production of fewer movement responses. To test the hypothesis that paraplegics tend to suppress movement in their projections, each subject in both groups was asked to draw a picture of a man and of a woman. While elaborate inferences may be made from the size, placement, facial expression, line pressure, continuity; and other elements of these drawings (2, 4, 5), the writer restricted himself to an examination of the expression of movement of the lower extremities in the figures drawn. Of the 21 paraplegics whose injuries did not prevent them from drawing, only 6 executed drawings in which the legs of *both* figures were functional, i.e., they stood with legs apart or walked. Of the AVC sample 12 of the 25 drew two figures in which "movement" was evident. The remainder of the drawings exhibited other differentiating characteristics—in the paraplegic group, for example:

1. The drawing of only the head for both man and woman,
2. The representation of only a head for the man but a full-length drawing of the woman,
3. Profile or frontal views of both figures, the man with nonfunctional legs, the woman in a "movement" pose,
4. Both figures with rigid or flaccid, but nonfunctional, legs, or
5. A complete rejection of the task when the subject was asked to complete the figure.

Even one figure which was apparently drawn by a mental defective demonstrates this realization of the inutility of the lower portion of the patient's body.

4

In the affective sphere many differences in emotional relationships with the environment are immediately evident. The writer employed the weights for C, CF, and FC customarily utilized in obtaining a ΣC score, but it must be realized that since these responses were not spontaneously elicited, the ΣC cannot be interpreted in the traditional Rorschach manner. Nevertheless, it can be utilized here as a relative index of the degree of affective stimulation and response. This difference, significant at the .1 per cent level, depicts the paraplegic as one who, in comparison with the nonparaplegic world, responds primarily to the emotional elements of his environment. Thus, while the nonparaplegic's strivings are most readily stimulated from within, the paraplegic is motivated most easily by external stimuli.

If we analyze the nature of the color responses, we can observe other striking differences. While many paraplegics are capable of mature, adult types of emotional rapport, the more prevalent emotional pattern is one of adolescent egocentricity. This is reflected in Table 1 in the difference in CF means. While this seems to be the most characteristic mode of emotional adjustment, elements of infantile, uncontrolled affective reactions are much in evidence, as indicated in Table 1 by the difference between means for the pure C response. We find manifestations of this potential explosiveness both in the number of pure color responses and in the number of Fire responses. The latter include all such responses as "smoke," "an erupting volcano," and "an exploding firecracker."

In his treatment of the Y responses, Beck (1) refers to them as expressions of an "anergic" state and a "dysphoric" mood in the individual, amounting in the pure Y responses to passivity or total absence of activity. A priori we should expect to discover both conditions in the paraplegic population, and this is indeed the case. More Y responses were elicited from this group, and of these the largest difference is manifest in the pure Y responses, the indicators of what Beck terms a "washed-out" feeling.

An inspection of the content of the responses yields further illuminating aspects of the paraplegic's adjustment. We have previously discussed the importance of the Fire content in relationship to the patient's affective experiences. Human

5

responses reflect a need for relationships (not necessarily healthy ones, however) with other people. The AVC group exhibits a greater gregariousness, a greater facility for forming associations with other people. Table 2 gives the means for the AVC and paraplegic groups at 6.48 and 3.64, respectively, the difference being significant at the 1 per cent level. There is in this statement no implication, however, that paraplegics are less able to conform to group standards or to adhere to the modes of thinking of the social milieu. Comparison of the A and P categories for both groups shows no significant difference and confirms this essential respect for social convention and cliché.

Specific personal needs crop out in the content designations. The Multiple Choice Test records of the paraplegic are rife with Anatomy, Blood, and Dirt responses, the latter category embracing such responses as "something squashed," "a black mess," and "dirty water." These responses likely reflect their preoccupation with their injuries, with the incessant treatment, and with the "messiness" of their conditions, especially with respect to incontinence.

With respect to intelligence and intellectual efficiency, little, unfortunately, can be deduced because of the very nature of the testing instrument used. Since many of the responses were not scorable in terms of W and D, we could not form any opinions regarding Approach and Sequence, but we do know that the groups did not differ in attention to small details. We might expect that intellectual efficiency would remain unimpaired, and the writer believes that this conjecture is not contradicted by the data. Why then should there exist a statistically significant difference in $F+$ response? We must recall that this is the mean of the $F+$, not the mean of the $F+ \%$, and consequently not a measure of intellectual integrity but rather an indication of interest in the formal aspects of the blots. By this we mean that the construction of the test can be made to account for this discrepancy; since the number of responses was limited for each individual, it is obvious that if the paraplegic group were primarily responsive to color, they could not simultaneously select $F+$ percepts. This appears to be the most reasonable explanation for our data. Yet this does not explain the difference in the $F-$ category. Examination of the $F-$ responses, however, reveals that most (69 per cent) of these temporary breakdowns occur in conjunction with Anatomy responses. Thus, the pressing personal needs related to concern over health are apparently responsible for the distortion of reality and the corresponding difference in the $F-$ means.

The evasions constitute the last group of responses we shall consider. These include the Card Descriptions and the Card Rejections, and if we group these categories together, little difference in evasive behavior can be said to exist. It is interesting to note in this respect, however, that none of the paraplegics disguised their names, although the instructions permitted them to do so, while seven of the AVC group did. Nevertheless, the paraplegic sample, by virtue of its extreme stimulation by color, apparently selected a "Just colors" response in preference to a "Nothing at All" response whenever it had an opportunity to do so.

SUMMARY
The Harrower-Erickson Multiple Choice Test was administered to volunteer groups of 25 paraplegic patients and 25 nonparaplegic veterans. Each of the responses was scored both numerically and in terms of determinants and content. Significant differences were discovered for the numerical scorings as well as for 13 of the scoring categories. The paraplegic may be characterized as one who is motivated with greater ease by stimuli external to himself and whose emotional makeup is primarily egocentric. However, the potential for mature emotional response as well as for explosive affect is still present. He is intensely preoccupied with his own condition and the "messiness" of his life, is constantly aware of the inutility of his legs, but knowing that protest will not alter his condition, has become passive in his relationships. The facility for association with other people has decreased, but he still observes group mores.

REFERENCES

1. BECK, S. J. *The Rorschach test.* New York: Grune & Stratton, 1946.
2. BUCK, J. N. The H-T-P technique: A qualitative and quantitative scoring manual. *J. clin. Psychol.,* 1948, 4, 317-396.
3. HARROWER-ERICKSON, MOLLY R., AND STEINER, M. E. *Large scale Rorschach techniques.* Springfield, Ill: Charles C. Thomas, 1945.
4. MACHOVER, K. *Personality projection in the drawing of the human figure.* Springfield, Ill.: Charles C. Thomas, 1949.
5. WOLFF, W. *The personality of the pre-school child.* New York: Grune & Stratton, 1946.

Selective Perception in the
Interpretation of Symbols*

In the development of psychoanalytic theory much has been made of analogy and allusion to validate or to illustrate certain Freudian hypotheses. The use of allusion finds prominent expression in the interpretation of symbols, e.g., fire is often treated as a symbol of male sexuality, and to confirm this interpretation, allusion is frequently made to the Prometheus myth. Although Freud in his early writings formulated a system which included fixed symbols (1), he later modified his position so that greater use was made of the patient's personal associations in the interpretation of symbols. Nevertheless, a perusal of psychoanalytic writings would reveal that symbols are often interpreted as having fixed meanings independent of the personality of the person who expresses these symbols—in dreams, in literature, in art, or in advertising. When such interpretations are made, it is our hypothesis that a process of selective perception occurs and that the symbol interpreter responds only to those elements which confirm his biases and neglects or rejects those aspects which are counter to his own values.[1] That such a process occurs has been experimentally demonstrated by Postman, Bruner, and McGinnies(2). In order to point out how this process operates we cite the following illustration:

Recently at a case conference a psychoanalyst, in discussing the case, referred to the automobile as a fixed masculine symbol. To lend further emphasis to this interpretation he alluded to

---

[1]We can discover this selective process in the ordinary use of proverbs where to believe "Absence makes the heart grow fonder" contradicts "Out of sight, out of mind." Those who accept "Haste makes waste," of course, neglect the attitude that "He who hesitates is lost."

*Reprinted by permission from THE JOURNAL OF ABNORMAL AND SOCIAL PSYCHOLOGY, 1952, 47(2), 255-256. Copyright 1952 by the American Psychological Association, Inc.

phrases used in automobile advertisements. The writers consequently examined current automobile advertisements describing thirteen makes of automobiles. In support of the analyst's interpretation we found such statements as the following:

"power-packed with plenty of zoom"
"double rigid"
"the abundant performance of Fireball valve-in-head power"
"blazing get-away—entirely new command of the road at any speed"
"stronger, *twice* as rigid, lasts longer"

However, further examination of these advertisements demonstrated that the same sort of validity could be attributed to the interpretation of the automobile as a feminine symbol for we find such language as the following:

"rich . . . in the spaciousness of its interior—roominess"
"more value in beauty and comfort . . . more value in safety protection"
"leads in those things that make driving *easier, safer, more comfortable*"
"has more room in it than any other standard 6-passenger sedan on the market."
"when you find how much room and restful comfort [in the] spacious interior . . ."
"with these bodies . . . you'll enjoy a far safer, quieter, more comfortable ride."
" . . . gives you 'Fashion Car' styling. From the sweep of its lines and the soundness of its coachwork . . . to the last detail of its 'jewel box' interior . . . it's America's best dressed car."
". . . started with a spacious interior and practically built the rest of the car around it! Here is room 'to roam around in'—plenty of room to let the human body take the positions that are *natural* and therefore *comfortable.*"

Finally one advertisement which urges one to "feel the surging power of the high compression 'Get-Away' engine!" follows this with the contradictory statement, "see how smoothly *she* rolls along . . . and see how wonderfully easy *she* is to handle" (italics ours).

On the basis of this limited survey it seems apparent that an equally valid case for attributing feminine qualities to the automobile as a symbol could be formulated. Examination of the cited phrases would indicate that advertisement writers seem to stress both masculine and feminine attributes in exploiting their wares, masculine traits including power, rigidity, and size, while feminine attributes include roominess, comfort, protection, and glamour. From this, several conclusions are possible. It would seem that symbols cannot always, if indeed ever, be interpreted independently of the individuals employing the symbols. It is altogether possible, moreover, in this specific illustration that the advertising phraseology employed is a reflection of the individual advertisement writer's unconscious processes rather than a universal expression. Possibly because the advertiser must appeal to both men and women, he unconsciously plays up both aspects. This would also suggest that the private meaning that the automobile has for the individual is important. For some it may represent a symbol of power, prestige, wealth, or beauty, in which case an interpretation along Adlerian lines might equally "explain" the symbol. It also becomes evident that caution may be exercised in using allusory material for validation of symbolic interpretation since selective perception may seriously distort these interpretations.

REFERENCES

1. FREUD, S. *The interpretation of dreams.* New York: Carlton House, 1950.
2. POSTMAN, L., BRUNER, J., & McGINNIES, E. Personal values as selective factors in perception. *J. abnorm. soc. Psychol.,* 1948, 2, 142-154.

Problems in the Definition and Measurement of Success in Psychotherapy[1,] *

CRITERIA OF SUCCESS

IN INVESTIGATING THE NATURE of psychotherapy the problem of criterion selection invariably arises. In its simplest formulation the problem becomes one of determining how we know when a patient is improving or is cured and of designating the factors which have contributed to such an evaluation. The purpose of this chapter is to raise some of the major pertinent problems related to the concept of progress in psychotherapy.

Hiterto there has been no dearth of reports of "successes" or "cures" claimed for various therapeutic approaches, reports bolstered by statistics and testimonials, by recourse to traditional learning theory, and by the application of words which have taken on colored meanings such as "permissive," "flexible," "warmth" and "consistency," and finally by the use of such socio-philosophical concepts as "democratic" versus "authoritarian," "respect for the individual" and "social interest." Unfortunately for the progress of research in psychotherapy, the definition of cure and the criteria of progress are two subjects too frequently glossed over. When the terms have been defined, a perusal of the literature will confirm that they have been worded extremely vaguely and without consideration of the numerous issues involved. In many instances the basis for judgments of cure is not reported except for the occasional statement that the judgments were made by the

[1]Portion of a dissertation submitted in partial fulfillment of the requirements for the degree of Doctor of Philosophy in the University of Chicago. Reviewed in the Veterans Administration and published with the approval of the Chief Medical Director. The statements and conclusions published by the author are a result of his own study and do not necessarily reflect the opinion or policy of the Veterans Administration. This study was completed at the VA Hospital, Hines, Ill.

*Reprinted by permission from W. Wolff & J.A. Precker (Eds.), *Success in Psychotherapy*. New York: Grune & Stratton, 1952.

therapist or by judges. For example, although Rosen (52) makes explicit his criteria for recovery in his description of the results of his therapeutic efforts with direct analysis with schizophrenic patients, he receives critical comment from the discussants of his paper for ignoring a basic issue, that of the permanence of the cure.

Hendrick, to cite another illustration, offers a compilation of results of psychoanalytic therapy carried on at the Berlin, London and Chicago psychoanalytic institutes. For the Berlin institute, cure denotes (27) "an essential personality-change resulting from a fundamental redistribution of instinctual energy formerly exploited by neurosis," while "'much improved' denotes an essential and worthwhile change, but with considerable evidence of neurosis persisting . . ." This would seem to imply that the success of a therapy can be appraised in terms of the neurotic residual; that is, how much neurosis is left after psychoanalysis. Remaining to be answered is the question of how one measures "neurosis" except very grossly. Can we define "cure" as a little bit less of neurosis; failure, as a little bit more of neurosis? Further, we must inquire concerning such phrases as "essential and worthwhile." What changes occurring during therapy or as a result of therapy are "essential and worthwhile?" "Worthwhile" for whom? And who shall determine the worth of changes? The value judgments implied in a pronouncement of success or failure form one of the major questions to which this chapter is addressed.

Among those advocating somatic procedures in therapy, conditions are essentially similar. Taylor and von Salzen (67) rely upon the "ability of the patient to be paroled and the ability to complete successfully a full year on parole." Such a criterion is, however, an indirect one in that prior criteria for parolability must be assumed. Moreover, the phrase "to complete successfully" implies that a value judgment of success must be made by some interested or disinterested observers. Finally, the writers insist that the "recovery" be sustained for a full year. Does a judgment of success entail the assumption of permanence as in the medical "five year cure" or is this issue irrelevant for psychotherapy? This raises the second question with which this chapter will concern itself.

Despite the significant progress made by the nondirective school, its proponents have also occasionally followed the pattern of their more directive confreres. Comparing one unsuccessful with four successful cases, Snyder (61) describes the failure by stating: "At the end of treatment both the counselor and the client agreed that the seven interviews had not been successful in producing any desirable change of attitude on the part of the client." And of the successful cases, they "were judged to be examples of successful nondirective counseling by three judges who were trained clinical psychologists." Snyder's failure to describe the basis for this evaluation ignores a crucial problem for psychologists.

A satisfactory definition of success would assist us in clarifying still another aspect of this problem of criteria, that of the depth of the treatment. Alexander and French (3) distinguish between two types of therapy—supportive and insight. The latter type has often been regarded as the special province of psychoanalysis, while other therapies have been termed symptomatic, supportive and superficial. The adherents of this viewpoint suggest that there are several levels of adjustment, that only insight therapy, which they equate with psychoanalysis, is "deep" therapy, and that other therapies are superficial and the cures claimed for them equally so. The theme of depth of adjustment constitutes the third problem to be treated in this discussion of evaluation in therapy.

From the foregoing, it should be evident that satisfactory research in therapy has lagged because of the lack of attention devoted to constructing adequate criteria of success. Blair epitomizes the confusion regarding criteria in a pertinent statement (5). "We shall see, when reviewing the literature, the use of such terms as 'recovery,' 'complete recovery,' 'social recovery,' 'recovery with deficit,' 'much improved,' 'improved,' etc., varying in number and meaning from one article to another."

The problem of defining criteria of progress, it must be recognized, is a complex one. After we have defined progress as the difference, either qualitative or quanititative, between the patient's adjustment at two points of therapy, our problem is reduced to defining the latter concept. Vexing not only clinical psychologists, this definition of adjustment poses difficulties in other applied fields. In the educational and vocational fields when the object of prediction is to divide a population into groups based upon such part-criteria as passing grades, work output, or speed of operation, the criterion choice is not too difficult. Even in the clinical field, when our sole purpose is that of screening individuals, for example, adjusted from maladjusted, normal intelligence from feeble-minded, we do not meet serious obstacles, although with the unrefined instruments we ordinarily use for such purposes, we do encounter false positives and false negatives. When other applied psychologists, however, attempt to define criteria which are more comprehensive, they discover that the current practices are somewhat less than satisfactory. Lurie and Weiss (36), in their analysis of the concept of occupational adjustment, perceive four ways in which criteria in the occupational field have been employed. We might profit from a review of these procedures since they closely parallel the practices in the clinical field.

One criterion may be selected as an approximation of total adjustment. Consonant with this view are the methods, if not the philosophies, of a number of investigators in the clinical area. The Discomfort-Relief Quotient of Dollard and Mowrer (15) which reflects changes in tension and the PNAvQ of Kauffman and Raimy (31) based upon the classification of self-referring statements are two measures based upon this assumption. In the psychoanalytic orientation the necessary condition for success may reside in the resolution of the Oedipus Complex or as Reich (46) maintains, in the achievement of orgasm with a tenderly loved mate. Sachs (54) takes issue with the use of a single criterion:

> When is an analysis finished? . . . It is comparatively easy to construct a norm representing what perfection a successfully analyzed person should have attained and what imperfections eliminated, but such models are useless for practical purposes. The answer to the question cannot be gained from one simple criterion. Several different psychological considerations and factors in reality have to be weighed and cautiously assessed to arrive at a dependable solution.

Since no single criterion of adjustment is infallible, several writers rely upon a combination of several part-criteria by formula. The mechanical view of adjustment toward which this procedure is inclined furnishes one of the reasons why this approach has been greeted with little enthusiasm. Roughly, it suggests that adjustment consists of a *summation* of several contributory factors. Although rarely formulated explicitly in

15

theoretic discussions, this viewpoint is quite frequently encountered as the rationale underlying certain psychologic tests purporting to measure adjustment. Its proponents' claims to global evaluation of personality notwithstanding, even the Rorschach falls heir to this shortcoming when the instrument is fragmentized in the extant "sign" approaches. Hoffman (30), too, in his study of behavior changes in counseling, resorts to a criterion of this nature, defining success as "the difference between first and last interviews in the standard scores of the average of four interview-analysis measures: attitudes towards self, acceptance of and respect for self, understanding and insight and defensiveness."

A third manner of viewing adjustment is to regard it not as a mere *summative* arrangement but as an *integration* of various part-criteria. Ratings of adjustment based upon analysis of case histories or of therapy interviews often take this form.

The last of the prevailing attitudes mentioned by the above authors requires an assumption that there exist infinite varieties of occupational adjustment. The clinician's application of this viewpoint would necessitate destroying the concept of adjustment and advancing in its stead such substitutes as interpersonal relationships, dominance-submission, defensiveness, reactions to frustration and attitudes toward the self as independent entities without consideration of their interrelationships. This approach might be more defensible if primary personality variables could be demonstrated somewhat in the fashion of Thurstone's primary mental abilities.

Since, as we have already indicated, progress can only be defined as the disparity between two estimates of adjustment made at two temporal points, it is apparent that any measure of progress will depend upon the type of definition we assign to adjustment. And since the goals of therapy are a derivative of our definition of adjustment, any measure we employ for gauging progress must be designed with the goals of the particular therapy in mind. Thus, if the goal of therapy is to arrange that (21) "where id was, there shall ego be," then we will have recourse to different measuring devices, or at least interpret the results of our measures quite differently, than when the goals are to "unmask" the fallacies in the style of life (1). Or if the goals should be expressed in terms of the "organization and the functioning of the self" (51) yet another type of measure might be preferred. The value systems, then, of various schools, as to what constitutes a legitimate therapeutic goal, play an important role in the definition of success.

SUCCESS AS A VALUE JUDGMENT

Success is often treated in the literature as if it were an objective concept and this aura of objectivity is sometimes reinforced through the use of so-called objective measurements. Actually, however, we are compelled to recognize that the essential quality of our judgments is that they are value judgments and intrinsically subjective. These valuative pronouncements may emanate from the client himself or they may be judgments obtained from external sources—the therapist, test and typescript interpreters, or other outside observers. From the former point of perception, that of the client, the judgment is based primarily upon an individual norm, although the client may incorporate social values in making his decision. Judgments expressed by external observers would primarily reflect social values, either of society as a whole or of the society of therapists engaging in a specific brand of therapy. Indeed, Adler (2) maintains that the goal of therapy should be the development of "social interest," a concept which he equates with social empathy and cooperation with others.

The issue of frames of reference, that is, of deciding who shall exercise judgment upon the matter of progress, warrants our careful consideration. Shall we accept the decision of the person undergoing treatment, concurring with Ovid that "I know myself better than any doctor can," or with Sir Thomas Browne who advises, "Weigh not thyself in the scales of thy own judgement, but let the judgement of the judicious be the standard of thy merit?" In clarifying this issue we shall observe that much will depend upon the orientation of the therapy and of the therapist. If a therapy is phenomenologic and "client-centered," we can anticipate such attitudes as that of Taft (66), who believes that therapy "is a purely individual affair and can be measured only in terms of its meaning to the person, child or adult, of its value, not for happiness, not for virtue, not for social adjustment but for growth and development in terms of a purely individual norm." The tendency in research will be to analyze verbatim interviews for evidence of the client's satisfaction or dissatisfaction with his status after receiving psychotherapy or, like Lipkin (35), to request the client after therapy has been terminated to evaluate the therapeutic benefit he has derived.

Assuming that we accept the patient's estimate of improvement after counseling, what factors must be weighed in assigning validity to this opinion? The first set of factors revolves about the patient's need to escape or to cling to the therapy. Fenichel (18) refers to the former phenomenon as "flight into health," while Bergler (4) describes it as "success because of unconscious fear," that is, the patient gives up his symptoms temporarily so that he may escape analysis and insulate himself against further threats to his ego. Any estimate by such a patient regarding his improvement would necessarily be suspect. At the other extreme we discover very dependent individuals who cling to the therapy and to the therapist as crutches. These patients might tend to minimize or even negate some of the improvement, as externally judged, realized in therapy. Schmideberg (56) generalizes this reaction to other than dependent individuals:

> Patients who have been severely ill have to make quite a readjustment when they get better and, paradoxically, this is often very upsetting. Even people who suffered from physical pain over a long period of time told me they quite missed it when it stopped. "It somehow did not seem natural." When a patient's neurosis has lasted some time it has acquired a secondary significance.

A second set of factors centers about the presence of symptomatic improvement. Frequently, patients are beguiled by temporary symptomatic relief and assure their therapists, perhaps by discontinuing therapy, that they are now cured. Transference phases may further distort the patient's judgment in psychoanalytic therapy. During the course of therapy the patient's enthusiasm may reflect an effort to ingratiate himself with the therapist or to manipulate him. It may result from the patient's fear that he may incur the therapist's wrath, lose his love or be deserted. The possibility of the patient's judgment being associated with temporary moods should also not be overlooked. Postman and Bruner (43) give an excellent account of the disorganizing effect of stress upon perception which may be applicable to therapy. "The major dimensions of perceptual function are affected: selection of percepts from a complex field

18

becomes less adequate and sense is less well differentiated from nonsense: there is maladaptive accentuation in the direction of aggression and escape; untested hypotheses are fixated recklessly." When periods of stress are experienced, the patient's perception of the counseling process may thus be affected considerably, and if measures are applied during these periods of stress, their accuracy with regard to the general status of the patient might well be challenged.

Further complicating the picture is the need of some patients to placate, manipulate or express hostility toward the therapist. The "good little boy" self-concept is inimical to expression of aggression, while the patient who feels that he cannot accept anything from others, and the patient who, deeming himself worthless, feels that he does not deserve to improve, each may conceal whatever personal benefits have accrued to them. This constitutes one of the major deficiencies of the testimonial, especially when solicited.

The recent experiment by Bruner and Goodman (9) in which school children were asked to judge the sizes of coins of various denominations may hold some interesting implications for us. These investigators observed that children from lower economic groups had a tendency to overestimate the coin sizes while the judgments of economically secure children more nearly approximated the actual coin sizes. Transposing these results to therapy, we might surmise that the greater the need of the patient for improvement the greater the possibility of his overestimation of the changes which do occur.

Similar factors are operative when the judgments are made from an external frame of reference. The "judgment of the judicious" has customarily been assumed to refer to the judgment of the therapist. While often regarded as near infallible, these assessments must be appraised in the light of what Krech and Crutchfield (32) term the "functional" factors of perception. By this we mean that the needs, biases and tensions of the therapist mold the outcome of therapy as surely as do the formal "objective" aspects of therapy. Freud recognized these functional components, maintaining (20) that "analysts do not in their own personalitites wholly come up to the standard of psychic normality which they set for their patients. . . The analyst . . . because of the peculiar conditions of his work is really prevented from discerning his patient's situation correctly and reacting to it in a manner conducive to cure." The experiment by Weingarten (72) on selective perception in clinical judgments tends to corroborate Freud's opinion with respect to the contertransference.

We must next question whether the therapist can really ever interject himself into the internal frame of reference of the patient. Adler (2), Reik (47), Rogers (50) and Rosen (52) answer this question affirmatively. In his facile literary style, Reik describes the process of one unconscious talking to another, a premise upon which Rosen's direct analytic therapy rests. Rogers' view is more similar to that of Adler, who writes (2), "We must be able to see with his [the patient's] eyes and listen with his ears."

Another source of error resides in the lack of opportunity most therapists have had in observing and treating many types of cases. No therapist ever treats a statistically valid sample of neurotics. To the contrary, many therapists acquire reputations for treating certain types of patients, and patients falling in this category gravitate to their offices. Consequently, these therapists are not, in all likelihood, in a position to evaluate other types of cases adequately. It is altogether possible that some therapists, in selecting their area of operation, satisfy their own needs in the countertransference. Indeed, we may speculate whether these therapists, in specializing, do not exhibit their own repetition compulsions.

The therapist's own theoretic prejudices may cast further doubt upon the reliability of his judgment. We have already mentioned in another connection that the therapist's concepts of adjustment and of therapeutic goals will influence his decisions. These biases are often so well entrenched that when observations and biases clash, the therapist may sooner reject the observation than question his prejudices. Thus, those therapists who subscribe rather *rigidly* to systematic formulations of the nature of personality or of psychotherapy may develop a form of psychologic scotoma and make their observations fit a Procrustean bed of theory. Reik (47) inveighs against his fellow analysts on just this score. The sparsity of research upon and treatment of psychopathic individuals spotlights what may occur when a therapist considers a condition untreatable. Some therapists will even shirk from applying certain diagnoses because prognosis for these cases is poor, which leads Freyhan to comment (23):

> This situation must be traced to fear of therapeutic paralysis. Fears, of course, are no scientific criteria and science must discover facts regardless of the therapeutic prospects. . . No neurologist would shirk from diagnosing Huntington's chorea, no internist hesitate to diagnose leukemia because of fear of therapeutic limitations.

When judgment involves administrative considerations, as it does in institutional practice, the decision regarding cure may become encumbered by bias and fear. The psychotic in a "hospital for the criminal insane" would very likely be required to meet more rigorous standards than would an ambulatory schizophrenic receiving outpatient care.

These, then, are some of the major issues involved when success is recognized to be a value judgment. Let us now proceed to a second vital issue, that of the depth of adjustment, of therapy and of cure.

THE DEPTH OF ADJUSTMENT

As a result of the introduction of projective technics into the United States, diagnosticians have begun to speak of levels of adjustment. Workers in the field of therapy, however, have long recognized that these levels existed and have engaged in vituperative controversy over this issue. Fundamental to psychoanalytic theory is the dichotomy between conscious and unconscious levels of operation. Psychoanalysts have, therefore, differentiated between cures and illusions of cure, cures occurring where the patient has undergone deep therapy, illusory cures occurring when the patient has not resolved certain basic unconscious conflicts. Apropos of this distinction is Bergler's observation (4):

> A witty patient characterized every psychotherapy as eternal fight between the couch and the door. The question is in what state the patient decides that fight. He can run away; he can establish a new defense mechanism, or—even be cured.

Another variation upon the theme of levels of adjustment in therapy is evident in the distinction between cure and the

21

"flight into health." Still a third nuance is visible in the differentiation between symptomatic, superficial and deep therapies. Bergler (4) distinguishes between "psychotherapy aiming at destruction of neurosis" and "psychotherapy aiming at temporary conscious improvement of the patient's suffering." Real success, he maintains, can only be achieved by "changing the underlying neurosis."[1] Commenting at a symposium on psychotherapy, Bretnall (7) adopts a similar attitude:

> If the behavior changes exist at more than the verbal intellectualistic level, one probability is that the change resulted from deepened defenses against unyielding unconscious material . . . [This] might bring, temporarily, a relief from symptoms, but not a genuinely therapeutic personality reorganization.

With this distinction as a weapon nondirective therapy is accused of being superficial because it does not control the transference relationship. Adlerian therapy, from this standpoint, becomes an "ego therapy" because it neglects the deeper instinctual sources of human nature. Kubie (8), in discussing this controversy, makes an astute observation:

> Some psychiatrists believe that psychotherapy can never go beyond this limited goal [palliation] and should never aim at more. Others maintain that whether or not any psychotherapeutic process can achieve more than this depends entirely on the "depth" or "orthodoxy" of the treatment . . . The fact of the matter is that it has never been possible to establish a clear correlation between the extent, or degree or depth of the treatment or of the insight attained.

Characteristic of the intrusion of this thinking in terms of level of operation or levels of defense into the diagnostic area are the writings of Shneidman (59), Stein (63) and MacKinnon (37). Arey[2] is conducting a tachistoscopic study to investigate the unconscious factors in Freudian symbolization.

---

[1] Cf. Wyatt (6): "Nor do we know enough about personality to presume to change it fundamentally. It does not make biological sense that an organism moulded into a certain pattern under innumerable influences over many years, should be changed profoundly through an influence within a few months. A therapist who insists on the rebirth of his patients may have missed his calling."
[2] Personal communication.

If levels of personality exist, and we believe that they do, then our probe tools must be geared to the levels of personality we intend to explore. However, the current descriptions of personality in terms of traits, attitudes, and goals are devoid of real meaning unless the levels at which these express themselves are designated.

THE PERMANENCE OF CURE

In psychology, the question of the permanence of cure has received scant attention. Follow-up studies which might give us the requisite information are difficult to carry out on many scores. The mortality rate from the mail-questionnaire type of follow-up is great. Questioning of friends, relatives or other observers regarding the patient's adjustment might violate the confidential aspects of psychotherapy. Disregarding the ethical question for the moment, it remains doubtful whether external observers are capable of giving accurate and meaningful descriptions of the patient's behavior. The fact that patients are unwilling or unable to present themselves for evaluation at specific intervals after therapy also poses problems for the follow-up study.

Aside from these practical considerations many theoretic issues are involved. In somatic medicine the practice in assigning the label of permanence to a cure is based upon the patient's ability to remain symptom-free for a period of five years after treatment. Gottschalk (24) endorses this practice as it is applied to psychotics because he feels that "since the proper dosage of psychotherapy for psychotics is not clearly established, the criteria for recovery, as far as time is concerned, should certainly be no less than the familiar and arbitrary five-year remission used in statistical evaluation of treatment in other diseases." This attitude is not universal among psychotherapists, for we find Eisenbud (52) dissenting. "It is doubtful whether life can guarantee five years of stability to any person." This inability to properly assess environmental stress in the post-therapeutic period militates against differentiation between recurrence and new disease. Let us suppose that a "cured" neurotic returns later for treatment of schizophrenia. Does this constitute new illness or has the old illness assumed more maligant proportions? In the midst of this controversy, Rosen (52) voices his unconcern.

This leads to the next inevitable question: Will these results withstand the test of time? That question cannot be answered at present; time alone will tell. In the meantime, however, 37 persons, who, according to prognoses, might face lives of institutionalization, have lived comfortably with society if only for a time. Even if it should be necessary for these patients to return to mental hospitals tomorrow, at least they have been able to enjoy their periods of happiness.

QUANTITATIVE PROBLEMS

The testing literature is replete with reports of endeavors to lend the adjustment concept to quantitative treatment. The problems which have received major attention are those of establishing the reliability of tests, ratings and raters and the validity and standardization of tests. In this connection, Webb (71) has pointed out some of the cautions which must be observed in defining populations, in sampling and in establishing reliability. In the projective testing area reliability and validity studies have been conducted by a number of writers (25, 26, 28, 29, 33, 45, 53, 60, 68, 73). It is not our purpose here to recapitulate these discussions. We intend instead to present some of the more general quantitative problems related to evaluating adjustment. First, there is the problem of the quantifiability of behavior and the units to be used. Schafer (55), in his discussion of diagnostic testing, delineates one of the problems here:

> Many aspects of the organism's behavior appear to be intrinsically not quantifiable. How can we, for example, quantify without artifice a mode of coping with passive needs? Or a mode of verbalizing one's thoughts? Or an egocentric mode of concept formation?

Zubin (74) acknowledges similar difficulties with regard to the personality correlates of projective scores and the methods of measuring such variables. The lack of facility in quantifying personality variables is evident in the numerous attempts to objectify projective technics. Let us cite several illustrations relating to the inequality of units on the Rorschach. The questions which arouse concern here are twofold. Does an increment on one scale correspond psychologically to an equal numerical increment on a second scale? Second, are steps on a single scale equally spaced, that is, can the increment from 3M to 4M be interpreted as equal to that from 7M to 8M? The answer to both of these questions is in the negative, and this is of special significance in the so-called "sign" approaches to the Rorschach. Yet Muench (38), after specifically referring to the principle of interrelationship of Rorschach variables commits exactly this error. Carr (10) repeats this error in his revision of the Muench scoring although he, like this writer, finds the same objections to Muench's study. This situation is recified to some extent by Munroe (39) who includes in her instructions for sign scoring certain corrections based upon the number of responses elicited and other adjustments for the presence, absence or magnitude of related factors.

Although we are bound to recognize that sign scoring may provide us with convenient methods for large scale testing, we must also admit that fractionation of the Rorschach does not take advantage of the concept of the unity of the personality upon which it users rely. The interrelationships between factors are obscured or distorted. In the Munroe scoring (39), when only the total number of "bad" signs are used, the quantitative score may remain constant even when the test configuration is radically altered. Thus, when the Total Color: Total Movement ratio is 2:1, we score one plus sign. If this ratio should be reversed after therapy, the subject receives one minus sign. Nevertheless, in computing the total score, only the *absolute* values are summed, in this case belying the actual change which occurred.

What are some of the other quantitative problems associated with such projective instruments as the Rorschach? Let us consider the use and interpretation of the ratios which are so characteristic of the test. In comparing two ratios it is obviously unsuitable to use the difference between numerator and denominator because of the inequality of the scalar units. Thus, a ratio of 7:6 is not equal to one of 5:4, although the difference in each case is 1. Mathematical principles govern the interpretation of ratios, but unfortunately, their psychologic meaning does not conform to these mathematical principles. For example, in mathematics $8:4 = 4:2 = 2:1$. In Rorschach "mathematics" it is immediately evident that W:M $=$ 8:4 would require a somewhat different interpretation than a W:M ratio of 4:2 or of 2:1. Treating ratios as fractions in which one can divide the

25

numerator by the denominator is also unsuitable in the extreme case when either the numerator or the denominator is zero. We can readily observe that an M:Sum C of 0:1 does not equal one of 0:6, although they are mathematically equivalent. When the denominator is zero, the division is, of course, impossible.

Spurious results may also be obtained when averages are applied to Rorschach data. An oversimplified illustration will help clarify this point. Two subjects, A and B, take the test in a before and after sequence. Examining their psychograms we discover that A's W score has increased by 2W while B's score decreases by 2W. If we average the change scores, we find no change for the total group (a too small group statistically, it is true, but adequate for illustrative purposes) despite the fact that each member of the group has demonstrated either a positive or negative change. Thus, group statistics disguise the actual changes in the therapy. Our inference from the average might lead us to find no changes in therapy when in actuality each individual in the group might have changed from his pretherapy position. Nor is this problem unique to the projective test. Group MMPI profiles provide another illustration of group treatment of data minimizing or even negating the presence of change when change actually exists. Pacella and his collaborators (40) treat the MMPI in this fashion in investigating the effects of electroshock and discover that the test has little diagnostic value.

Group treatment of data may contribute toward fallacies in interpretation. The MMPI group profiles again afford us illustration when we consider the writings of certain psychologists. Where Wundt founded a psychology based upon the "generalized, normal adult," these writers seem to have extended the Wundtian viewpoint to the "generalized, abnormal adult." Du Mas' implementation of this view (16) by his suggestion that his coefficient of profile similarity will assist psychologists in comparing the profiles of individuals with those for various diagnostic groups commits this fallacy of resorting to such a nebulous concept as the "average neurotic." Let it be said at this point that the group profile, valid though it be, is in the majority of instances unlike that of any member of the group. Averages are excellent statistical tools when they are not used in contexts for which they are inappropriate. The characterization of the "average American" as "nine-tenths white, 50 per cent male and slightly pregnant" emphasizes the inutility of averages as descriptive measures in certain contexts. The use of group statistics presents another difficulty. Fundamentally, our present group statistics make it only possible for us to predict for groups, but this is not the problem which confronts the therapist or the patient. Each is interested primarily in the prognosis for the patient seated in the therapist's office, not for some group joined by the ties of certain diagnostic labels or symptoms.

The failure to use the most appropriate statistical tests when working with the Rorschach has resulted in unwarranted inferences. While the nature of the Rorschach makes excessive demands upon our present statistical technics, there are certain guides for optimal use of these tools. Cronbach's excellent review of Rorschach research (13) is particularly revealing of the number of studies where faulty inferences have been made. Certain encouraging signs may be discerned, however. A drive to enlist the aid of statisticians in the solution of complex clinical problems is gaining momentum. Indicative of this effort to effect a rapprochement between clinical and experimental psychology are the American Psychological Association symposia devoted to common problems of both fields, a trend which can have salutary effects.

VERBAL LEGERDEMAIN

Therapy, as a form of communication, is largely dependent upon an exchange of words. Using this as a starting point, investigators have examined the words used in the therapeutic sessions not only to evaluate progress but also to clarify process. Studies by Porter (41, 42), Curran (14), Snyder (62), Kauffman and Raimy (31), Sheerer (58), Seeman (57) and Stock (65) provide ample illustration of this tendency. From a semantic viewpoint words can prove very tricky. No word possesses a uniform meaning for all people, although many investigators treat words as if they did. Hence, words like integration, acceptance, socialization, regression, nondirective, and, needless to say, adjustment and progress often find their way into print under the investigator's tacit assumption that these words possess universal connotations. Because of this assumption of universal

27

meaning many concepts go undefined, and experimental "results," while sometimes present, are often ambiguous. This is also partially explanatory of many apparently contradictory results based upon seemingly identical assumptions.

Reik's indictment of other psychoanalysts for their use of "psychoanalese" focuses attention upon the use of words (47):

> . . . not as a means of scientific communication but for adornment and decoration . . . Many apply those terms to save themselves the trouble of thinking independently and others to save themselves the effort of thinking at all . . . We suspect that these names aim less at enlightenment than at creating an impression. We could endure the absence of many of these figures comfortably. We can afford to lose quite a few more. Sometimes we wish that most of them would go to He—to Hades, I mean, of course.

Those who work with personality inventories will recognize a problem in this area. The MMPI, for example, bases its norms upon conformity with the views of a standardizing group. Yet, we have no assurance that the statements possess the same meanings for all individuals taking the test.

Users of the Rorschach have complicated the problem further by introducing an esoteric vocabulary including such non-universal concepts as "creative fantasy" and "intra-psychic tension." Thurstone (69) criticizes this practice recommending: "The first step in removing the Rorschach test from its isolation must be in translating the specialized jargon into currently known and accepted concepts, or else in the introduction of such new psychological concepts as may be necessary and with such discussion that psychologists generally can understand the new concepts."

With the introduction of electrical recording equipment verbatim records of interviews became available (11, 12, 49), making the analysis of interviews a more convenient and more accurate procedure. In analyzing interviews some investigators have been prone to point to certain phrases employed by patients as evidence that a certain therapy was relatively more efficacious than a second therapy or that a therapeutic method such as reflection was more advisable than interpretation. Hence, if the patient responded to a therapist's statement with a remark like "Yes, that's exactly the way I feel," it might be construed as demonstrating the counselor's understanding of the patient's feelings. Such uncritical acceptance of the patient's statement may prove misleading for as Forer (19) has indicated, corroboration of personality description may be greatly influenced by what he calls the patient's "gullibility." He concludes from a validation experiment (19):

> A naive person who receives superficial diagnostic information especially when the situation is prestige-laden tends to accept such information. He is impressed by the obvious truths and may be oblivious to the discrepancies. *But he does more than this. He also validates the instrument and the diagnostician.*

Thus, a patient given a superficial interpretation by the therapist may validate the interpretation by whole-hearted acceptance, yet we cannot accept his validating statement at face value.

Errors of personal validation may reflect, as Forer suggests, the patient's gullibility or naivete, but it is also possible that other personal needs may affect the patient's validating responses. When a patient fears to offend the therapist or when he confirms a statement because he feels, unconsciously or otherwise, that confirmation will conceal more basic conflicts from the therapist's scrutiny, we may discover validating responses that reflect less of real acceptance of the therapist's statements than distortion due to personal need. Naivete and need may also conspire to mislead the therapist. Half-facetiously this writer once differentiated between nondirective and directive therapies in the following manner. The goal of the former is to get the client to accept his own rationalizations; in the latter, he is expected to accept the therapist's rationalizations. Or as an unknown psychologist phrased it: "A patient demonstrates insight when he comes around to the viewpoint of the therapist." The study of perception by Postman, Bruner, and McGinnies (44), while it does not offer conclusive results, points toward increased sensitivity for words which are consonant with the perceiver's values. Bergman (8) appreciates this possibility and cautions against this tendency when evaluating patients. In those therapies where dream interpretation is an accepted procedure, therapists may also succumb to this temptation, as Stekel points out (64):

29

. . . it [is] plain to me that patients dream in the dialect of whatever physician happens to be treating them. The dreams are "made to order," are produced in the form that will best please the analyst. That is why the dreams of a patient who is familiar with his doctor's pet theories must never be taken as confirmation of these theories. Badgar's patients will dream about urinary eroticism; mine, perhaps, of the symbolisms of death and religion; Adler's of "top-dogs" and "underdogs" and of the "masculine protest." My friend Svoboda's student will dream of beautiful periodicity; Silber will be provided with fascinating instances of threshold symbolism and functional symbolism. I do my utmost, therefore, to obtain from my patients "pure" dream material, uncontaminated by my personal influence. To this end I treasure the dreams that are dreamed in the early days of analysis . . .

CONCLUSIONS

In the preceding sections we have discussed some of the major issues which psychologists encounter, but sometimes do not meet, in their investigations of progress in psychotherapy. It is true that the problem permits no simple solution. Nevertheless, there are certain guides which the investigator of the therapeutic process might profitably heed. Too often in the past theory, practice and research have been regarded as alienated foci. However, it must be realized that these three are mutual processes and a "reciprocal trade agreement" should be initiated and implemented. Theory and practice can provide the hypotheses for research investigation. Improvements in methodology would undoubtedly open wide vistas for additions to personality theory. The testing of new hypotheses will necessitate clarifying our thinking about personality concepts and making them amenable to fruitful investigation. Many of the major problems in evaluation have already been raised. That certain areas of agreement in psychotherapy can be found has been amply demonstrated in the literature (70).

But practice also has something to contribute. Only in experiencing the process of therapy, in the give and take between therapist and client, do certain aspects of therapy acquire significance. The therapist, while motivated to help the patient, has additional responsibilities. He has a responsibility for contribution to the broad field of therapy as a consequence of his therapeutic endeavors. He must be ever alert to the processes he is observing. This, of course, implies that he will have at his disposal adequate technics for observation. Recent research in recording of interviews and such efforts as that of Brenman and Gill (6) to extend this recording to visual observation offer promise despite Freud's contention that the psychoanalytic interview, at least, does not admit of a third person (22). The round tables conducted by the American Orthopsychiatric Association each year (6, 8) offer many constructive suggestions for improving observational technics. Kubie's discussion of the establishment of a neurosis center, although perhaps somewhat idealistic at present, furnishes several excellent ideas for controlling variables in therapy.

The therapist also has the responsibility to observe *himself* in the course of therapy. Until now our emphasis in therapy has consisted of examining *what the therapist did* and *what happened to the patient.* Unfortunately, we have neglected, with the exception of the psychoanalytic school, to remember that therapy is a two way street. Studies of the character of the perceptions and the learnings of each participant would seem to be in order.

Third, the practitioner owes his psychologic colleagues the duty of remaining as scientific as possible within the therapeutic framework. This is probably not possible within the therapy *per se,* but it should be characteristic of the reporting of therapeutic management and research in therapy. Ellis' article on improvement of psychoanalytic research (17) presents some glaring illustrations of the unscientific attitude of several psychoanalytic studies along with some gratifying examples of other studies which are more accurately reported with respect to, and for, facts and inferences. Another practice in reporting which would be conducive to more effective communication would consist of explicitly designating the criteria by which therapeutic results are assessed. If this were done, two readers might arrive at different conclusions based upon their own value systems, but they would at least possess the basic data for making these value judgments.

With respect to research—we need more of it! But a mere increase in output does not completely solve the problem. We must construct meaningful hypotheses to test and while rigid experimental controls may not be feasible, the slipshod methods of the past should be rejected. Our statistical and experimental technics undoubtedly need development and refinement, but investigations such as those conducted by Cronbach (13) and Lewis and Burke (34) demonstrate that we are not utilizing even those technics which we are fortunate enough to possess in the fashion in which they were designed to be employed.

If we intend to employ tests in the investigation of therapy, then we ought perhaps to devise "tailored tests," that is, tests which possess validity for the specific task of measuring therapeutic benefit. Our reliance upon tests constructed for other purposes depreciates the value of our present studies. In addition, it would seem that clinical psychology could bear more investigations of the normal (defined very broadly) personality. Our academic courses in personality, in testing, and in many instances, in therapy reflect our present emphasis upon the deviant rather than the normal personality. However, if we are to make progress in the study of personality, we might do well to heed Roe's admonition (48):

> We have not explained the etiology of maladjustment if we do not know the etiology of adjustment. This problem is as crucial for diagnosis and therapy as it is for theory, and it is a problem which can be solved only by clinical studies of large numbers of normal persons. Adjustment is not just a result of the lack of factors which lead to non-adjustment.

Thurstone's plea for a less esoteric Rorschach terminology (69) applies equally to other areas. Unless we define our variables more adequately, we shall continue to measure vague concepts with inapplicable technics, and come up, not so strangely, with ambiguous results. The definition of the goals of therapy and the determination of the degree of adjustment which is desired or desirable must fare better at our hands than they have until now. Otherwise we face the dilemma of Alice in Wonderland when she met the Cat.

> "Cheshire Puss . . . Would you tell me, please, which way I ought to go from here?
> "That depends a good deal on where you want to get to," said the Cat.
> "I don't much care where—" said Alice.
> "Then it doesn't matter which way you go," said the Cat.
> "—so long as I get *somewhere*," Alice added as an explanation.
> "Oh, you're sure to do that," said the Cat, "if you only walk long enough."

REFERENCES

1. Adler, A.: The Practice and Theory of Individual Psychology. Translated by P. Radin. Totowa, N. J., Littlefield, Adams, 1925.
2. ——: What Life Should Mean to You. New York, Capricorn, 1931.
3. Alexander, F. and French, T. M.: Psychoanalytic Therapy. New York, Ronald Press, 1946.
4. Bergler, E.: Prognosis in psychotherapy. Psychoanalyt. Rev. 36: 115-122, 1949.
5. Blair, D.: Prognosis in schizophrenia. J. Ment. Sc. 86: 378-477, 1940.
6. Brenman, M., Kubie, L. S., Rogers, C. R., and Gill, M. M.: Research in psychotherapy. Round Table, 1947. Am. J. Orthopsychiat. 18:92-118, 1948.
7. Brettnall, P.: Psychotherapy and counseling: Summary of discussion. J. Consult. Psychol. 12: 88-91, 1948.
8. Bronner, A. F., Kubie, L. S., Hendrick, I., Kris, E., Shakow, D., Brosin, H. W., Bergman, P., and Bibring, E.: The objective evaluation of psychotherapy. Round Table. Am. J. Orthopsychiat. 19: 463-491, 1949.
9. Bruner, J. S. and Goodman, C. C: Value and need as organizing factors in perception. J. Abnorm. & Soc. Psychol. 42:33-44, 1947.
10. Carr, A. C.: Evaluation of nine psychotherapy cases by the Rorschach. J. Consult. Psychol. 13:196-205, 1949.
11. Covner, B. J.: Studies in phonographic recordings of verbal material: I. The use of phonographic recordings in counseling practice and research. J. Consult. Psychol. 6:105-113, 1942.
12. ——: Studies in phonographic recordings of verbal material: III. The completeness and accuracy of counseling interview reports. J. Gen. Psychol. 30: 181-203, 1944.
13. Cronbach, L. J.: Statistical methods as applied to Rorschach scores: a review. Psychol. Bull. 46: 393-429, 1949.
14. Curran, C. A.: Personality Factors in Counseling. New York, Grune & Stratton, 1945.
15. Dollard, J. and Mowrer, O. H.: A method of measuring tension in written documents. J. Abnorm. & Soc. Psychol. 42: 3-32, 1947.
16. Du Mas, F. M.: The coefficient of profile similarity. J. Clin. Psychol. 5: 123-131, 1949.
17. Ellis, A.: Towards improvement of psychoanalytic research. Psychoanalyt. Rev. 2: 123-143, 1949.
18. Fenichel, O.: The Psychoanalytic Theory of Neurosis. New York, W. W. Norton, 1945.
19. Forer, B. R.: The fallacy of personal validation: A classroom demonstration of gullibility. J. Abnorm. & Soc. Psychol. 44:118-123, 1949.
20. Freud, S.: Analysis, terminable and interminable. Internat. J. Psycho-Analysis. 18: 373-403, 1937.
21. ——: New Introductory Lectures on Psycho-Analysis. Translated by W. J. H. Sprott. New York, W. W. Norton, 1933.
22. ——: The Question of Lay Analysis. Translated by N. Procter-Gregg. London, Imago Publishing Co., 1947.
23. Freyhan, F. A.: Psychiatric realities. J. Nerv. & Ment. Dis. 106: 482-492, 1947.
24. Gottschalk, L. A.: Systematic psychotherapy of the psychoses. Psychiatric Quart. 21: 554-574, 1947.
25. Harrison, R.: Studies in the use and validity of the T. A. T. with mentally disordered patients, II. A quantitative validity study. III. Validation by the method of "blind analysis." Charac. & Pers. 9:122-138, 1940.
26. ——and Rotter, J. B.: A note on the reliability of the T. A. T. J. Abnorm. & Soc. Psychol. 40:97-99, 1945.

27. Hendrick, I.: Facts and Theories of Psychoanalysis. New York, Knopf, 1947, p. 253.
28. Hertz, M.: The reliability of the Rorschach ink-blot test. J. Appl. Psychol. 18: 461-477, 1934.
29. ——: Validity of the Rorschach method. Am. J. Orthopsychiat. 11:513-516, 1941.
30. Hoffman, A. E.: A study of reported behavior changes in counseling. J. Consult. Psychol. 13:190-195, 1949.
31. Kauffman, P. E. and Raimy, V. C.: Two methods of assessing therapeutic progress. J. Abnorm. & Soc. Psychol. 44:379-385, 1949.
32. Krech, D. and Crutchfield, R. S.: Theory and Problems of Social Psychology. New York, McGraw-Hill, 1948.
33. Krugman, J. I.: A clinical validation of the Rorschach with problem children. Rorschach Res. Exch. 6:61-70, 1942.
34. Lewis, D. and Burke, C. J.: The use and misuse of the chi-square test. Psychol. Bull. 46: 433-489, 1949.
35. Lipkin, S.: The client evaluates nondirective therapy. J. Consult. Psychol. 12: 137-146, 1948.
36. Lurie, W. and Weiss, A.: Analyzing vocational adjustment. Occupations. 20:1-5,1942.
37. MacKinnon, D. W.: Clinical practice and personality: A symposium. II. Psychodiagnosis in clinical practice and personality. J. Abnorm. & Soc. Psychol. 44: 7-13, 1949.
38. Muench, G. A.: An evaluation of non-directive psychotherapy by means of the Rorschach and other tests. Appl. Psychol. Monogr. No. 13, 1947.
39. Munroe, R. L.: Prediction of the adjustment and academic performance of college students by a modification of the Rorschach method. Appl. Psychol. Monogr. No. 7, 1945.
40. Pacella, B., Piotrowski, Z., and Lewis, N. D. C.: The effects of electroconvulsive therapy on certain personality traits in psychiatric patients. Am. J. Psychiat. 104: 83-91, 1947.
41. Porter, E. H., Jr.: The development and evaluation of a measure of counseling interview procedures. I. The development. Educational & Psychological Measurement. 3: 105-126, 1943.
42. ——: The development and evaluation of a measure of counseling interview procedures. II. The evaluation. Educational & Psychological Measurement. 3: 215-238, 1943.
43. Postman, L. and Bruner, J. S.: Perception under stress. Psychol. Rev. 55: 314-323, 1948.
44. ——, ——, and McGinnies, E.: Personal values as selective factors in perception. J. Abnorm & Soc. Psychol. 2: 142-154, 1948.
45. Ramzy, I. and Pickard, P. M.: A study in the reliability of scoring the Rorschach ink blot test. J. Gen. Psychol. 40:3-10, 1949.
46. Reich, W.: The Function of the Orgasm. New York, Orgone Institute Press, 1942.
47. Reik, T.: Listening with the Third Ear. New York, Farrar, Straus & Co., 1948.
48. Roe, A.: Integration of personality theory and clinical practice. J. Abnorm. & Soc. Psychol. 44: 36-41, 1949.
49. Rogers, C. R.: Counseling and Psychotherapy. New York, Houghton Mifflin, 1942.
50: ——: Some observations on the organization of personality. Am. Psychologist. 2: 358-368, 1947.
51. ——: The attitude and orientation of the counselor in client-centered therapy. J. Consult. Psychol. 3: 82-94, 1949.

52. Rosen, J. N.: The treatment of schizophrenic psychosis by direct analytic therapy. Psychiatric Quart. 21:3-37, 1947.
53. Rotter, J. B.: Studies in the use and validity of the T. A. T. with mentally disordered patients. I. Methods of analysis and clinical problems. Charac. & Pers. 9: 18-34, 1940.
54. Sachs, H.: Observations of a training analyst. Psychoanalyt. Quart 16: 157-168, 1947.
55. Schafer, R.: On the objective and subjective aspects of diagnostic testing. J. Consult. Psychol. 12: 4-7, 1948.
56. Schmideberg, M.: The fear of getting well. Psychoanalyt. Rev. 35:185-187, 1948.
57. Seeman, J.: The process of nondirective therapy. J. Consult. Psychol. 13:157-168, 1949.
58. Sheerer, E. T.: The relationship between acceptance of self and acceptance of others. J. Consult. Psychol. 13: 169-175, 1949.
59. Shneidman, E. S.: Some comparisons among the Four Picture Test, Thematic Apperception Test, and Make a Picture Story Test. Rorschach Res. Exch. 13: 150-154, 1949.
60. Siegel, M. G.: The diagnostic and prognostic validity of the Rorschach test in a child guidance clinic. Am. J. Orthopsychiat. 18: 119-133, 1948.
61. Snyder, W. U.: A comparison of one unsuccessful with four successful non-directively counseled cases. J. Consult. Psychol. 11: 38-42, 1947.
62. ——: An investigation of the nature of non-directive psychotherapy. J. Gen. Psychol. 33: 193-224, 1945.
63. Stein, M. I.: Personality factors involved in the temporal development of Rorschach responses. Rorschach Res. Exch. 13: 355-414, 1949.
64. Stekel, W.: Interpretation of Dreams. Vol. I. New York, Liveright, 1943.
65. Stock, D.: The self concept and feelings toward others. J. Consult. Psychol. 13: 176-180, 1949.
66. Taft, J.: The Dynamics of Therapy in a Controlled Relationship. New York, Macmillan, 1933.
67. Taylor, J. A. and Von Salzen, C. F.: Prognosis in dementia praecox. Psychiatric Quart. 12: 576-582, 1938.
68. Thornton, G. R. and Guilford, J. P.: The reliability and meaning of Erlebnistypus scores on the Rorschach test. J. Abnorm. & Soc. Psychol. 31: 324-330, 1936.
69. Thurstone, L. L. The Rorschach in psychological science. J. Abnorm. & Soc. Psychol. 4: 471-475, 1948
70. Watson, G., Adler, A., Allen F. H., Bertine, E., Chassell, J. O., Rogers, C. R., Rosenzweig, S., and Waelder, R.: Areas of agreement in psychotherapy. Am. J. Orthopsychiat. 10: 698-709, 1940.
71. Webb, W. B.: Some considerations concerning the use of statistics in abnormal psychology. J. Gen. Psychol. 40: 95-102, 1949.
72. Weingarten, E. M.: A study of selective perception in clinical judgment. J. Personality. 17: 369-406, 1949.
73. Williams, M.: An experimental study of intellectual control under stress and associated Rorschach factors. J. Consult. Psychol. 11: 21-29, 1947.
74. Zubin, J.: Personality research and psychopathology as related to clinical practice. J. Abnorm. & Soc. Psychol. 44: 14-21, 1949.

Patient-Therapist Relationship in Multiple Psychotherapy. I*

Its Advantages to the Therapist

Multiple psychotherapy has been defined by Dreikurs as "all forms of therapy where several therapists treat a single patient simultaneously (1)." Perhaps the earliest use of the method was in Adler's child guidance clinics in Vienna where, beginning in the early 20's, Adler used the method for its therapeutic effectiveness. Children responded, when their problems were discussed sympathetically in front of them, sometimes better than they did when the discussion was directed to them (2). A technique called the "joint interview" was developed in a hospital clinic in Cleveland by Reeve (3). Reeve started this procedure for teaching purposes for social workers, but soon perceived its value as a therapeutic method. Adults responded with an acceleration and expansion of therapeutic progress. Hadden describes the use of multiple psychotherapy for teaching purposes (4). Whitaker et. al. successfully used the technique of bringing in a second therapist to handle the psychotherapeutic impasse (5). Haigh and Kell mention that there is a therapeutic advantage in the use of this method, but in their study were interested in its value for training and research (6).

The purpose of this paper is to show how the technique of multiple psychotherapy is of special advantage to the therapists in their treatment of the patient. A subsequent paper will show what the advantages are to the patient when this technique is utilized.

At the present time, the writers' general procedure is as follows: The patient is seen at his first interview by one of the therapists, usually the senior psychiatrist. He assigns the patient to another therapist and continues as consultant therapist. The second therapist now becomes the active therapist and starts by investigating the patient's early

---

*Reprinted by permission from THE PSYCHIATRIC QUARTERLY, 1952, 26, 219-227.

childhood, the formative period of life. The writers have found this method useful in overcoming resistance to the introduction of a second therapist, since its similarity to a referral for a laboratory or psychological work-up is understandable to the patient. Collecting the necessary information usually requires two interviews, during which a good therapeutic relationship with the patient is established. The first multiple interview then takes place. In this session, both therapists discuss the significance of the material that has been obtained, using care and good sense in the interpretations offered to the patient. The patient mostly listens but is encouraged to participate. The active therapist then continues with the patient, according to a therapeutic plan which evolves in each multiple interview. Frequent multiple interviews are scheduled regularly, ranging from every alternate interview to every fourth or fifth, depending upon the requirements of the therapeutic situation. Sometimes it is helpful to have several consecutive multiple interviews, and sometimes it is helpful for the active and consultant therapists to switch roles. The techniques used and relationships developed are described more fully by Dreikurs (1).

The writers have found multiple psychotherapy to be of value to the therapist in the following ways.

I

Multiple psychotherapy has the obvious advantage of offering the opportunity of constant consultation between two therapists. The therapists can be more sure of their accuracy in diagnosis, interpretation, and choice of procedure. There is constant opportunity to check one's work with patients. This is invaluable for all therapists no matter what the extent of their experience. The consultant therapist can always bring a new, and perhaps corrective, perspective into the therapeutic situation, regardless of whether he is more or less experienced than the active therapist. Multiple psychotherapy is therapeutic teamwork. Its advantages can be seen in the following example:

Patient A. was the younger of two sons. He was ambitious but discouraged at his inability to live up to his high ideals. He had strong feelings of inadequacy in relation to his brother who was a success by conventional standards. The patient had compensated for his feelings of inadequacy by developing higher moral and intellectual standards which, he felt, made him superior to his brother. He made rapid progress in the early stages of therapy, began to work enthusiastically, improved his relationship within the family and was having dreams in which he was successful and aggressive. Progress stopped, although neither patient nor active therapist knew why. In the multiple interview, the consultant recognized something the active therapist had missed. The patient had made progress because he had stopped trying to live up to his "ideal image," but he had not relinquished his assumption that he was inferior. Progress began again after this interview.

II

Individual psychotherapy takes place in an artificial atmosphere which may permit the patient to adjust to the limited relationship with one person, often through an emotional involvement. The introduction of a third person upsets this equilibrium and may result in the patient's revealing more of his natural reactions. This permits both therapists to evaluate the patient's attitudes and progress. Patients sometimes remain on very good behavior through a desire to please the active therapist. The presence of the second therapist is often disturbing enough to the structure of the situation so that the patient is more likely to exhibit more fully his disturbed relationships with people. Example:

Patient B. was the baby in her family. Being unsure of her own strength she was exceedingly dependent on other people for approval. She was in her late 20's and rather attractive. She had been dating a man for several years. She felt she did not like him well enough to marry him, but could not bear to hurt his feelings by letting him down. In therapy she had difficulty in verbalizing, since she was never sure of the therapist's reaction to what she might say. She was "making progress" in therapy, trying to behave the way she felt the therapist wanted her to. In one of the multiple interviews, the two therapists disagreed on a minor point, and as is their custom, asked the patient to state her opinion. The patient was completely blocked and confused. It was then pointed out to her that she could not talk for fear of displeasing one or the other of the therapists. She could see that the therapists could disagree without hurting each other's feelings, but her single, and typical, response was an apology for not being able to say anything. This incident provided the patient with a dramatic experience and permitted her to recognize more fully her faulty attitude.

III

When a therapeutic impasse arises because of the patient's strong resistance or because the therapist has inadvertently gone up a blind alley or fallen into a non-productive rut, the multiple interviews offer a fresh approach, a disruption of a relationship which has become too rigidly set, a reconsideration of issues, and, if necessary, a switch in therapists.

Patient C. suffered from feelings of personal inadequacy in any situation in which he could not maintain a position of superiority. After first making progress and improving his personal relationships, he became depressed. At a multiple interview, both the patient and the consultant therapist recognized the sibling rivalry that the patient felt to the active therapist, who was the same age as the patient. The consultant therapist was able to clear the air, and, by taking over the role of active therapist, continued to work with the patient until his antagonism was dissipated and he no longer felt that he had to be "more intelligent" than the active therapist, whom he identified with a younger sibling.

IV

Many patients are adept enough to put the therapist into their own service, a performance which is often interpreted as countertransference. They thus trick the therapist into confirming their own opinions of themselves, while the therapist is trying to help the patient change these self-concepts. To successfully understand and treat the patient, the therapist must understand the "private logic" by which the patient actually operates, as opposed to the common sense which he consciously thinks he is using (7). When a therapist has "fallen for the patient's trick," the multiple interview is often effective in bringing about recognition and correction of this situation.

Patient D., an only child of overprotective and demanding parents, was constantly making a mess of his jobs, his friendships, and his marriage. His interviews usually consisted of a dissertation on the disappointments and failures that he knew he had brought about himself. The active therapist would patiently point out the meaning of his behavior, and how it followed logically from his concept of himself as a person who had no chance in life and who could find glory only in catastrophe. In a multiple interview, the consultant therapist saw that the patient had succeeded in provoking the active therapist into telling the patient what he was doing that was wrong. The patient had utilized the therapist's responses as further evidence that he was "a guy who couldn't do anything right" and who was "doomed to failure."

V

Even didactic analysis—of whatever kind—does not completely remove a therapist's bias and emotional blocking; and his strong desire for a patient to get well, or his need to impress a patient (other forms of countertransference) often interfere with what is therapeutically better indicated. Whenever the therapist becomes emotionally involved with the patient for his own satisfaction, the consultant therapist helps to solve this difficulty through the multiple interview, or through taking over the role of active therapist.

Patient E. was a depressed young woman who was extremely ambitious and felt "stupid" in spite of her above average accomplishments in her own profession. She could stand no criticism from her husband, responding to his slightest remark with feelings of inferiority and consequent angry outbursts. Her competitiveness with men extended itself to the active therapist, who reacted by feeling irritated by the patient and being disinclined to work with her. The consultant therapist could show the active therapist the nature of his reactions, and the therapists switched roles. The former active therapist, now in the role of consultant, no longer responded to the rejection by the patient, and the therapy could proceed.

One important element in disrupting the emotional involvement of the therapist is that in the multiple interview the casual and objective discussion of the patient's problems almost always clears the air and provides a more impersonal atmosphere for any active therapist who has become overprotective, oversympathetic or hostile.

VI

One of the chief values of multiple psychotherapy is found in the numerous opportunities it offers the therapists to play different roles in relation to the patient. Through watching how another therapist meets a situation, the therapist's own vista is broadened, and he can grow through the experiences of another therapist. It is a reciprocal process, in which even a more experienced therapist can benefit from the fresh view of a younger man.

In the multiple interviews the therapists can provide a variety of experiences for the patient. One therapist can be more directive, another more non-directive; one may be forceful, the other permissive. A special type of situation is one in which one therapist actively interprets to the patient the meaning of his actions, while the second therapist "argues" from the point of view of the patient's "private logic" (7) as if trying to disprove what the first therapist has stated, or as if making the excuse that the patient himself has made. In such a situation, the patient often recognizes his own faulty perception as he sees the therapist using his own mechanisms.

Patient F. was an overprotected child who had felt rejected by her parents and especially by her father. With a permissive and supportive therapist she made very slow progress in gaining insight into the nature of her depressions. The consultant therapist, on the other hand, would make pointed interpretations of the patient's own dynamics, to which the patient reacted with strong resentment and depression. She would have discontinued therapy but for her relationship to the permissive active therapist. The latter refrained from making the interpretations which might be upsetting to the patient. Within this structure, the patient utilized the relationship with the active therapist to work out her reactions to the consultant therapist and to assimilate eventually his evaluation of the dynamics involved.

VII

A patient who refuses to accept an interpretation is more likely to consider it if he finds that a team of therapists in open discussion agree on this same point. His reliance on authority is thus more related to *people* than to a single *person*.

Patient G., a successful business man, was having marital difficulties. He did not see that his rigid critical attitude and assumption of righteousness were significant disturbing factors in the marital relationship. He did not at first believe that what he called "facts" were his own biased perceptions. When, in a multiple interview, both therapists concurred on this point, the patient was impressed enough by the similar and mutually supplementing opinions to consider that perhaps the "facts" were not as he saw them.

VIII

Multiple psychotherapy facilitates termination. The constant inclusion of the second therapist prevents too dependent a relationship on one therapist and makes it easier for the patient to carry over his newly found relationship to people other than the therapists. The consultant therapist may, moreover, see aspects of progress or lack of progress that the active therapist has overlooked because of his more intense relationship.

Patient H. had been a pampered child who was hampered by his own self-indulgence. He made considerable progress in therapy, changing and improving his attitude and actions. However, he continued to suffer from mild depressions which prevented him from functioning at his to-be-expected level. The consultant therapist saw that the patient was actually prepared to meet his problems on his own, but preferred to use the excuse of being in therapy to avoid unpleasant tasks and situations. A time was then agreed upon with the patient which was to mark the end of his self-indulgence, and the rest of the interviews were spent in summarizing the dynamics and progress of the therapy. After discharge the patient was able to rely on himself adequately.

IX

For reasons already cited, multiple psychotherapy makes it easier for the patient to accept group therapy at the therapist's request, since he has already had the experience of having therapy with more than one person.

X

Multiple psychotherapy is an invaluable teaching and research method. The reasons for this are obvious. Its use opens new possibilities for investigation into the nature and technique of psychotherapy.

* * *

Both Reeve (3) and Dreikurs (1) point out that preparation of the patient for multiple psychotherapy is less difficult than anticipated, if it is carefully explained to the patient that this is a regular therapeutic procedure, and if the therapist himself is convinced of the value of the method. When this is done at the beginning of therapy, the resistance encountered is negligible; if individual therapy has been carried on for some time, an attempt to introduce a second therapist may meet objection.

The writers have noticed that the chief difficulty which arises in multiple psychotherapy is in regard to the relation the therapists have to each other. Multiple psychotherapy requires a complete lack of competition between the therapists. Each therapist should be on guard for an antagonistic attitude by the patient to the other therapist, so that such feelings may be dealt with at an early stage. Antagonism to one therapist is sometimes expressed by excessive praising of the other therapist. If the junior of a therapeutic team has problems in relation to authority (either in pleasing or in fighting the senior therapist), or if the senior feels it necessary to maintain his prestige, the therapists will not be able to work well with each other. Incidental resentments may be carried over into the multiple interview with resulting loss of effectiveness. It is also important for each therapist to refrain from pressing the other into giving opinions or interpretations before the latter is prepared to do so; and each one should be careful not to push the other into any particular role which may hamper his freedom of action. The two therapists should be able to speak in front of the patient freely, neither being afraid to make mistakes. This freedom of expression which the therapists display is helpful to the patient.

Summary

The following advantages have been found in multiple psychotherapy:

1. The use of two therapists offers the benefit of their combined knowledge and experience.

2. The multiple interview may reveal more of the patient's personality than the individual interview.

3. The consultant therapist is useful in preventing or breaking up the therapeutic impasse.

4. The use of two therapists hinders either therapist from falling into the patient's service.

5. The use of two therapists hinders development of countertransference.

6. Multiple psychotherapy offers the therapists more opportunity to manipulate the relationship and provide therapeutic experiences for the patient.

7. Interpretations given by one therapist are reinforced by the concurring interpretations of the second therapist.

8. Multiple psychotherapy facilitates termination of therapy.

9. Introduction of the patient to group therapy is facilitated.

10. Multiple psychotherapy's implications in the fields of teaching and research are obvious.

Some precautions in using multiple psychotherapy are discussed.

When multiple psychotherapy is compared with individual psychotherapy, the former shows significant advantages in facilitating therapy and in decreasing the chances of error.

REFERENCES

1. Dreikurs, Rudolf: Techniques and dynamics of multiple psychotherapy. PSYCHIAT. QUART., 24:788, 1950.
2. Adler, Alfred and associates: Guiding the Child. Greenberg Publishers. New York. 1930.
3. Reeve, George H.: A method of coordinated treatment. Am. J. Orthopsychiat., 9:743, 1939.
4. Hadden, Samuel B.: The utilization of a therapy group in teaching psychotherapy. Am. J. Psychiat., 103:644, 1947.
5. Whitaker, Carl A.: Warkentin, John; and Johnson, Nan: The psychotherapeutic impasse. Unpublished paper read at the 26th annual meeting of the American Orthopsychiatric association, Chicago, 1949.
6. Haigh, Gerard, and Kell, Bill L.: Multiple therapy as a method for training and research in psychotherapy. J. Abnor. and Soc. Psychol., 45:659, 1950.
7. Dreikurs, Rudolf: Psychological differentiation of psychopathological disorders. Indiv. Psych. Bull., 4:35, 1944.

Patient-Therapist Relationship in Multiple Psychotherapy. II*

Its Advantages for the Patient

Multiple psychotherapy as a routine method of treatment is of very recent vintage. The term itself was first used by Dreikurs to designate a specific type of therapeutic relationship in which more than one therapist treated a patient simultaneously (1). The technique had been used previously for training purposes (2), to resolve certain types of difficulties in treatment (3), and subsequently as a method of research (4), but not as an established procedure in office practice. A recent paper by the writers describes the advantages accruing to the therapists using the multiple approach (5). The present paper will be devoted to discussing the value of multiple psychotherapy for the patient undergoing treatment.

Contrary to expectation, the writers have found that their patients accept multiple therapy very easily. At first, many are reluctant and others somewhat suspicious. The best way to overcome this resistance is to start multiple therapy immediately by establishing the roles of the two therapists at the beginning of treatment. The writers' findings are that once the patient has experienced the technique, he sees its value and accepts the approach. In fact, many patients express satisfaction that more than one person is concerned with their welfare. They feel that they are receiving more service and more variety. Multiple therapy, moreover, prevents the patient from feeling misunderstood or abused by one therapist, in that he can always discuss such apprehensions and feelings in the "multiple session." He is, consequently, less fearful of antagonizing the therapist and can "open up" with a greater feeling of security.

This discussion of values for the patient might be prefaced by pointing out that anything which helps the therapist possesses the possibility of being beneficial to the patient. Consequently many of the points which were made in the authors'

*Reprinted by permission from THE PSYCHIATRIC QUARTERLY. 1952, 26, 590-596.

previous paper (5) may apply equally here. However, there are, in addition, some aspects of multiple therapy which bear more directly upon the patient.

A.

Patients often enter treatment with the feeling, whether it be expressed or not, that the therapist is or should be a powerful person. He should be both omnipotent and omniscient. They exhibit the feeling that the therapist should, figuratively, wave a magic wand and cure them completely and near-instantly. Many request pills or hypnosis or shock treatment—some quick-acting technique. Many do not necessarily want to learn anything about themselves; they just want alleviation of their symptoms. They often ascribe ideal qualities to the therapist and rebel against the idea that the therapist is ungodlike—a human being who makes mistakes, who also has problems. Such concepts are counteracted when two therapists disagree, for the disagreement destroys the projection of omniscience onto the therapist. It makes, of the therapists, not superior beings (human or otherwise), but human beings with perhaps a superior knowledge of psychological dynamics, who are interested in helping the patient to arrive at a new understanding of himself with a subsequent reorientation in his behavior.

B.

True learning is an *experience* rather than a mere *accumulation* of "facts" (6). This experience is provided by multiple therapy in various ways. It permits the introduction of two personalities with two different approaches to whom the patient can react and with whom he can interact. In this fashion, he learns to modify his expectation about people. His fallacious perceptions of social interaction can be pointed out and evaluated on the spot. He can work out his own interpersonal conflicts in his interaction with the therapists. For example, the writers have observed situations in which the patient works out his attitudes toward authority by making the senior psychiatrist a father figure and by, simultaneously, attempting to set up a sibling rivalry situation with the junior therapist. The expansion of therapeutic roles can thus aid materially in the resolution of certain prominent conflicts which trace their origin to the formative years of family life.

Patient A. was the older of two brothers. His father was physically weak, a poor provider, who played a subordinate role in the family. While the younger brother resembled the father, the patient was able to overrun him, being the confidant and helper of mother, and assuming a protective attitude toward his brother. He was in competition with all men he encountered, trying to elevate himself above them. In therapy, he rebelled against the senior therapist whom he put in the role of his father, and was constantly surprised to find himself unable to push him down. The junior therapist was cast in the role of the brother, with the patient attempting to remain one step ahead and resenting the therapist when the latter could hold his own.

The introduction of fresh viewpoints keeps the therapy from getting into a rut and allows the patient to select, to compare, and to assess the material that is discussed in his presence. In fact, even such a simple procedure as one therapist's rephrasing of the other therapist's remarks can make the material more understandable, and, consequently, more acceptable to the patient. The patient may gain new insights from the "correction" of one therapist by the other, as has been pointed out previously. Certainly, the probability of interpretations being accepted is greater when one therapist independently validates the opinion of the other.

Further, multiple therapy permits the patient to be both spectator and participant. He can be the subject of the discussion and at the same time a more objective viewer of the proceedings. One patient described it as "like watching a ping pong game, only you're the ping pong ball." The patient can observe one of the therapists, for example, play his (the patient's) role and evaluate himself without becoming so emotionally involved that he cannot assess his behavior accurately. It is not implied here, however, that this lack of emotional involvement does not permit a corrective emotional experience for the patient. Much of his own resistance is minimized, since he can perceive the purpose of his resistance in the playing of roles by the two therapists.

Patient B., a college senior, an only child, who became discouraged in his efforts "to be a genius," had become thoroughly pessimistic during his senior year in college, when he was confronted with the intense competition and the uncertainty of his future. However, he was unable to recognize the defeatist and pessimistic attitude he had assumed. During a multiple interview, the active therapist assumed the patient's role and "argued" with the consultant, using all of the patient's rationalizations which seemed to justify his defeatism, while the consulting therapist offered interpretation of the actual motives involved. The patient became able to recognize his motives and his reluctance to participate in life, and became aware of his own resistance against facing his actual and unfounded attitudes. This was a turning point in his development of better social orientation and of an increased ability to function in school.

C.

In individual therapy, should patient and therapist not "hit it off," the patient may become discouraged sufficiently to terminate therapy. This occurs less frequently in multiple therapy, since the introduction of a second therapist permits resistances to be analyzed more easily in the multiple sessions before they attain this magnitude. In the event that resistance becomes so great, all such efforts notwithstanding, that the patient's hostility or distrust prevents positive movement in therapy, the patient can be transferred to the other therapist without feeling rejected or discouraged, or feeling that he has to start all over again.

D.

Dependency, as a factor in therapy, provides many crucial problems for the therapist. These dependency problems require solution throughout the several phases of treatment. In the initial phases, the problem for the therapist revolves about the necessity of helping the patient recognize his own responsibilities in therapy. The patient, on the other hand, partly due to his own neurosis and partly because of a cultural pattern which proclaims that the "doctor knows best," seeks to rely on the therapist and to be cured by him. During the middle stages of therapy, the patient may vacillate between dependence and rebellion against it; and even the shrewdest therapist occasionally becomes ensnared in the cleverly-set traps of the patient. In the final phases of therapy, the problem of termination become prominent. Here the patient must become convinced that he is "graduating" and not being "expelled," that he is ready to meet the world on his own. He must come to realize that, while he and the therapist have been participants in a good relationship, he can now stand by himself.

Multiple therapy facilitates the resolution of these dependency problems. The "doctor knows best" attitude may be discouraged very early, when detected, by a discussion of this attitude by both therapists. It may be pointed out that while the therapist possesses certain professional skills, the patient will play a major role in the therapy; and he comes to assume some responsibility for his own therapeutic growth through his participation in the discussion.

When dependence upon the therapist is intensified in the middle stages of therapy, multiple discussions may serve to dissolve this impasse to further therapy. In fact, since the patient deals at the start with two therapists, dependence upon a single person is immediately eliminated. It may be indicated to the patient that he need not rely on any single person, that he can consider "going it alone." The patient may thus be guided from an attitude of dependence to one of interdependence. The writers have found special merit for their method in dealing with those intense emotional reactions to the therapist which are often called transference attitudes. Here, by shifting to the "neutral" therapist, these attitudes may be uncovered and faced by the patient with a minimum of fear or guilt. They may be carefully analyzed and interpreted and the transference dissolved.

Patient C. reached a point in therapy where she seemed unable to communicate with the therapist. She felt she was in love with him but felt guilty for having such feelings. After confessing this love to the therapist, she reacted with shame which, in turn, provided another barrier to communication. She had a number of interviews with the consulting therapist, during which she realized that her attitude toward the active therapist was merely a repetition of her attitude toward her father. After this problem was worked out, she was again able to communicate with the active therapist.

Should the active therapist become ill or take a vacation, the patient's dependency needs are less apt to lead to feelings of "desertion." The absence of the therapist merely means that the patient will be consulting with the other therapist for a longer time than usual.

Since all of these emotional attachments can be analyzed and clarified and viewed with proper perspective, termination can be more easily accepted by the patient. Undoubtedly, there may be some regrets about giving up therapy and some experiencing of doubt about functioning on his own. Nevertheless, the "break" is smoother, for his attachment is to the *situation* rather than to an *individual*. While he cannot carry the therapist with him when he leaves, he can still take with him much of what he has learned in the therapeutic experience.

Patient D. had reached the stage in treatment where he understood the basic motivational patterns in his behavior. When he recognized this during a multiple interview, he was asked how much longer he was going to indulge himself in his emotional dependence upon the active therapist. The patient immediately saw that he was now using his relationship with the active therapist chiefly for self-indulgent gratification. He consequently set his own termination date for the near future.

E.

Finally, the interaction of the therapists provides a social situation of paramount importance. It shows the patient a good human relationship where two individuals can and do have an interpersonal relationship based upon mutual respect. He can observe the co-operation of two individuals, a co-operation which transcends competitiveness, "power politics," and prestige-seeking. He can see how this co-operation can exist even when the therapists disagree; and, above all, he may learn that one can be wrong without loss of status. This lesson may indeed be of more far-reaching significance for the patient's reorientation than any interpretations referring to his mistaken assumption that to err implies inadequacy or failure.

This procedure has implications beyond individual improvement. It affects the cultural pattern to which the patient has succumbed when he assumes that deficiency is degrading in our contemporary competitive culture. This therapeutic procedure exemplifies democracy in action.

SUMMARY

In a previous paper (5), the writers discussed the advantages of multiple psychotherapy for the therapist. The present paper discusses the advantages for the patient. Briefly these may be summarized as follows:

1. Multiple therapy creates an atmosphere which facilitates learning.

2. The patient can interact with two different personalities with two different approaches.

3. Therapeutic impasses are avoided by the introduction of fresh viewpoints, thus accelerating the therapy.

4. The patient may view himself more objectively, since he is both spectator and participant.

5. In the event that the therapist and patient do not "hit it off," the patient does not become a therapeutic "casualty" and is merely transferred to the second therapist.

6. The many problems related to dependency in treatment are solved more easily. These include the responsibility for the self, absence of the therapist, transference reactions, and termination.

7. Multiple therapy is an example of democratic social interaction and is thus a valuable lesson for the patient.

REFERENCES

1. Dreikurs, Rudolf: Techniques and dynamics of multiple psychotherapy. PSYCHIAT. QUART., 24:4, 788, 1950.
2. Reeve, George H.: A method of co-ordinated treatment. Am. J. Orthopsychiat., 9:743, 1939.
3. Whitaker, Carl A.: Warkentin, John; and Johnson, Nan: The psychotherapeutic impasse. Unpublished paper read at the 26th annual meeting of the American Orthopsychiatric Association, Chicago, 1949.
4. Haigh, Gerard, and Kell, Bill L.: Multiple therapy as a method for training and research in psychotherapy. J. Abnor. and Soc. Psychol., 45:659, 1950.
5. Dreikurs, Rudolf; Shulman, Bernard H.: and Mosak, Harold: Patient-therapist relationship in multiple psychotherapy. I. Its advantages for the therapist. PSYCHIAT. QUART., 26:2, 219, 1952.
6. Cantor, Nathaniel: The Dynamics of Learning. Foster & Stewart. Buffalo. 1946.

The Psychological Attitude in Rehabilitation*

One day a patient of mine was bewailing her fate—a long nose which she maintained restricted her social participation and made her unattractive to men. As she spoke there flashed to mind the name of Jimmy Durante who, with the same physical handicap, had achieved a position of national prominence and public acclaim. Other names—Franklin D. Roosevelt, Helen Keller, Beethoven, Steinmetz, Edison—joined this mental procession and confirmed a fundamental thesis long held that there is no necessary correlation between actual inferiority and inferiority feelings. In each instance what is more important than the nature and extent of a handicap is the individual's attitude toward his handicap and the use he makes of it. He may with courage face the tasks of social living or, feeling inferior, he may retreat, become hostile to the world, put others into his service or feel sorry for himself and thus avoid social participation.

Since the inferiority feeling is the basis for the individual's compensation or withdrawal, let us examine how the inferiority feeling develops. I should like to elaborate upon the concept life style. This is a group of attitudes which may be categorized as follows:[1]

1. The first component of the life style is the self concept which includes all attitudes referrable to the self, e.g. "I am intelligent," "I am a real man," "I like Mozart," "I am conservative," "I am attractive," "I generally do the right thing."

2. A second group of attitudes comprises all of the things which the individual feels he should be or do or like and is known as the self ideal. The discrepancy between the self concept (what the individual *feels* he is) and the self ideal (what the individual *feels* he should be) is the inferiority feeling.

---

[1]This discussion is an extension of a classification made by Coleman, J.C. *Abnormal Psychology and Modern Life.* Chicago: Scott, Foresman & Co., 1950

*Reprinted by permission from AMERICAN ARCHIVES REHABILITATION THERAPY, 1954, 2, 9-10.

Thus, among the handicapped there are many far less incapacitated than some nonhandicapped individuals who do possess strong inferiority feelings. This discrepancy is expressed in such attitudes as the following:

"I should not be handicapped."

"I should be able to care for myself."

"I should function like a real man."

"I should support my family."

"I should not have been so stupid (or careless or reckless) as to have incurred my injury."

3. Each individual also has an environmental evaluation, a group of attitudes which describes how the individual sizes up the world and people. The discrepancy between the individual's self concept and his environmental evaluation is again the inferiority feeling, e.g.

"It's a dog eat dog world—and I'm the dog that gets eaten."

"People are out for themselves and no one cares for me."

"Nobody wants a cripple."

"All they'd have for me is pity."

4. Finally, each individual has his *personal* moral code comprising all of his "right-wrong" attitudes. The discrepancy between the individual's self concept and his moral code, i.e., when an individual does something which he feels is wrong or when he fails to do something which he feels is right, constitutes a special kind of inferiority feeling known as the guilt feeling. This was a commonly observed feeling in the Air Forces among sole surviving members of combat crews who felt guilty that they had not met the fate of the remainder of the crew. Among certain patients with intense religious backgrounds and among others who have drifted from their faiths, one also occasionally discovers the feeling that the injury is punishment visited upon them for their "sins."

All of these inferiority feelings result in a loss of self esteem, a loss of sense of personal worth. And since inferiority feelings always imply a comparison with others, possession of such feelings is coupled with a feeling of social isolation, of not belonging. The goal, then, of any psychological rehabilitation program would be to decrease inferiority feelings or, to put it another way, to increase the individual's feeling of belonging. Is psychotherapy, then, the answer? I think not. While psychotherapy might be advisable, with the current scarcity of trained psychotherapists, psychotherapy for all would hardly be feasible. On the other hand, anything which reduces inferiority feelings is psychotherapeutic and in this sense, every rehabilitation therapist, to the extent that he accomplishes this goal, is a psychotherapeutic agent. The specific techniques the rehabilitation therapist might utilize to achieve this goal are perhaps better known to you than to me. However, all of the techniques are based upon the following psychological attitude—*acceptance of the patient as he is*. This implies no pity for the patient, no looking back for what has been lost but rather a looking forward to what the individual can do with what he has. Overambition on the part of the patient with its resultant defeatism must be diminished. We as therapists must keep in check our tendencies to be overambitious for the patient and not push him into activities which he cannot perform or which are premature. And finally, any rehabilitation program, for that matter any educational program, must be based upon encouragement. We must help the patient overcome his discouragement since a demoralized individual rarely possesses the motivation to learn. Building and restoring faith is often a difficult task. For some patients the reassurance of belonging supplied by clergymen, by family, and by friends may be sufficient; for other patients our acceptance of them as individuals with worth may assist them in accepting themselves as worthwhile individuals. It is this faith in self which makes the crucial difference in whether or not the patient will be rehabilitated.

To summarize, anything which encourages the patient, which gives him the feeling of belonging, which removes his feeling of social isolation, restores his faith in himself, and permits him to accept himself as he is may be considered therapeutic. Techniques which discourage, which permit pity and self pity, and which permit the patient to indulge himself in his feelings of inferiority should be avoided. And, although it was said in another context we must remember that the Good Book does not say,

> "There is none so blind as he who
> *cannot see*" but rather
> "There is none so blind as he who
> *will not* see."

Language and the Interpretation of "Sexual" Symbolism*

In current psychoanalytic practice the interpretation of symbols is accorded two types of treatment. There are those psychoanalysts who believe that certain symbols are fixed symbols while others tend to regard these symbols as possessing meaning only when interpreted in the context of the individual or group using these symbols. Freud advocated the first position in his statement (2, p. 246) that "there are (symbols) which preponderantly, or almost exclusively, designate one of the sexes, and there are yet others which so far as we know, have only the male or only the female signification. To use long, stiff objects and weapons as symbols of the female genitals, or hollow objects (chests, boxes, etc.) as symbols of the male genitals is not permitted by the imagination."

If we were to accept Freud's premise, then we might expect that language, which is also a symbolic form, should bear the stamp of these unconscious processes (4). Consequently a group of symbols to which sexuality has been attributed[1] were translated into three languages—French, Spanish, and German—which designate gender for nouns. Tables 1 and 2 present the translation and the gender designation for each translation of a symbol. In each instance the first applicable dictionary definition was selected.

RESULTS

If Freud's statement is valid we might assume that symbol and gender designations would coincide. From Tables 1 and 2 it is immediately apparent that Freud's contention is not borne out symbolically in language. In French 15 of the 33 "male"

---

[1]The writer selected symbols from Gutheil's list (3) although many other lists of such symbols exist.

*Reprinted by permission from JOURNAL OF CONSULTING PSYCHOLOGY, 1955, 19, 108.

TABLE 1
TRANSLATIONS AND GENDER OF "MASCULINE" SYMBOLS

Symbol	French		Spanish		German	
umbrella	parapluie	m*	parasol	m	Schirm	m
hat	chapeau	m	sombrero	m	Hut	m
necktie	cravate	f	corbata	f	Krawatte	f
sail	voile	f	vela	f	Segel	n
flagpole	hampe du drapeau	f	asta del pabellón	m	Flaggenstange	f
key	clef	f	llave	f	Schluessel	m
fishing pole	canne à pêcher	f	càna de pescar	f	Angelrute	f
fountain pen	plume à reservoir	f	pluma fuente	f	Fuellfederhalter	m
pencil	crayon	m	pincel	m	Bleistift	m
rifle	fusil	m	carabina	f	Gewehr	n
gun	fusil	m	arma de fuego	f	Kanone	f
sword	épée	f	espada	f	Schwert	n
knife	couteau	m	cuchillo	m	Messer	n
arrow	fleche	f	flecha	f	Pfeil	m
pipe	tuyau	m	tubo	m	Rohr	n
syringe	seringue	f	jeringa	f	Spritze	f
tail	queue	f	cola	f	Schwanz	m
squirrel	ecureuil	m	ardilla	f	Eichhoernchen	n
rat	rat	m	rata	f	Ratte	f
fish	poisson	m	pez	m	Fisch	m
bird	oiseau	m	ave	f	Vogel	m
horse	cheval	m	caballo	m	Pferd	n
bull	taureau	m	toro	m	Stier	m
udder	mamelle	f	ubre	f	Euter	n
banana	banane	f	banana	f	Banane	f
pear	poire	f	pera	f	Birne	f
flower	fleur	f	flor	f	Blume	f
finger	doigt	m	dedo	m	Finger	m
nose	nez	m	nariz	f	Nase	f
hair	cheveu	m	cabello	m	Haar	n
arm	bras	m	brazo	m	Arm	m
tooth	dent	f	diente	m	Zahn	m
female breast	sein	m	pecho	m	Brust	f

*m = male; f = female; n = neuter

TABLE 2
TRANSLATIONS AND GENDER OF "FEMININE" SYMBOLS

Symbol	French		Spanish		German	
bag	sac	m*	saco	m	Tasche	f
wound	blessure	f	herida	f	Wunde	f
nest	nid	m	nido	m	Nest	n
cavern	caverne	f	caverna	f	Hoehle	f
ring	bague	f	círculo	m	Ring	m
target	cible	m	rodela	f	Ziel	n
muff	manchon	m	manguito	m	Muff	m
door	porte	f	puerta	f	Tuer	f
window	fenêtre	f	ventana	f	Fenster	n
pot	pot	m	marmita	f	Topf	m
box	boite	f	boj	m	Schachtel	f
cage	cage	f	jaula	f	Kaefig	m
stove	fourneau	m	estufa	f	Herd	m
water pool	étang	m	charco	m	Tuempel	m
boat	bateau	m	bote	m	Boot	n
drawer	tiroir	m	aguador	m	Schublade	f
shell	coque	f	cáscara	f	Schale	f
oyster	huitre	f	ostra	f	Auster	f
kitten	chaton	m	gatillo	m	Kaetschen	n
fig	figue	f	higo	m	Feige	f
peach	pêche	f	melocoton	m	Pfirsich	m
cabbage	chou	m	berza	f	Kohl	m
leaves	feuilles	f	hojas	f	Blaetter	n
rose	rose	f	rosa	f	Rose	f
mouth	bouche	f	boca	f	Muna	m
eyes	yeux	m	ojos	m	Augen	n

*m = male; f = female; n = neuter

57

symbols possess feminine gender while 12 of the 26 "female" symbols are designated by masculine articles. Spanish, which contains common etymological origins with French, assigns feminine articles to 19 "male" symbols and masculine articles to 12 "female" symbols. In German symbol-gender reversals occur for 11 of the "male" symbols and 9 of the "female" symbols. However, since German utilizes a neuter gender, these results are not directly comparable to those given for the Romance languages. It is also interesting to note, in the light of Freud's statement, that the designation of such "long, stiff objects and weapons" as *sword, rifle* and *arrow* as "feminine" and "hollow objects" as *box* as "masculine" is indeed "permitted by the imagination."

No consistency in gender appears for the three languages. In fact, only 21 of the 59 symbols are consistently used with the same gender in all three languages, and of these 21, 8 demonstrate consistent symbol-gender reversals.

DISCUSSION

The entire question of symbolism has always proven stimulating and thought provoking, and in view of its importance in several systems of psychotherapy, is worthy of critical examination. If it were true that certain symbols are fixed and sexual, as many psychoanalysts would maintain, it would follow that language, as another symbolic form, would express this same fixedness and this same sexuality. This our results do not confirm, and we would seriously question whether these symbols are either fixed or sexual. We might further draw the inference that such symbols can only be interpreted with reference to the symbolizing individual or group (5). It might be argued, however, that Freud's theory of symbols was based on his expressed feeling that dreams and dream elements are preponderantly visual images and therefore would not possess parallelism with language symbolism. Freud himself confutes such a possible argument when he uses etymological evidence to corroborate his theory of dream symbolisn (1).

In the area of psychotherapeutic investigation such results as ours confront us with an anomalous condition. For despite lack of theoretical foundation or experimental verification, certain therapeutic techniques may nevertheless prove effective under certain conditions. This effectiveness might even be utilized to demonstrate the validity of the assumptions underlying the use of the technique. In actuality this effectiveness demonstrates no more than the utility of the technique. The ability of the medieval healer to exorcise the devil from the mentally ill was frequently curative but did not establish the presence of the devil. In the framework of psychoanalytic theory, Freud's hypothesis might possess such utility. The presence of so many "sexual" symbols in dreams of analysands, however, is no demonstration of validity but is probably a function of three variables—(a) the analytic framework within which such dreams are interpreted, (b) the biases of the analyst (5), and (c) the ability of patients "trained" in the rules of Freudian interpretation to produce "sexual" symbols and dreams to order (6). For other schools of psychotherapy the theory of fixed, sexual symbols would presumably possess little utility or validity.

Summary

Fifty-nine symbols to which a sexual reference is ascribed were translated into three foreign languages which designate gender for nouns to test Freud's statement concerning fixed, sexual symbols. Symbol-gender reversals occurred sufficiently to warrant questioning Freud's viewpoint.

REFERENCES

1. Freud, S. A general introduction to psycho-analysis. New York: Permabooks, 1953.
2. Freud, S. The interpretation of dreams. New York: Carlton House, 1950.
3. Gutheil, E. The language of the dream. New York: Macmillan, 1939.
4. Hitschmann, E. Sexual symbolism, and typical dreams. In Woods, R. L. (Ed.). The world of dreams. New York: Random House, 1947.
5. Mosak, H. H. and Todd, F. J. Selective perception in the interpretation of symbols. *J. abnorm. soc. Psychol.* 1952, 47, 255-256.
6. Stekel, W. Interpretation of dreams. Vol. I. New York: Liveright, 1943.

Early Recollections as a Projective Technique*

Early recollections have been the subject of psychological interest since G. Stanley Hall (33) published his paper on this topic in 1899. Most of the subsequently published reports have fallen into three categories. The first consists of a group of taxonomic and statistical studies which classify the age of the recollection, the affective character of the memory, and other aspects of the memory content (16, 17, 20, 21, 31, 34, 40, 48, 53). A second group takes as its starting point Freud's views of earliest recollections as screen memories which cover up infantile sexual conflicts or traumata. Freud's early work convinced him that such incidents were repressed but were revealed in disguised form in the patient's early recollections (25, 26, 27). The recollection, then, repressed rather than expressed (10, 13, 14). Investigators in this second group largely restricted themselves to the study of the hedonic tone of the early memories in an attempt to validate the Freudian theory of repression[1]; few attempted to interpret the content dynamically. Rapaport (50) and Zeller (56) have pointed out that most studies in this latter group did not fulfill the conditions for a true test of repression, while Waldfogel (53) indicates that studies which did appear to verify Freudian repression theory contained erroneous interpretations. In the third group are found those students of perception whom Krech (38) labels as the "New Look" psychologists who feel that perception and memory are both related to the individual's frame of reference or attitudinal set, that is, to his personal values and needs (22, 46, 47, 54).

---

[1]Summaries of this body of literature appear in Cason (15), Dudycha and Dudycha (20), Gilbert (30), and Meltzer (39).

*Reprinted by permission from JOURNAL OF PROJECTIVE TECHNIQUES, 1958, 22(3), 302-311. Copyright 1958 by the Society for Projective Techniques and Rorschach Institute, Inc.

Many of the historical antecedents of the last viewpoint can be discovered in the writings of Alfred Adler (2, 3, 4, 5, 6, 7, 8, 9). His followers (1, 10, 11, 12, 14, 18, 24, 28, 29, 36, 41, 42, 43, 44, 45, 52, 55) fall in the third group. Adler differed from Freud in holding that early memories were retained because of a selective factor in memory, and that this selective factor was not repression but rather consistency with the individual's attitudinal frame of reference, the life style. [2] Of the manifold experiences of childhood one only retained at the level of consciousness those few experiences which expressed one's approach to life. These incidents did not mold the individual's future life and therefore could not be regarded as causal incidents. They were neither necessarily traumatic incidents nor innocuous camouflage for such incidents, neither pleasant nor unpleasant, although both could be present in some individual's reported memories. The recollections merely reflected the person's perceptual framework within which he interpreted life's experiences. Adler wrote, "Thus his memories represent his 'Story of My Life'; a story he repeats to himself to warn him or comfort him, to keep him concentrated on his goal, to prepare him, by means of past experiences, to meet the future with an already tested style of action" (9, p. 73). Although Adler anticipated by almost three decades the current interest in the relationship between frame of reference and behavior, his work on early recollections has received scant recognition. Yet an experimental study by Purcell concludes with a "special note. . . of the general support for Adler's views on early memories. Exception was taken only to Adler's opinion concerning the fundamental importance of the very earliest incident an individual can recall" (49, p. 440)[3].

Accepting Adler's assumptions, the earliest recollections could be treated as a projective technique. It should be possible to deduce from them some clues as to how the individual perceives himself in his relationship to his perceived environment.

---

[2]For a more extensive discussion of the Adlerian viewpoint the articles by Ansbacher (10) and Dreikurs (18) are especially valuable.

[3]This exception is clarified in a note by Ansbacher (12).

The earliest recollections, in common with the dream and such projective techniques as free drawings and fingerpainting, have the advantage of being completely unstructured. The individual does not respond to some external stimulus as in the Rorschach or TAT, the properties of which may influence his production. With the exception of the possible influence of the examiner or therapist, the production is influenced only by the individual's perceptual framework which selectively focuses upon the particular memories which he produces.

All memories contain omissions and distortions. The individual colors and distorts, emphasizes and omits, exaggerates and minimizes in accordance with his inner needs. The fact of omission or distortion possesses the same significance as in dream interpretation. The following recollection was elicited from a man who had been raised in a Christian Science home where it was imperative to deny the existence of evil, illness, and death.

ER—My family and two neighbors were sitting around the dining room table. It was a festive occasion. Every one smiling, every one pleased. Father was home.

Interpretation—This is a relatively innocuous account of a pleasant episode as the recollection is reported. However, what is the significance of the last sentence? Upon further inquiry the subject recalled that his father had just returned home from the sanitarium. While the subject in adulthood had broken with this childhood faith, the recollection indicated his still present involvement in his religious precepts and the need not to recognize the existence of illness.

Several studies have attempted to verify the accuracy of the incidents which the respondents related. From our experience, whether the recollection is accurate or not is not germane in interpretation. The significance of the recollection lies in the fact that it has been remembered or thought to be so. As Bartlett (13) suggests, remembering is more a process of construction than one of reproduction. Our experience has indicated that recollections range from what are obvious fabrications, although rarely deliberate lies, to rather accurate portrayals of situations.

Adler recounts one of his recollections which he discovered to be completely fictitious but which reflects "my longing to overcome death" and is consistent with his choice of profession.

Shortly after I went to a board school. I remember that the path to the school led over a cemetery. I was frightened every time and was exceedingly put out at beholding the other children pass the cemetery without paying the least attention to it, while every step I took was accompanied by a feeling of fear and horror. Apart from the extreme discomfort occasioned by this fear I was also annoyed at the idea of being less courageous than the others. One day I made up my mind to put an end to this fear of death. Again (as on my first resolve), I *decided upon a treatment of hardening.* (Proximity of death!) I stayed at some distance behind the others, placed my schoolbag on the ground near the wall of the cemetery and ran across it a dozen times, until I felt that I had mastered the fear (4, pp. 179-180).

In exchanging reminiscences with a schoolmate when he was in his mid-thirties, Adler discovered that such a cemetery had never existed and other acquaintances corroborated this information. Two other fictional memories in which subjects describe their births may be found in Adler (7) and Hadfield (32). "Recollections" which others have told the respondent may not be interpreted as recollections. If the subject can visualize the incident, it is interpretable; if he proves unable to do so, the incident is not treated as a recollection.

Assuming the consistency of the self as a frame of reference, the memories, since they reflect the self concept, should all be consistent with each other. This does not imply that each memory will convey exactly the same meaning as every other memory produced by the subject (12). As with other projective techniques, interpretations from recollections will supplement, complement, and elaborate upon each other. Thus, the early recollections may be regarded, as personality is, as theme and variations. As Plewa says, "It is not always easy to extract the entire content of a recollection. One recollection can have so many facets, and it is only when one is able to study an individual for a long time that one notices in him the tendencies to be seen in the recollections with their multitude of variations. Therefore no matter how many interpretations one recollection lends itself to, each of these substantiates the unity of the personality" (44, p. 97). Later recollections in a series may furnish details and specifications for generalized attitudes expressed in earlier recollections. Where contradictions appear in the recollections, they exist only as surface phenomena which can be reconciled interpretatively. The technique of reconciliation will be illustrated in the section below.

THE INTERPRETATION OF EARLY RECOLLECTIONS

The interpretation of early recollections requires a careful distinction between a recollection and a report. Some clinicians ascribe equal significance to memories which report single incidents and to memories which report general occurrences of childhood. For example, the "I remember one time . . . " memory is accorded the same treatment as the "I remember I used to like to read when I was little." For this writer the former would be termed a recollection while the latter would be regarded as a report. A recollection pertains to a single incident which can be reduced to a "one time" format while the report cannot (18). The recollection, therefore, generally contains more specific detail than is possible in the report and is similar to a TAT story. Second, the recollection can be visualized, whereas the report cannot since it involves a collection of incidents whose individuality has been lost. Frequently, in the clinical situation, in order to verify that the subject is producing a recollection rather than a report, we ask him to close his eyes, to visualize the scene, and to report the incident as he visualizes it with all of its details. While reports are clinically significant, we only interpret recollections projectively.

Early recollections may be regarded as a prototype of the individual's fundamental attitudes (6). Consequently, they are first interpreted thematically and second with respect to specific details. In the latter instance enlargement upon the incidents may be requested of the patient. The characters incorporated in the recollection are not treated in interpretation as specific individuals but as prototypes. They represent people or men or women in general or authority figures rather than the specific individuals mentioned. In this respect our interpretation differs from that of Brodsky (14) who uses the memories as a means of reconstructing the subject's interpersonal relationships during his formative years or that of Eisenstein and Ryerson (23) who see the recollections as the "earliest, perhaps clearest, derivative of forgotten infantile conflicts."

> ER—We had a cookie jar on the top shelf in the kitchen. I couldn't reach it by myself, so my uncle lifted me up, and I got the cookie jar.

Interpretation—This memory, given by a woman, is suggestive of a feeling of smallness on her part. In order to get the "goodies" of life, she must rely upon the assistance of bigger people. From a diagnostic viewpoint dependency upon the uncle may be significant. However, the recollection expresses a more generalized dependency feeling either toward all people or with respect to men specifically. Subsequent recollections might inform us which of these two alternatives is more valid. Nevertheless, even were the above incident an isolated occurrence in the subject's life history or perhaps even fictitious with no actual dependency upon the uncle possible, the *retention* of the incident would point to an underlying, generalized feeling of dependency.

While the content of the recollection is given primary consideration, a sequential analysis provides a more rounded picture of the individual, adding some nuances of the personality. In any event, the diagnosis of the self-concept from a single recollection is extremely hazardous. Generalization from a single case is as unreliable here as in other logical and scientific endeavors. The second recollection given by the woman who reported the cookie jar incident demonstrates the additions which sequential analysis makes to the personality picture.

ER—I was sitting on top of a fence. Suddenly I lost my balance, fell off, and broke my jaw.

Interpretation—In the first recollection the patient describes her dependency upon others, especially men. In the above she describes what happens if she relies upon herself. Only disaster can ensue; she cannot stay "on top." This woman felt that she could only be elevated, "lifted up," by a man, and she married one who gave her status and material possessions, the "goodies." When her husband left her and deprived her of her status and his strength, she could not bear living alone and made a suicidal attempt.

We have already mentioned that when apparent contradictions occur, they must be understood in their total context. Occasionally the contradiction merely states that under a certain set of conditions, actual or perceived, the individual will respond in one manner and to another set of circumstances in a second way. An illustration of this type of "contradiction" appears in the following recollections of an adult woman.

ER—I remember that I was under three and the lady next door picked me up over the fence to take me home.

ER—My uncle gave my sister ten cents to kiss him. Then he made me the same offer. I ran out the back door and all the way home.

Interpretation—In the first ER people are depicted as supportive while in the second, they appear to be threatening. Actually the contradiction is resolved when one observes that the supportive person is a woman while the threatening person is a man. Thus, this woman only has a place in the woman's world. The masculine world, especially because it involves sexual behavior, is threatening and she must avoid it.

In interpreting early recollections it should be understood that what is elicited are the individual's attitudes and not a mere description of his overt behavior. Although these attitudes are predominantly unconscious perceptions of the environment and the individual's role in the world, the individual nevertheless operates in accordance with this attitudinal frame of reference. The recollections describe a *modus vivendi* rather than a *modus operandi*. The characteristic outlook rather than the characteristic behavior is portrayed. In the following recollections, among other things, the subject characterizes life as dangerous.

ER—Another child was riding on my bike. He fell off on some glass, cut his arm, and had to be taken to the hospital.

ER—A boy fell off the slide in the school yard. They took him into the school and waited for the doctor to come.

Such a person, behaviorally, may see danger where none exists. He may exaggerate the dangers of life. He may retreat from these perceived dangers with anxious or phobic behavior. Or he may call upon certain defense mechanisms to cope with the omnipresent threat. In the compulsive individual, for example, one observes reliance upon ritual and feelings of omnipotence and the necessity to control as response to this danger. Many compulsives are preoccupied with death because this is the greatest threat—the one force which cannot be controlled. Hypochondriacs may exaggerate each body symptom as expressing their conviction that life is fraught with danger. Other individuals may develop into towers of strength or become dependent upon or identify with "strong" people or groups in order to minimize the dangers of life. Still others may actually court or provoke personal disaster in order to confirm their basic attitude. Some flirt with danger in order to prove that they possess a charmed life. While these reactions do not exhaust the repertoire available to people who feel that life is dangerous, they do serve to exemplify the variety of reactions which are possible within a single dimension of an individual's perceptual frame of reference.

Frequently behavioral response is elicited as well as basic attitudes.

ER—I saw a street car coming. I lay down on the tracks to stop it. The motorman got out and chased me down the street. I ran home.

Interpretation—The subject makes mischief, provokes the world, and tries to get by with it. He is willing to risk his life to make mischief and to demonstrate his power and right to do as he pleases, to control the others. He hits and runs.

ER—Mother always spanked us with a hair brush. This day she couldn't find it, so she spanked me with the handle of a scissors. I was frightened and screamed, "I'll be good!"

Interpretation—In addition to certain basic attitudes, this recollection also indicates the subject's behavioral response. He will only promise to behave (whether he will actually behave we can only guess) under the threat of punishment.

To fill out the personality picture thematic analysis is accompanied by an analysis of the details in the ER. Consider the following recollections given by two women.

ER—My mother was nursing my younger brother. I ran over and bit her breast.

ER—My mother made me mad. I don't know why. I went to the closet and bit a hole in her favorite dress.

Interpretation—Both recollections on the surface are similar, yet the details make them different. One recognizes the sources of her frustrations; the other does not. The first expresses her aggression directly; the second displaces her anger and attacks circuitously.

APPLICATIONS

Numerous applications of early recollections may be made. Inasmuch as they constitute a quick device for uncovering an individual's unconscious attitudes, they may be used in situations where rapid screening of individuals is desirable. A study by Kadis, Greene, and Freedman (36) indicates that the ER possess validity for this purpose. A second application occurs in the area of educational and vocational guidance (6, 8, 9). One clue with respect to vocational preparation is offered by Adler (7, 9) who noticed that physicians generally produce a recollection concerning death and illness. He is of the opinion that this ER serves as a directive that death must be fought. Several of Adler's own ER fell within this category. At the age of two he recalls being bandaged with rickets. At age four or five he was run over twice by vehicles; at age five he had pneumonia and " ... the doctor who had been suddenly called in, told my father that there was no hope of my living" (3, p. 10). His daughter also recalls that one of Adler's ER is concerned with the death of his brother (1).

Some sequences of recollections are primarily concerned with observation and others participation, some with motor activity and others with complete passivity, some with seeing and some with hearing (16, 34, 48), all of which have vocational implications. Take, for instance, the following recollections of a physiologist of the senses.

ER—It was the first time I saw the sea. I don't remember seeing the sea first. I only smelled it and heard it; then I saw it.

Orgler (42) cites similar early recollections of a mathematician and of a motion picture director.

The usefulness of ER in psychotherapy is enhanced by their emergence almost as a matter of course in the analytic psychotherapies without interfering with the continuity of the therapy. They permit the therapist to make initial hypotheses in treatment much before all of the significant material has emerged. Predictions of the patient's reaction to treatment and to the therapist may be formulated at a very early stage in treatment. The three recollections which follow serve to illustrate this point.

ER—I was in my baby carriage. People were looking at me. I was just lying on my back being a baby.

ER—The teacher was talking to us. It was the first day of school. I was trying to be good. I wasn't talking to anyone, wasn't doing anything.

ER—I won a prize in first grade, but I don't know for what. Don't remember my feeling. The teacher just called me up in front of the class and gave it to me.

Interpretation—The passivity of the patient is immediately obvious. He will very likely place the onus of responsibility upon the therapist for the progress of the therapy. He will probably try to be a "good" patient and try to gain the therapist's approval. Overt resistance should not be expected. Expression of feeling will rarely occur. Being the center of attention in therapy will be consistent with his needs. His emphasis is upon getting rather than upon doing.

DISCUSSION

Although the ER constitute a relatively simple projective technique, there are still many unsolved problems. Among the theoretical problems is the question as to whether the recollections can be utilized for differential diagnostic purposes. Rephrased, the question may be stated as—"do people of diverse personality types produce characteristic recollections?" Eisenstein and Ryerson (23), and Friedmann (27) and Feichtinger (24) indicate that the ER may be used for diagnostic purposes although most other writers are silent on this point.

Another question centers about the "dramatic" recollection. This recollection consists of a vivid, dramatic or traumatic incident—death, disaster, an accident, a unique happy experience—which most people, if it had occurred to them, would probably remember. We have in such instances a rule of thumb—the more "dramatic" an incident, the less significance is attached to the interpretation of the incident since the retention of the incident is at least partially dictated externally; the more innocuous an incident, the greater likelihood the recollection is dictated by the individual's needs. That an incident is not merely remembered because it is dramatic or traumatic is well illustrated by Orgler (43). Even in these "dramatic" incidents the individual's basic attitudes determine how the story will be told, the details that will be emphasized and those which will be omitted.

ER (dramatic)—There was a fire in the town we lived in. Three quarters of the town burned down at night. All kinds of homeless people were brought to my house. There was an old man, a Parkinsonian, burned all over. He was treated in my house. I felt sorry for him.

Interpretation—This recollection would probably be retained for its vividness and the impression it must have made on all who experienced the fire. Yet this recollection, given by a physician, still reveals the uniqueness of the subject's perception of the situation.

ER (innocuous)—I was sitting in the alley playing with some boxes. How nice it felt to sit and arrange the boxes.

Interpretation—Why should a person remember an incident which on the surface is so trivial? Many adults have had similar experiences as children and do not remember them. The recollection becomes more comprehensible when we learn that the patient is compulsive.

Until what age is an ER "early"? Why do not later recollections possess the same significance as earlier recollections? The second question is more easily answered than the first. It would appear that later recollections change with the present mood while early recollections reflect the basic attitudes to life. In line with this we have arbitrarily set age eight as the cutoff point for early recollections. An exception to this procedure is made when the subject's position in the family constellation has changed in childhood. Thus, for example, in a two child family, if the older child should die, the younger would suddenly be catapulted into the position of an only child. In such instances the underlying attitudes may change very radically. From limited clinical observation it appears that the subject "forgets" his early experiences and only retains memories from the period subsequent to his altered life status.

If ER are consonant with the individual's frame of reference, another question is posed. When the individual's attitudes change in psychotherapy, do his ERs also change? Clinical reports (18, 51) indicate that they do. The patient either (a) produces new memories, (b) "forgets" some of the old memories, i.e. they are not spontaneously produced or sometimes even remembered, (c) furnishes the same memory but divested of the original emotional tone, or (d) recasts the original memories with additions and omissions so that while the incident remains the same, the message it provides the

70

patient is different. As an illustration of the last point, below is the same incident as related by the individual at the beginning and end of treatment.

ER (pre-therapy)—We went to visit these friends of my family. I sat on a man's lap and he did something which was not very nice. I don't know what but I was afraid and wouldn't go back on subsequent family visits.

ER (post-therapy)—My sisters took me to visit a man. I was on his lap, his hand in my bloomers. I didn't think it was right but I didn't do anything about it.

Occasionally the ER may give clues to underlying insidious processes which may not appear clinically. Such signs appeared in the recollections of the following patient who entered treatment in a deep depression. After several months of treatment the depressive symptoms disappeared and the patient on the surface seemed quite well, so well that she discontinued treatment. Yet the ER she gave prior to the termination of treatment indicated she was not as well as she assumed.

ER—I was sick one day. The teacher had all the kids write to me. I felt good.

ER—I had whooping cough. We were waiting for the bus to come to go to the doctor. Each time a bus came I threw up. This happened four times. When we got on the bus, I threw up out of the window.

ER—My parents were having a party. I caught the measles. I looked at myself in the mirror which I shouldn't have done. I looked terrible. Remember lying in bed, a candle in the room, and the party going on in the next room.

Interpretation—One can still detect in these ER the consciousness of sickness of the patient, her feeling of not belonging, and the secondary gains from being ill.

As can be readily seen the numerous possibilities for the application of the ER have just been tapped and subsequent research should add to the fruitfulness of the technique. To illustrate the many types of interpretation to which ER lend themselves, a complete set of recollections given by a hospitalized male patient is here reproduced.

ER 1—In church with my mother standing next to me singing hymns. It was as if her voice were directed toward me, as if she were singing to me only. I felt like something special.

Interpretation—ER 1 reveals the individual's need to be something special Cf. Adler's "drive for significance" (9) and Horney's "search for glory" (35). However, the recollection does not indicate that he does anything to be something special. Instead he is the passive recipient of the attention of others. He is probably an egocentric individual who likes to be the center of attention. Observe also his mention of the singing voice. Perhaps he uses his voice vocationally or avocationally.

> ER 2—Age 5 when my mother died. She was lying in the coffin. Suddenly she picked herself up and hugged me.

Interpretation—Here is a bizarre recollection giving us a clue that this individual may be psychotic. Although this memory is fabricated, we observe that he is again the center of attention, the passive recipient of the affection of others, and an individual who is so special that even the impossible is not denied him. Since his mother died when he was five years old and he hardly remembers her, why does she appear so significantly in these recollections? Is he merely revealing his passive—dependent needs? Is he attempting to say in essence, "Others could not possibly give me the special attention a mother would"? It seems in any event that one can only be special through passively receiving the affection of a woman. We might also surmise that this patient holds no fear of death. According to Horney (35), this patient would be revealing how his demands for uniqueness exempt him from the "rules" of life.

> ER 3—I remember the first time it snowed in.................. It was the first time any of us had seen snow. Mother dressed us and sent us out to play in the snow. We scooped the snow out of a can and made snowballs. It was fun.

Interpretation—If life is special, out of the ordinary, he can enjoy it. He probably cannot accept mediocrity in himself or routineness in life. Both he and life must be out of the ordinary. For the first time he introduces figures other than his mother which would indicate that his dependency needs do not eliminate social interaction.

> ER 4—This was in school. The teacher punished me for something by putting me in a dark closet. I guess she forgot about me, so when I got hungry, I ate her lunch. After a while I had to go to the toilet. I was frantic and didn't know what to do. So I tried the door and it was open, so I went home. On the way I filled my pants

and I thought that when I got home, my mother would be angry with the teacher for causing all this. Then three boys appeared and wanted some money from me. I didn't have any, so they got out a knife and cut three slits in my belt. I went on home but don't remember what happened when I got there.

Interpretation—This is a rather complex recollection in which the patient commits certain anti-social acts but does not accept responsibility for his mischief making. His teacher is responsibile for "causing all this." The mechanism of projection comes to the fore here and affords us a clue to a possible paranoid process when taken together with ER 2. Again he is exempt from the usual rules. He has a special privilege of nonconformity, and if others do not respect this privilege, they are unfair. The masculine world is depicted as hostile and threatening. Hospital records indicate that the patient was actually diagnosed as paranoid schizophrenic. Although he is engaged in overt homosexual activity (contrary to classical Freudian theory), he did not regard himself as a homosexual, but as something special—a "bisexual." Prior to hospitalization he had been employed as a radio announcer (confirming our guess in ER 1) in a city known for its thrilling atmosphere.

Early recollections lend themselves well to other interpretive frameworks than that illustrated above (9, 31, 67). For example, a Freudian might see in ER 4 a recapitulation of the psychosexual development of the patient. The boy is put in a dark closet (the womb). Later he eats the teacher's lunch (oral stage), fills his pants (anal stage), goes toward mother (beginning of the oedipal phase), and meets three boys (three is the symbol for the male genitalia and could be representative of the father) who cut slits in his belt (since the belt is a long, pointed object, he is symbolically castrated).

SUMMARY
Although early recollections have received much attention in the literature, most writers have not treated the recollections projectively. A method for such interpretation is presented with a discussion of the problems involved in interpretation. The technique is useful in rapid psychiatric screening, differential diagnosis, vocational guidance, and in the analytic psychotherapies. Further research would undoubtedly uncover many more uses for this rather simple technique.

REFERENCES

1. Adler, Alexandra. *Guiding human misfits*. Millwood, New York: Kraus, 1976.
2. Adler, A. Erste Kindheitserrinnerungen. *Int. Z. Indiv. Psychol.*, 1933, 11, 81-90.
3. Adler, A. How I chose my career. *Indiv. Psychol. Bull.*, 1947, 6, 9-11.
4. Adler, A. *The practice and theory of Individual Psychology*. Totowa, N.J.: Littlefield, Adams, 1963.
5. Adler, A. *Problems of neurosis*. New York: Harper & Row, 1964.
6. Adler, A. *The science of living*. New York: Doubleday, 1969.
7. Adler, A. The significance of early recollections. *Int. J. Indiv. Psychol.*, 1937, 3, 283-287.
8. Adler, A. *Social interest*. New York: Capricorn Books, 1964
9. Adler, A. *What life should mean to you*. New York: Capricorn Books, 1958.
10. Ansbacher, H. L. Adler's place today in the psychology of memory. *J. Pers.*, 1947, 3, 197-207.
11. Ansbacher, H. L. and Ansbacher, Rowena. *The Individual Psychology of Alfred Adler*. New York: Basic Books, 1956.
12. Ansbacher, H. L. Purcell's "Memory and psychological security" and Adlerian theory. *J. abnorm. soc. Psychol.*, 1953, 48, 596-597.
13. Bartlett, F. C. *Remembering: a study in experimental and social psychology*. New York: Macmillan, 1932.
14. Brodsky, P. The diagnostic importance of early recollections. *Amer. J. Psychother.*, 1952, 6, 484-493.
15. Cason, H. The learning and retention of pleasant and unpleasant activities. *Arch. Psychol.*, 1932, 21, No. 134.
16. Colegrove, F. W. Individual memories. *Amer. J. Psychol.*, 1899, 10, 228-255.
17. Crook, M. N. and Harden, L. A quantitative investigation of early memories. *J. soc. Psychol.*, 1931, 2, 252-255.
18. Dreikurs, R. The psychological interview in medicine. *Amer. J. Indiv. Psychol.*, 1952, 10, 99-122.
19. Dudycha, G. J. and Dudycha, M. M. Adolescents' memories of preschool experiences. *J. genet. Psychol.*, 1933, 42, 468-480.
20. Dudycha, G. J. and Dudycha, M. M. Childhood memories. A review of the literature. *Psychol. Bull.*, 1941, 38, 668-682.
21. Dudycha, G. J. and Dudycha, M. M. Some factors and characteristics in childhood memories. *Child Developm.*, 1933, 4, 265-278.
22. Edwards, A. L. The retention of affective experiences—a criticism and restatement of the problem. *Psychol. Rev.*, 1942, 49, 43-53
23. Eisenstein, V. W. and Ryerson, Rowena. Psychodynamic significance of the first conscious memory. *Bull. Menninger Clin.*, 1951. 15. 213-220.
24. Feichtinger, F. Early recollections in neurotic disturbances. *Indiv. Psychol. Bull.*, 1943, 3, 44-49.
25. Freud, S. A *general introduction to psychoanalysis*. New York: Garden City, 1938.
26. Freud. S. Repression. In *Collected papers*. Vol. 4. London: Hogarth, 1925.
27. Freud, S. The unconscious. In *Collected papers*. Vol. 4. London: Hogarth, 1925.
28. Friedmann, Alice. Early childhood memories of mental patients. *Indiv. Psychol. Bull.*, 1950, 8, 111-116.
29. Friedmann, Alice. First recollections of school. *Int. J. Indiv. Psychol.*, 1935, 1, 111-116.
30. Gilbert, G. M. The new status of experimental studies on the relationship of feeling to memory. *Psychol. Bull.*, 1938, 35, 26-35.

31. Gordon, K. A study of early memories. *J. Delinqu.*, 1928, 12, 129-132.
32. Hadfield, J. A. Reliability of infantile memories. *Brit. J. med., Psychol.*, 1928, 8, 87-111.
33. Hall, G. S. Note on early memories. *Pedagog. Sem.*, 1899, 6, 485-512.
34. Henri, B. and Henri, C. Earliest recollections. *Pop. Sci. Mon.*, 1898, 53, 108-115.
35. Horney, Karen. *Neurosis and human growth.* New York: Norton, 1950.
36. Kadis, Asya, Greene, Janet S., and Freedman, N. Early childhood recollections—an integrative technique of personality test data. *Amer. J. Indiv. Psychol.*, 1952, 10, 31-42.
37. Kahana, R. J., Weiland, I. H., Snyder, B., and Rosenbaum, M. The value of early memories in psychotherapy. *Psychiat. Quart,* 1953, 27, 73-82.
38. Krech, D. Notes toward a psychological theory. *J. Pers.*, 1949, 18, 66-87.
39. Meltzer, H. The present status of experimental studies on the relation of feeling to memory. *Psychol. Rev.*, 1930, 37, 124-139.
40. Miles, C. A study of individual psychology. *Amer. J. Psychol.*, 1893, 6, 534-558.
41. Opedal, L. E. Analysis of the earliest memory of a delinquent. *Int. J. Indiv. Psychol.*, 1935, 1, 52-58.
42. Orgler, Hertha. *Alfred Adler. The man and his work.* London: Daniel, 1939.
43. Orgler, Hertha. Comparative study of two first recollections. *Amer. J. Indiv. Psychol.*, 1952, 10, 27-30.
44. Plewa, F. The meaning of childhood recollections. *Int. J. Indiv. Psychol.*, 1935, 1, 88-101.
45. Plottke, P. First memories of "normal" and of "delinquent" girls. *Indiv. Psychol. Bull.*, 1949, 7, 15-20.
46. Postman, L. and Schneider, B. H. Personal values, visual recognition, and recall. *Psychol. Rev.*, 1951, 58, 271-284.
47. Postman, L. and Murphy, G. The factor of attitude in association memory. *J. exp. Psychol.*, 1943, 33, 228-238.
48. Potwin, E. B. Study of early memories. *Psychol. Rev.*, 1901, 8, 596-601.
49. Purcell, K. Memory and psychological security. *J. abnorm. soc. Psychol.*, 1952, 47, 433-440.
50. Rapaport, D. *Emotions and memory.* Baltimore: Williams and Wilkins, 1942.
51. Saul, L. J., Snyder, T. R., and Sheppard, Edith. On earliest memories. *Psychoanal. Quart.*, 1956, 25, 228-237.
52. Thatcher, P. An early recollection in a case of juvenile delinquency. *Indiv. Psychol. Bull.*, 1944, 4, 59-60.
53. Waldfogel, S. The frequency and affective character of childhood memories. *Psychol. Monogr.*, 1948, 62, No. 4 (Whole No. 291).
54. Watson, W. S. and Hartmann, G. W. The rigidity of a basic attitudinal frame. *J. abnorm. soc. Psychol.*, 1939, 34, 314-335.
55. Way, L. *Adler's place in psychology.* London: Allen and Unwin, 1950.
56. Zeller, A. F. An experimental analogue of repression. I. Historical summary. *Psychol. Bull.*, 1950, 47, 39-51.

The Getting Type, a Parsimonious Social Interpretation of the Oral Character*

Characterologies have occupied the attention of writers and psychologists almost since the dawn of time. Each era has seen the emergence of one or more descriptions of the nature of man. Undoubtedly, the most prominent set of such descriptions and the one most influential on the current psychological scene is Freud's theory of psychosexual development which should perhaps be attributed equally to Karl Abraham (1). One of the cornerstones of classical Freudian theory, it provides a description of certain character types which develop in accordance with the assumptions of psychic energy (libido theory) and of psychic determinism.

The present paper will attempt to demonstrate that the so-called "oral traits," while accurately described, may be explained more parsimoniously in social terms. The oral character has been selected not because it is more significant than other aspects of the theory, but merely to illustrate how the Freudian concepts lend themselves to advantage to social, non-libidinal interpretation.

The Oral Character

According to Freudian theory, the earliest cathexis of the libido is vested in the mouth: Through incorporating, holding, biting, spitting out, and closing, tension reduction occurs. Calvin S. Hall describes these as prototypes of later personality traits. He says:

> Taking in through the mouth is the prototype for acquisitiveness, holding on for tenacity and determination, biting for destructiveness, spitting out for rejection and contemptuousness, and closing for refusal and negativism. Whether these traits will develop and become part of one's character or not depends upon the amount of frustration and anxiety which is experienced in connection with the prototypic expression (5, p. 104).

*Reprinted by permission from JOURNAL OF INDIVIDUAL PSYCHOLOGY, 1959, 15, 193-198.

Through coping behavior (i.e., sublimation and displacement) and through the use of defense mechanisms, expecially projection, reaction formation, fixation, and regression, these prototypes may be elaborated to include certain behavioral modes, interests, and vocational choices. Thus the "oral erotic person" may become a gourmet, a nurse, a singer or fat, while the "oral sadistic person" may become a cigar chewer, a drama critic or a nail biter. The "oral incorporator" especially may be extremely acquisitive, more for the sake of acquisition than for its content, because it is "only a substitute for what he really wants, namely, food from a loving mother" (5, p. 105) The oral personality is also alluded to as an "oral dependent individual." The alcoholic, for example, falls within this category and is often explained as a person who has substituted one bottle for another.

THE GETTING TYPE

From the point of view of social interaction, the oral personality might more appropriately be called the "getting type." This term is taken from one of Adler's last papers in which he briefly attempted a typology based on characteristic ways in which individuals may relate themselves to others. Adler spoke of a "ruling type," a "getting type," an "avoiding type" and a fourth, ideal type, "prepared for cooperation and contribution" (2, pp. 6-7, and 3, p. 168).

With respect to child rearing practices, there have always been family constellations in which a child was encouraged to get. Most frequently, these roles fell to the youngest in the family, to the ill or handicapped, and to only children, although training in getting was not necessarily restricted to these.

Since World War II, however, cultural trends have encouraged more than previously the emphasis on getting. With the highest standard of living in American history and with depression-bred parents compensating through their children, we train children not only to get but to *demand*. The traditional pressures upon children to "get ahead," which implied doing, have been altered to getting material things, to getting more than the others (otherwise you are a sucker), and to getting a thrill. Getting without doing is considered a triumph; doing and getting reward is merely for suckers.

Another factor operating to encourage getting is the trend in some circles, lay and professional, toward permissiveness and indulgence in the training of children in order not to "frustrate" the child, not to injure the child's psyche. The parents' insecurity in holding their ground in facing the child's demands, and their desire for his approval, make them easy victims of the child's retort, "You don't love me," when they fail to submit to his demands.

A third factor contributing to the emphasis on getting is our age of anxiety, which encourages us to get as much as we can before the hydrogen bomb falls, or the draft catches up with us, or life, the arena of responsibility, must be tackled. After all, parents believe, "You are only young once," or "There is plenty of time for a child to grow up."

Children growing up with the "getting" complex encounter very little opportunity or necessity to do things. Consequently, they have little awareness of their own abilities to contribute, to be productive, to create, or to give. Thus lacking self-reliance and faith in themselves, they train themselves to get, to get served rather than to serve, to get love rather than to love, and of course, to get by and to get out of things, to avoid responsibilities.

Since getting depends on others, the "getter" attempts to surround himself with people who are willing to comply. He is frequently gregarious, but conditionally; feels comfortable in social situations and uncomfortable alone; and often develops special social skills.

The getter, very frequently, is a self-indulgent person. "Eat, drink and be merry for tomorrow we die." Therefore, it is incumbent on him to get as much as possible and to get it *now*. Immediate gratification becomes a primary goal.

If one examines the self-indulgent person's credo closely, one can detect the source of his insistent demands. "For tomorrow we die," betrays his pessimism. Without abilities to rely upon should he be left without people to gratify his demands, how much faith can he have in himself or in life? Many getters resort to alcohol or narcotics because, in typical getter fashion, they either can get high or get less tense, or get some kicks, or because this facilitates social interaction, or conditions the environment (it gets others to take care of them).

Frequently, the pessimistic getter, unable to face his pessimism, covers up by radiating a superficial optimism. He believes, "In the long run, nothing will happen anyway; therefore, I might as well take the easy way now." The chronic gambler, for example, falls into this group. Covering up the pessimism with optimism is the nuclear process of manic-depressive psychosis and explains why the cycloid personality has been associated with the oral character.

Since getting seems so important, getting more and more becomes even more desirable. "Necessary" is perhaps a better word than "desirable" since the individual feels that his personal worth, upon which his feeling of belongingness rests, depends upon acquiring more. If getting ever stops, nothing is left. Therefore, the getter often eats too much, drinks too much, bites off too much business, tries to learn everything or gain as much fame or money as possible. Naturally the getter feels one should get as many kicks out of life as possible.

Unfortunately for the getter, life very frequently says "no" to him. Therefore, he often feels that life is unfair; for after all, does not life owe something to him? Life appears as cruel, and people just do not love him. When a person feels this way, he is particularly sensitive to criticism. This is the so-called projection onto others of one's own "oral aggressive needs," and one is prone to be depressed. Actually, it is the feeling that life is unfair that makes the individual susceptible to depressive episodes. Such individuals operate according to the German proverb, "*Wenn man dir gibt, nimm; wenn man von dir nimmt, schrei.*" ("If they give to you, take; if they take from you, holler"). And is not depression merely a silent form of hollering?

THE QUESTION OF PARSIMONY

Compared to the Freudian "oral character," the Adlerian "getting type" is undoubtedly the simpler construct. While both describe essentially the same behavioral phenomena, as we have attempted to show, the latter assumes only the self-consistency of the individual which would link his early experiences and interpretations of his social situation with his present behavior. The Freudian concept, on the other hand, assumes libido, its early cathexis in the mouth, and its frustration at that stage together with anxiety, plus the reflection of all these in the present conduct of the individual—all assumptions which have not been verified and probably are unverifiable.

The proofs furnished by the Freudians are unconvincing. While it is undeniable that in later life sensual gratification may occur through activities of the mouth, especially the lips, as kissing or sucking one's thumb, does this fact really necessitate the assumption of the lasting significance of an oral phase of development? After all, people receive gratification from scratching their ears, or by stroking their children or pets, or by olfactorily savoring a good wine. In these instances no one assumes an olfactory or tactual phase of development. Similarly, there is no need to connect an assumed early libidinal gratification with later character development, even when similar traits occur in adulthood.

As evidence of the prominence of the oral zone in character development, psychoanalysts very frequently allude to such universal expressions as, "I could eat you up," "I can't swallow it," "Let me chew on it for a while," etc. But such evidence, however reasonable on the surface, does not account for other expressions which might more properly be attributed to some zone of the body outside the scope of the erogenous zones. For example, the grasping personality is very frequently attributed either to the holding-on oral personality or to the retentive anal personality. But could we not also make a case for the grasping personality to be one who has fixated at the manual or tactual level of development? Could we not also say that the manipulative person is one who, as a child, enjoyed playing with his blocks?

When we regard character not as a mere mechanistic outcome of certain infantile libidinal experiences, but as an expression of the manner in which an individual contemporaneously experiences himself in relationship to life, the Freudian concept does not furnish greater explanatory value regarding dynamics, in spite of its greater complexity. The greater value of the Freudian concept would lie only in its genetic implications, doubtful as these are. The deprivation of the love object, the breast, which the Freudians use as explanation of the genesis of depression, is probably no more than an expression of the observation that people who are trained to get become angry when others do not give or are not around to give. Likewise, an "oral dependent person" is merely one who has learned to put others into his service through such "oral traits" as charm or by manipulating others. Such traits as independence, on the other hand, are often seen by psychoanalysts as reaction formations against the desire for dependence.

Also by the criterion of prediction, does the Freudian concept fail to be superior. From the theory of psychosexual development, at best postdictive statements can be made. Assuming the fact that "oral characters" exist, one cannot predict such a character development from a knowledge of an infant's experience.

CONCLUSION

While the observations made by the Freudians on the oral character may be accurate, the development of this particular personality structure may be explained more parsimoniously in the social rather than libidinal terms of Adler's getting type. The Freudian concept of character in general is a reflection of the individual's psychosexual experiences during infancy. In our conception, character is an expresssion of the manner in which an individual contemporaneously experiences himself in relationship to life, and a reflection of his interpretation of the cultural values of his society (4).

REFERENCES

1. ABRAHAM, K. *Selected papers on psychoanalysis.* London: Hogarth, 1927.
2. ADLER, A. The fundamental views of Individual Psychology. *Int. J. Indiv. Psychol.,* 1935, 1(1), 5-8.
3. ADLER, A. *The Individual Psychology of Alfred Adler.* New York: Basic Books, 1956.
4. DREIKURS, R. Psychotherapy as correction of faulty social values. *J. Indiv. Psychol.,* 1957, 13, 150-158.
5. HALL, C. S. *A primer of Freudian psychology.* New York: Mentor Books, 1955.

Effect of Time Limits: A Comparison of Two Psychotherapies*

This is a report on work with a particular structure in therapy, and some of the findings when that same structure is employed by therapists of two different orientations. The particular structure is the imposition of time limits, when termination is set in advance. The two different therapies are Client-Centered and Adlerian.

THEORY

Experiments with time limits need to be understood in their proper light. On the evidence, there seems to be much to recommend them, but with reservations. Time-limited or deliberately brief therapy is being employed more and more in various clinical settings and it worries us to think that this should be given premature impetus by our research work. This experimental work takes its impetus from the clinical and theoretical work of earlier figures in the field, particulary Otto Rank and Jessie Taft. In essence, the theory is that time limits place the emphasis where it belongs; on quality and process, rather than upon quantity. Time does not heal, because it cannot. Only activity can heal, and the more activity, the shorter the time required. This theory holds that limits, in effect, increase energy, choice, wisdom, and courage, and so they heighten the essential process while they reduce the largely unessential time. Such theory is hard to grasp and hard to hold on to, partly because of general human evasiveness. We say that, "Time flies," but what we really mean is, "I am too slow." Our conventional thinking leads us to consider time as if *it* were active, and an event in itself. We even say that people die of old age. Actually they die of some malfunction which could and often does appear at an earlier age.

*Reprinted by permission from JOURNAL OF COUNSELING PSYCHOLOGY, 1962, 9(1), 31-34.

This theory deserves serious consideration, partly because of the intelligence it represents, and partly because of the empirical results in current research. At the same time, it is important to remember that while Taft called time limits "one of the most valuable tools ever introduced into therapy," she also warned that this tool could never be used as a "mechanical salvation" to be employed as a resort of the desperately incompetent or inexperienced therapist. It is that latter caution that makes us want to say firmly that we are not trying to promote "instant therapy" or apply a mass production technique, or anything of that sort.

CONDITIONS

In this research, the structural intervention of time limits are employed by therapists of considerable experience, and the research itself, we hope, is a partial demonstration of their competence. The conditions are simply described as follows: clients or patients are offered therapy when they apply for it, with the provision that (1) they would participate in research and (2) that the therapy would be limited to a maximum to 20 interviews at the suggested rate of two per week. Fifteen client-centered therapists and eight Adlerians participated.

RESULTS

Figure 1 shows the results in terms of the self-ideal correlation using an 80-item modified Butler-Haigh Q sort. The Q sort was administered before therapy, after seven interviews, at the end of therapy, and after a follow-up period averaging 12 months. The follow-up period is represented by the shaded area. The other intervals are shown on the base line. There are five population lines on this chart; each one shows the mean self-ideal correlation for one of the control or experimental groups. The lower line of "z's" is a group of "own controls"—people who applied for therapy, who were tested, and then asked to wait for three months before therapy began. The mean correlation is zero, both at the beginning and at the end of the wait period. It indicates that without therapy, for people who see themselves as needing therapy, the mere passing of time does not on the average change the S-I correlation. The top line of "x's" represents another control group of people who did not apply for therapy but were so-called "normal" controls, asked to take part in "personality research." Neither does this control group change over time without therapy. (It should be mentioned that while the means are almost perfectly stable in the two control groups, there is variation in many individual "scores." Such variation simply cancels out in these averages.) These two control groups, for all their deficiencies, are useful. They suggest that time alone makes no difference, on the average, and they provide the levels of self-ideal congruence for two self-defined populations, one "needing therapy" and one "not needing therapy." These two control groups differ at the .001 level of significance, and thus provide a frame of reference for the experimental therapy groups, indicating the desired direction of change.

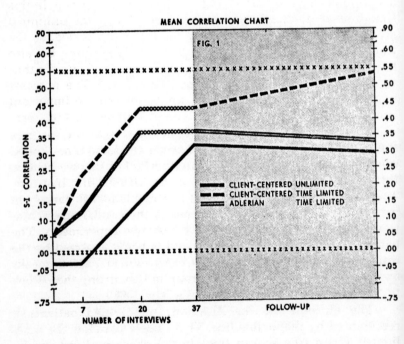

Fig. 1

There are three experimental groups. The first is the solid line, representing 30 individuals who applied for client-centered therapy, and were given the customary opportunity to begin and terminate therapy when they chose to do so, without limits in time or in number of interviews. They all voluntarily terminated, after an average of 37 interviews. The gain was significant at the .01 level (as are all the pre- to post or follow-up gains for the experimental groups) and it was an improvement—that is, in the predicted direction, with stability in the follow-up period. This was the first experiment. It offers evidence that unlimited therapy is effective.

The second experiment is represented by the broken line. It describes the average correlation of a group of 20 persons who applied for client-centered therapy, and who were offered therapy under the time-limited conditions, a maximum of 20 interviews. This group, for whom termination was set in advance, actually had an average of 18 interviews—half the number of actual interviews for the average in the unlimited group. In this time-limited group, the gain is the same as in the unlimited group. Again there is stability in the follow-up period, so the time-limited group may be said to be not only *effective*, but also twice as *efficient*. There was other supporting evidence for this, and also one contradiction among the criteria. The outcome might have been a "fluke." Time limits seemed too important and too radical a step for us to accept without further test.

The third experiment is a replication (that all too rare thing in social sciences) conducted under the same time-limited conditions of a maximum of 20 interviews. For this we have to thank our colleagues on the staff of the Alfred Adler Institute. These are a group of psychiatrists and psychologists, largely in private practice, and as homogeneous in their Adlerian orientation as were the Rogerians in the first two experiments. The battery of tests was administered and is being analyzed by the research staff at the Counseling Center, which I think speaks for the courage of the Adlerian group in submitting their work to "independent laboratory analysis."

The outcome for the Adlerian time-limited patients is represented by the double line. This closely parallels the time-limited group (the broken line) in the client-centered experiment. There is no point of significant difference between them, from pre-to posttherapy. The Adlerian group again shows that time-limited therapy is both effective and efficient. The sharp increment after the first seven interviews appears now to be a genuine and unique characteristic of time-limited therapy, not found in the unlimited cases shown here, nor in the average of a group of other longer unlimited cases. (The only cases approaching such early acceleration are those unlimited cases which were long ones designated the most successful according to other independent criteria.)

SOME CONCLUSIONS

1. First, we see that for the third time, the self-ideal correlation has shown significant improvement as the consequence of psychotherapy, when compared with controls. It is interesting to note, however, that no posttherapy group reaches the level of the "normal" controls.

2. Time-limited therapy, according to this measure of improvement, receives a second validation of its effectiveness and efficiency.

3. The therapist employing this particular intervention (of termination set in advance) can produce some results which are unique. We refer here to the early acceleration.

4. Though Adlerian and client-centered therapies have points of theoretical agreement, there are also differences, which show up sharply in the actual conduct of the therapist. The structure of time-limits seems to have effects which apparently outweigh the differences in the therapeutic conduct. At least, this is so for the over-all "score" made up of the self-ideal correlation. But the S-I correlation, it should be noted, is an abstract score which could be obtained in a number of different ways. Probably its abstract generality tends to mask some real differences in therapist effect. There is some evidence that this is so, since certain clusters of concrete Q sort items do differentiate Adlerian and client-centered effects in the self-sorts at posttherapy. Nonetheless, taking only the abstract S-I correlation itself, the research evidence is clear—the structure of time limits will promote certain similar effects even where the therapists are distinctly different in their behavior.

Predicting the Relationship to the Psychotherapist from Early Recollections*

An individual ordinarily behaves in a self-consistent manner consonant with his life style. In psychotherapy he brings this same life style to the therapeutic situation. Thus, what the Freudians refer to as transference attitudes are merely the expression of general convictions the patient has come to hold with respect to himself and the world. In 1913 Adler wrote:

> I expect from the patient again and again the same attitude which he has shown in accordance with his life-plan toward the persons of his former environment, and still earlier toward his family. At the moment of the introduction to the physician and often even earlier, the patient has the same feelings toward him as toward important persons in general. The assumption that the transference of such feelings or that resistance begins later is a mere deception. In such cases the physician only recognizes them later (1, pp. 336-337).

In order to avoid this "later" recognition it would be helpful to the therapist if he could predict early in treatment the patient's attitudes, whether referring to these as transference or not.

Such a possibility exists in the use of early recollections which Adler suggested as one of "the most trustworthy approaches to the exploration of personality" (1, p. 327). He explains the rationale of the diagnostic value of early recollections as follows: "[The individual's] memories are the reminders he carries about with him of his own limits and of the meaning of circumstances. There are no 'chance memories': out of the incalculable number of impressions which meet an individual, he chooses to remember only those which he feels, however darkly, to have a bearing on his situation" (1, p. 351).

Early recollections (ERs) permit the formulation of a thumbnail description of the individual's life style. The method has been described in detail by the present writer (3). For a

*Reprinted by permission from JOURNAL OF INDIVIDUAL PSYCHOLOGY, 1965, 21, 77-81.

method of rapidly ascertaining antecedent information concerning the family atmosphere, which Adlerians find congenial in their understanding of the development of the life style, the reader is referred to articles by Dreikurs (2) and Shulman (4).

CASE I

To illustrate, let us analyze the following ERs given by a man of 40 who has a history of poor interpersonal relations. He tries hard to be a "nice" guy but others treat him poorly in return. He cannot understand why this should be, but wants to discover the reason in psychotherapy.

1. I was lying on the floor listening to the radio while my parents and another couple were playing bridge. My father was running his hand over my aunt's leg. She pushed it away but my father put his hand on it again. I was angry with my father because he was wrong.

2. I fell down the stairs and landed on my head on a cement floor. I was conscious but insensible. My mother got excited and took me on the street car to my uncle's office. He was a dentist. I don't know why she took me to him.

3. This happened in first grade. I was a talker in school. This day the teacher was bawling out a kid and threatening to call his father. I said, "You always say it but never do it." She said, "What did you say?" I was scared but I repeated it. She marched me into a room with a lower grade. I was only trying to help her.

4. The maid took me home to her house and offered me beer. I hated it but drank it and didn't let on I didn't like it.

5. When I was seven, my mother was pregnant and my uncle and aunt took me out. They stopped somewhere because I had to go to the washroom. There were some puppies there, and I bent over to pet one, and the mother dog bit me in the behind. I screamed. My uncle laughed, took me into the restaurant, and applied iodine in public. I hated him for making me a laughing stock.

6. My mother sent me to the store with a $10 bill in my pocket and told me not to take it out. I did and lost it. I came home and lied that two men had held me up. My mother called the police, and I crossed myself up. My father beat hell out of me with a strap.

7. My father took us for a ride in his new car. When we got in front of our house, I jumped out before the car stopped and the door was torn off the car when it hit a pole. If my father could have killed me, he would have.

Life Style

Since ERs are assumed to reflect an individual's current mode of perception, we may use these to discern several major trends in his personality. We note that in all his ERs someone does wrong, intentionally or otherwise. People are constantly spoiling things for each other. The patient does not exempt himself from this category of wrongdoers. However, even when he endeavors to do the right thing, he winds up hurt. He tries to please but ends up suffering. He always gets "the short end of the stick." We arrive at the picture of a hypercritical individual who finds fault with all of life including himself although he has better intentions than others do. He does not believe in the possibility of good human relations. Anticipating suffering inevitably, he is a thorough pessimist who at times goes looking for his own beatings.

Predictions

How might this person perceive and use the therapy situation? The therapist can formulate several tentative hypotheses. The patient might

1. be critical of therapy, the therapist, and his progress;
2. perceive the therapist as another person who will make him suffer;
3. attempt to provoke the therapist (not intentionally, of course,) to make him (the patient) suffer; then he can be critical of the therapist and feel morally superior to him;
4. devote himself to the recitation of incidents, past and present, where others have abused him, humiliated him, and wronged him;
5. distrust the therapist and distrust the possibility of a good human relationship with him;
6. try to ingratiate himself with the therapist and then be disappointed when the therapist fails to meet one of his implicit or explicit demands;
7. caught in a tight spot, attempt to lie his way out, but would probably do so clumsily, since he expects to be found out;
8. fearing punishment and humiliation, withhold certain information from the therapist until he feels he can trust him with it.

Outcome

In the course of treatment, the patient's behavior confirmed several of the above hypotheses. He consistently inquired of the therapist whether therapy was *really* helping him (Hyp. 1). At other times he would attempt to ingratiate himself with the therapist by telling him that therapy had been helpful but that his wife and children really needed the treatment (Hyp. 6). He devoted most of the initial period of treatment to a recitation of how his mother abused him, how his wife and her family wronged him, how his children misbehaved, and how his employees took advantage of him (Hyp. 4). He withheld speaking of his own misdeeds until much later in treatment, and then with a sheepish grin, since he was apprehensive that the therapist might disapprove of him (Hyp. 8). When he terminated treatment, he grudgingly admitted making some gains but was still focusing on the world's abuse of him (Hyp. 1 and 4).

CASE 2

Occasionally the question as to whether a certain type of therapist is preferable for a particular patient assumes importance. Frequently we ask ourselves whether the patient might relate better to a male or female therapist, though there are differences of opinion as to how crucial a factor this may be. This decision is difficult to make at the initiation of therapeutic contact since we have so little reliable information about the patient at this time. Here again ERs can give us assistance.

The following ERs were given by a college student both of whose parents set excessive standards for him. His father was a man with questionable authority in his own family since the mother dominated him (and the son) through a self-sacrificing, martyr-like goodness. This domination of the patient was so thoroughly effective, that when he, soon after beginning treatment, was dismissed from college for deliberately obtaining poor grades, he boasted gleefully to his therapist, "That's the first decision I ever made on my own in my whole life." His ERs were:

1. My tonsils were being taken out. I remember someone putting a mask over my face. A woman was saying something to me. I felt like the breath was being drawn out of me.
2. I was playing ball with my sister. I bent over a wire to get the ball and my sister pushed me over it. I fell on a board and cut my hand on some glass. All the neighbors were throwing down towels to put around the wound but it kept bleeding through.
3. The first day of kindergarten. Our collie dog was going blind; it would defecate in the back yard. I stepped in it but didn't know it. When I came to school, I noticed the odor, looked down at my shoe, and scraped it off. When leaving the room, the teacher asked me to help her clean up the floor.

4. I was walking to school with a girl. I asked her, "Will you be my girl friend and I'll be your boy friend?" She slapped me. I came home and didn't want to ever go to school again.
5. My grandmother died and it was my first funeral. Everyone was crying, and I thought it was silly, and I laughed.
6. I called a girl a "whore." She cried and told my mother. My mother asked whether I knew the meaning of the word. I pretended I knew and wouldn't tell.

Predictions

From this brief diagnostic material it was possible to guess the patient's possible attitudes toward a female therapist. Consistently the ERs depict a little boy being overwhelmed and hurt by women. In addition, in ER 3, he attempts to cover up the malodorous part of himself, but even in this instance, a woman finds him out. As in the previous illustration we can phrase several hypotheses which in this case involve predictions as to what might occur were this patient assigned to a woman therapist. The patient might

1. see a female therapist as a threatening, potentially overwhelming person;
2. take perverse pleasure if something adverse happens to his therapist;
3. provoke the therapist to see whether she makes trouble for him since he feels he is the victim of women;
4. attempt to cover up his deficiencies, his "sins," and his "ignorance," at the same time expecting to be found out;
5. make some "innocent" sexual advances to the therapist; and if "accused" of such behavior, attempt to leave therapy;
6. devote much of his therapeutic time to elaborating upon the theme "You can't do business with women."

Outcome

In this case, acting upon the clear indications of the ERs, the choice of a male therapist was made. Consequently, the negative predictions for a female therapist were not directly checked by the course of events in therapy. This did, however, support the general conclusions drawn from the ERs regarding the subject's life style.

When the patient entered psychotherapy, he was unmarried and constantly involved with women with whom nothing worked out. His mother made life difficult for him and for his father. He dropped out of treatment and was performing successfully at a university when he married a willful and, by her own admission, "spoiled brat." They fought almost every day of their marriage. The patient returned to psychotherapy and the wife also sought treatment. Except for periods of discouragement when he gave full expression to his failure, he attempted to "look good" to the therapist, even resorting to lying to cover up his negative aspects.

SUMMARY

Prediction of the probable attitudes of a client toward his therapist would prove of considerable assistance to the therapist, whatever his theoretical orientation, and in the choice of a therapist. Early recollections, when understood as suggested by Adler as representative of the individual's life style and hence as reflecting his current mode of perception and attitudes, provide a means for such prediction. This is illustrated by two cases.

REFERENCES

1. ADLER, A. The Individual Psychology of Alfred Adler. H. L. & Rowena R. Ansbacher (Eds.) New York: Basic Books, 1956.
2. DREIKURS, R. The psychological interview in medicine. Amer. J. Indiv. Psychol., 1952, 10, 99-122.
3. MOSAK, H. H. Early recollections as a projective technique. J. proj. tech., 1958, 22, 302-311.
4. SHULMAN, B. H. The family constellation in personality diagnosis. J. Indiv. Psychol., 1962, 18, 35-47.

The Tasks of Life I. Adler's Three Tasks*

Work, society, and sex, Adler and subsequent Adlerians wrote, comprise the three life tasks with which each person must cope and attempt to find solutions.[1] However, like many other fundamental views shared by Adlerians, the concept of the life tasks is by no means clearly defined. The purpose of this paper is twofold-first, to indicate the subtle differences of opinion as they appear in the writings of Adler and his associates, and second, to enlarge the presently accepted formulations. *These extensions are logical derivatives of some cursory statements which Adler and other Adlerians have made but did not develop fully.*

Of more than historical interest is Adler's first formulation of the life tasks. He considered all problems confronting man as falling into three categories. "They make up reality for him ... He must always answer these problems, because they are questioning him" (4, p. 5). He considers the first as a consequence of our "living on the crust of this poor planet earth, and nowhere else. We must develop under the restrictions and with the possibilities which our place of habitation sets us. . .Every answer must be conditioned by the fact that we belong to mankind and that men are beings who inhabit this earth" (4, p. 5).

This formulation is exceedingly significant and too often overlooked by those who discuss the three life tasks. It designates in clear fashion the *field* in which man moves. All of man's problems are presented by his very existence *in a given field* which is "the fact that we are tied to the crust of this. . earth, with all the advantages and disadvantages which our position brings" (4, p. 6).

---

[1]For an outline of the problems included in the first three life tasks and a comprehensive bibliography of Adlerian writings in this area, the reader is referred to Mosak and Shulman (11).

*Reprinted by permission from THE INDIVIDUAL PSYCHOLOGIST, 1966, 4(1), 18-22.

The second set of problems in Adler's earliest formulation is presented by the fact that "there are others around us and we are living in association with them, and that we would perish if we were alone" (4, p. 6). The third set of problems results from the fact that we exist in two sexes, and that the preservation of individual and group life must take this fact into account.

In this formulation Adler makes no reference to work as a life task. Yet, when he summarizes the three problems, his position shifts to include it, for he continues, "how to find an occupation which will enable us to survive under the limitations set by the nature of the earth; how to find a position amongst our fellows so that we may cooperate; how to accommodate ourselves to the fact that we live in two sexes, and that the continuance and tolerance of mankind depends on our love life. We found no problems in life which cannot be grouped under these three main problems—occupational, social and sexual" (4, p. 7).

Adler is not always consistent in his designation of the primacy or relative importance of these tasks. Later in the same volume (4, p. 202), he considers the problem of relationship to other men as first task of life and the occupational task as second. Love and sex remain the third. Later he again calls the problem of occupation the first task, but he suggests that the best method of coping with it comes through the solution of the second problem, that of living in association with others, through friendship, social feeling and cooperation. "With the solution of this problem, we have an incalculable advance toward the solution of the first" (4, p. 239). The relative importance of the tasks alternates throughout Adler's lifetime; in his last book we learn that "all the questions of life can be subordinated to the three major problems—the problems of communal life, of work, and of love" (3, p. 42).

In the earliest expression of his viewpoint Adler finds all of the tasks interwoven, remarking, "none of these problems can be solved separately; each of them demands the successful approach to the other two" (4, p. 239). Continuing, he comments, "These three problems are never found apart; they all throw crosslights on the others; and indeed, we can say that they are all aspects of the same situation and the same problem—the necessity for a human being to preserve life and to further life in the environment in which he finds himself" (4, p. 241).

Way's formulation of Adler's position is that "Adler summarized into three main groups the practical demands which the society is all the time making upon the individual's capacity for adaptation. These three great sets of problems, of Society, of Occupation, of Love are closely interlocked" (13, p. 179). Way considers these three tasks as being nothing else than "those old friends of psychology, the three instincts of the Herd, of Nutrition, and of Sex. Only they appear in Individual Psychology no longer as urges of a subjective nature, but are seen from the other side, as external facts belonging to the logic of communal existence. They are absolutes, insofar as it would be difficult to conceive a society in which some form of adaptation along these lines would not be demanded of the individual. But the character, and the extent of adaptation as well, will vary with every generation and with every alteration in the structure of society. The problems they pose can never be solved once for all, but demand from the individual a continuous and creative movement toward adaptation" (13, pp. 179-180).

Observing the approach of an individual to these tasks, we can test an individual's training in cooperation. However, says Way, "the human being does not necessarily develop himself at all equally, and may find himself much better equipped for the solution of one of these problems than for the others. He may succeed in occupation but not in love; or love and social contacts may both be easy to him as compared with the difficulty of earning a living" (13, p. 180). It is apparent that Way, in contrast to Adler, recognizes different levels of "adaptation" or, perhaps better stated, different levels of fulfillment of one or the other of the life tasks. "There are often cases where one or the other of these demands remain deliberately unanswered" (13, p. 181). However, he does share Adler's view of the primacy of the occupational task in his observation that, "Most people manage a certain amount of adjustment to the problem of work, since their existence depends on it. The problem of love and marriage is not so immediately urgent. It may be postponed, or even be avoided altogether, especially, if work has been sufficiently successful to act as compensation" (13, p. 192).

Wolfe parallels Way's views. He states, "In contrast to the other two great problems, failure to solve the problem of sex need not result in personal disaster. For this reason, aberrations in the solution of the sexual problem are most numerous. The tyranny of our stomachs compels us to work lest we starve, and the tyranny of loneliness compels us to make certain gestures toward our fellowmen, lest we become insane. But men and women can evade the solution of the sexual problems and still live. . .It is the problem most frequently left unsolved. In no other problem does the seeker after guidance find so many obstacles in his way. Many false solutions of the sex problems are passively tolerated by society, despite their anti-social meaning" (14, p. 201).

Dreikurs (7), too, finds the love task comparatively rarely fulfilled at the present time. Defective social interest can more readily reveal itself in this task because this intimacy of love and sex, tests their capacity for cooperation to the utmost and destroys the distance which can usually be preserved in occupational and social relationships. Moreover, the newly emerging relationships of equality between the sexes presents problems in courtship and marriage which did not exist previously (5).

The above discussion demarcates clearly the difference of opinion centering about two points. In the first instance, there is the disagreement, Adler himself reversing his viewpoint, as to which of the tasks takes precedence over the others. With respect to the second, Adler assumes, with other Adlerians dissenting, that "none of the three problems of life can be solved separately" (4, p. 239). In an even stronger vein on the topic of the unity of the life tasks, he comments, "For the answer we give to these three questions, by virtue of our style of life, is seen in our whole attitude toward them. . .everyone's style of life is reflected more or less in his attitude toward all of them" (3, pp. 42-43).

This implies other issues which find Adlerians at variance. The third difference of opinion is as to whether a person's life style determines all of his approaches to the tasks of life. Adler seems to imply that this is the case. If this were really so, then a person could not be helped in his adjustment without parallel changes in his life style. Yet experience demonstrates that much help can be given to individuals within the framework of the existing life style. Dreikurs' work in child guidance, especially, (6, 9) resides upon the premise that many individuals fail in the life tasks because of lack of knowledge and training in effective methods of coping with contemporary problems rather than through ineffective life styles. Mosak (10) offers a rationale to explain why Adler feels these changes must involve a change in life style and Dreikurs does not. If the life style is seen as a *modus vivendi*, rather than as a *modus operandi*, then many types of behavior are possible within the same life style. These behaviors may be modified or changed even when the basic apperceptive mode remains relatively intact. Therefore, we are probably justified in saying that while a mistaken life style certainly is not conducive to successful fulfillment of any life task, in some instances the individual may even be able to operate adequately despite his mistaken concepts and limited social interest. Adler often pointed out that one can never be sure of a person's social interest, unless it is tested. If a person lives under particularly favorable conditions, he may not reveal his inadequacy until circumstances present more subjectively stressful problems for him to solve.

A fourth implication of Adler's discussion of the life tasks is that, were a man to be capable of solving them, he would be free of inferiority feelings and not fall victim to neurosis. A typical statement of this opinion reads, "If a man can be a good friend to all men, and contribute to them by useful work, by a happy marriage, he will never feel inferior to others or defeated by them" (4, p. 262). True enough, a person with such an amount of social interest is not likely to have any inferiority feelings. However, we should be forced to borrow Diogenes' lamp to find such a person. Even could such a person be found, Way would challenge Adler's statement. "An individual can succeed in solving all the elementary tasks of life, yet still become neurotic if he cannot succeed in reaching his subjective goal of perfection. Even successful persons thus fall into neurosis because they are not more successful. Moreover, success along any other line than that which fulfills the fictional goal has no influence on the person's estimate of himself. . Outward adaptation is no criterion in itself. One may be outwardly successful, yet a failure in one's own eyes. Conversely, one may be a failure from the world's point of view, yet sufficiently content in oneself" (13, p. 180). He proposes that "the individual's first duty is to himself, and the resolute independence is the only guarantee to his social usefulness" (14, p. 181).

If "the individual's first duty is to himself," is he really confronted only with these three tasks and can he be satisfied merely by solving the problems of occupation, association, and sex? Maybe we should recognize the existence of other tasks, all interrelated, and therefore, affecting the solution of the three tasks, but transcending them. Neufeld (12) offers such a proposal. He speaks of the "Four 'S' problems—Subsistence, Society, Sex, and Self." He refers to a statement by Adler which seems to indicate that the individual may be a problem to himself and thereby be part of the "outside world" with which he must deal. "The individual adopts a certain approach, a certain attitude, a certain relation toward problems of the outside world (the outside world includes the experience of one's own body, as well as the experience of one's psychic life)" (2, p. 7).

An earlier statement of Adler's emphasizes the same point. "This outside world includes the individual's own body, his bodily functions and the functions of his mind. He does not relate himself to the outside world in a pre-determined manner, as is often assumed. He relates himself always according to his own interpretation of himself and of his present problem" (1, p. 5). This makes it quite clear that man is a problem to himself. Everyone has to learn not merely how to get along with people, with a person of the opposite sex and how to keep a job; he also is required to learn how to get along with himself, how to deal with himself. This, then, seems to us to be the *fourth life task*.

And there seems to be a need to consider yet another task of life, besides those mentioned before. Each individual is confronted with the task to relate himself to the Universe, which is becoming more and more clearly an extension of our life on this earth. We are no longer merely "living on the crust of this poor planet earth" as Adler phrased it. We extend our life experience into the Universe, with the need to re-evaluate our place on this earth in relatedness to the Universe, to space and time, to eternity.

The problem is not new. Man always established his relationship with transcendental powers and forces in his religions. But our changing concepts of the Universe, of life and of ourselves makes it necessary to re-evaluate concepts and beliefs which were handed down to us throughout the ages. We can, therefore, speak of a *fifth life task*, the need to adjust to the problems beyond the mere existence on this earth and to find meaning to our lives, to realize the significance of human existence through transcendental and spiritual involvement.

REFERENCES

1. Adler, A., "The Fundamental Views of Individual Psychology," *Intl. J. Indiv. Psychol.*, 1935, 1 (1), 5-8.
2. Adler, A., "The Neurotic's Picture of the World," *Intl. J. Indiv. Psychol.*, 1936, 2 (3), 3-13.
3. Adler, A., *Social Interest: A Challenge to Mankind.* New York: Capricorn Books, 1964
4. Adler, A., *What Life Should Mean to You.* New York: Capricorn Books, 1958
5. Dreikurs, R., *The Challenge of Marriage.* New York: Hawthorn Books, 1974.
6. Dreikurs, R., *The Challenge of Parenthood*, New York: Hawthorn Books, 1958.
7. Dreikurs, R., *Fundamentals of Adlerian Psychology.* Chicago: Alfred Adler Inst., 1950.
8. Dreikurs, R., "Psychotherapy as Correction of Faulty Social Values," *J. Indiv. Psychol.*, 1957, 13, 150-158.
9. Dreikurs, R. and Soltz, Vicki, *Children: The Challenge.* New York: Hawthorn Books, 1964.
10. Mosak, H.H., "Early Recollections as a Projective Technique," *J. Proj. Tech.*, 1958, 22, 302-311.
11. Mosak, H. H. and Shulman, B. H., *Introductory Individual Psychology: A Syllabus.* Chicago: Alfred Adler Institute, 1961.
12. Neufeld, I., "Application of Individual Psychological Concepts in Psychosomatic Medicine," *J. Indiv. Psychol.*, 1955, 11, 104-117.
13. Way, L., *Adler's Place in Psychology.* London: Allen and Unwin, 1950.
14. Wolfe, W.B., *How to Be Happy Though Human.* London: Routledge and Kegan Paul, 1932.

The Tasks of Life II. The Fourth Life Task*

Adlerians have dealt extensively with attitudes which enhance or diminish a person's ability to meet the life tasks of work, social relationships, and sex. Now we propose to concern ourselves with the ways in which individuals deal with themselves. The requirements for success and the reasons for failure are fundamentally the same with regard to living in peace with others or in peace with oneself. The lack of social interest, of a feeling of belonging, reduces our tolerance level in dealing with the problems around us; its counterpart, a feeling of inferiority and inadequacy, prevents us from accepting ourselves as we are. To get along with oneself is thus the fourth life task.

One cannot attribute a person's failure to fulfill the tasks of life merely to individual maladjustment. We are faced with a cultural setting which makes the fulfillment of the life tasks difficult. We live in a neurotic society where nobody can be sure of his place and of his value. In an atmosphere of intense competition which violates the equality principle inherent in "The Ironclad Logic of Social Living" (2), man becomes man's worst enemy, and the more so the closer their relationships. Everyone tries madly—and in vain—to find a place for himself. If one does not realize that he has a place by the very reason of his existence, no success, power, education or wealth can provide a sense of security. Either one does not have place enough, or he can lose what he has. Only on the basis of equality,[1] of mutual respect, can we live in peace with others and with ourselves. Our failure lies in our inability to recognize our equality and to deal with each other as equals. Thus, we are culturally deprived of the realization that we are good enough as we are, and we instill this doubt in our children out of fear that satisfaction with what one is may prevent growth, effort and achievement. The

---

1. The concept of equality is difficult to grasp for most people. It has two aspects, equality of rights and equality of worth (7).

*Reprinted by permission from THE INDIVIDUAL PSYCHOLOGIST, 1967, 4(2), 51-56.

opposite is true. The more certain we are of our place, the stronger is our social interest, our feeling of belonging, the greater our ability to make useful contributions and to participate fully in the give-and-take which social living implies.

Getting along with oneself means nothing more nor less than to stop fighting with oneself. That may seem almost impossible to our contemporaries; but this is what we have to learn in order to adjust ourselves to a democratic society.

At the roots of all inner conflict lies a dualism, the assumption that there are two "I's," two opposing forces within us. Tradition and contemporary science have fortified such dualistic beliefs. There is God versus the Devil, good versus evil, the willing spirit and the weak flesh, sin versus virtue, the rational versus the irrational, reason versus emotion, objectivity versus subjectivity, consciousness versus the unconscious. Those who believe in such pairs of inner contradiction within themselves can never achieve peace of mind. Traditionally, the good in us fights against the base, or in psychoanalytic terms, the superego is in conflict with the id, and the irrational forces in us oppose our reason.

Most of us are caught in this inner struggle. There is, as it were, an "I" which observes the "Me"; we watch ourselves whether we do right or wrong, blaming ourselves for our shortcomings and mistakes and taking pride in our victories, mainly over ourselves. We are made to believe in will-power, in the need of "controlling ourselves," siding with one part of ourselves against the other.

The assumption of will-power is one of the most characteristic and, simultaneously, one of the most devastating fallacies in our general conception of human nature. We draw the analogy from our efforts to deal with objects outside of ourselves. Our ability to lift something with our hands depends on two factors: the weight of the object and our muscular strength. If I succeed in lifting it, I am strong; if I can't, I am weak. Thus, the concept of strength is appropriate enough when we deal with objects outside of ourselves. But is it equally applicable when we deal with ourselves? This is the crucial question.

If we fight with ourselves, we must be at the same time the one who wins and the one who loses. We constantly watch to see who will be stronger, "I" or "me." As a consequence, we only defeat ourselves, discourage ourselves, lose faith in ourselves, because we see the enemy within us. We treat ourselves as a bad teacher treats poor students—and with the same disastrous effects. We are conditioned to assume that if we do not fight with ourselves, we cannot control ourselves; and if we don't control ourselves, we will misbehave. In our slave mentality, we intimidate ourselves with the threat of failure, of humiliation. We cannot conceive that people would behave properly without such threats.

Before we can utilize all of our inner resources for the benefit of others and of ourselves, we need to reconsider the prevalent conceptions of human nature. Then, instead of seeing the good and bad at odds within ourselves, we may discover that we are one whole being with the ability to do anything we decide to do, be it good or evil. We can use the left and the right hand. A creature from another planet might assume that both hands constantly fight and oppose each other when we try to grasp something, because he may not realize that this opposition is part of a controlled function. In order to lift our arms we have to use the abductors as well as the adductors to maintain our balance. Equally, we use our reasoning *and* our emotional power, complementing one with the other according to our intentions. We become aware or remain unaware of whatever it is we want or need to know or not know. All seemingly contradictory functions are only self-deceptions. We have become free politically and socially—but we have not learned to recognize and embrace our freedom to decide for ourselves whatever we intend to do. We are one whole and indivisible human being who can use all faculties and abilities, be they physical or mental, reason or emotion, intelligence or ignorance, for our own self-determined purposes. This is a revolutionary conception of man, indeed. This conception, promoted by Adler, is in many regards in line with some aspects of religious thinking.

Subjectively, we may *feel* driven by emotions, by circumstances, and may respond with ambivalence. Scientific assumptions support such occurrences of ambivalence. However, ambivalence is always a self-deception, but self-deception with a purpose. It is an arrangement calculated to avoid responsibility, to demand service or to excuse inactivity. To the extent that ambivalence is perceived by us as "reality," so we find ourselves driven and torn by emotions and contradictions. Since we always move in one direction, one which we have chosen, ambivalence cannot in fact exist in reality because we cannot move in two directions at one time, regardless of how hard we may try. Even hesitation is a way of proceeding. And we use our emotions to fortify our intentions. They are not our masters but our servants (5). But we are only too willing to accept the assumption that man is driven by his emotions. For then we are not really responsible for our behavior—we can blame our emotions for it.

Of course, it is not easy to adopt the new conception of man, because we are so heavily trained to view ourselves as the victims of forces: victims of our hereditary endowment, of our upbringing, of our environment, of our society, of our emotions. We have yet to discover that man *is* a decision-making organism, that we decide every step we take, although not necessarily on the conscious level. What forces converge on us, what situations we find ourselves in, are less important than what we decide to do under the given circumstances. We decide upon the role we intend to play and often contribute significantly to the experience which we "make." We are not merely passive victims of circumstances. There is hardly any situation which does not offer us a better or poorer way to react.

In order, then, to get along with ourselves, we must first learn to recognize that we do only what we decide and what we prefer to do. There is a logic behind all our actions. However, we are not usually aware of our "private logic" or "hidden reason" (6). Here are some of the steps necessary to enable us to experience and utilize our freedom and our potentialities.

We must free ourselves from the prejudice which we have about ourselves. We must accept what we are instead of fighting it. Only then can we grow without the inner friction which drives *and* impedes us at the same time. It is sad that the only people who believe they are good enough as they are, are the mentally ill (9). The insane and the criminal are convinced that they are right—all the others are wrong. Naturally, we cannot be satisfied with everything we do. We all make mistakes. To make mistakes is human—the point is that we have to learn to live with ourselves *with* all our imperfections. We need the courage to be imperfect, to make and accept our mistakes graciously. It is less important what mistakes we make than

103

what we do afterwards. Unfortunately, most people become discouraged by their mistakes and thus are prone to make more mistakes.

Many of our contemporaries see only one purpose in living—to prove how good they are. In our competitive setting this seems to be most important. Therefore, they do not see any other meaning in their lives, except perhaps "to be happy." But neither worth nor happiness is obtainable by the direct striving for it. It is a byproduct of fulfilling one's life. We are here to be useful, to contribute, not to prove our value. Only if we realize that we have a place in life, can we forget about finding one and become responsive to the needs of the situation and not to the needs of our prestige or our desires (8).

In line with traditional conceptions of man as being small, weak, and limited in time and space, we fail to realize our strength, impressed as we are with our weaknesses. We focus our attention out of all reasonable proportion on what we cannot do, and fail to give ourselves credit for what we are or what we can do, except perhaps in rare moments of special achievement. But they do not prevent our fears or silence our doubts. We are constantly afraid of being failures or of being humiliated. Actually, humiliation exists only in the mind of a person who feels humiliated. A person whose self-evaluation is well entrenched cannot be humiliated by others. It is the opinion of ourselves which counts, and we must learn to respect ourselves. Only then can we influence ourselves constructively and utilize our inner resources.

Our present method of influencing ourselves is to fight ourselves. In this fashion we soon reach a deadlock and become powerless to accomplish the very thing we are striving for. And if we try harder and exert more pressure, we only increase the deadlock. While we torture ourselves in our attempt to control ourselves and force ourselves, we fail to observe that we act only as we decide, either "winning" or "losing" the battle with ourselves. We are always accuser, accused, state's attorney, defense lawyer, and judge at the same time—quite an assignment! If we decide to do something wrong, then no "control" and no anger nor fear will deter us. While such insight opens the door to freedom, many of us do not want it because then we would have to accept full responsibility for our behavior. We prefer a "good excuse" and are willing to suffer the pains of guilt feelings. But they, too, are only a pretense (3). Guilt feelings are the expression of good intentions which we do not really have. They always indicate an unwillingness to face up to a situation, using the excuse of past transgression.

Only when we admit to ourselves that whatever we do is based on our decision, thereby discounting all excuses and alibis, only then are we free to see alternatives and to change our decision and direction. We have the power to do so—without knowing it. We have freedom—without knowing how to use it properly. As a result, we all are afraid. We are a frightened generation, conditioned in the past to fear by centuries of autocratic control and now by fear of failure and humiliation. In the past, fear was instilled in the attempt to avoid sin; today, fear is the sin that keeps man from being truly free. As free men, we cannot afford it.

To free ourselves from fear, we have to recognize its fallacy. Far from preventing danger, fear increases it. Actually, it has no relationship to danger. Fear is present only when one thinks about danger, before or after its occurrence. An exception is the sensation of panic, which arises only if one feels lost, and it can bring about destruction.

One of the strongest motivations is anticipation. We all act in line with what we anticipate. We make a secret plan in our mind and move according to it. This is why fear is so dangerous, why the very fear of failure may bring failure about.

Inferiority feelings undermine and limit the all-important feeling of belonging, what Adler called *social interest* (1). In any given situation we must observe whether we increase our feelings of inadequacy or overcome it. This is the crucial factor in dealing with ourselves, as in all corrective efforts. Encouragement is a keynote, whether we wish to overcome deficiencies in others or in ourselves (4). If we want to get along with ourselves, we must not drive, criticize, frighten, or fight ourselves. Then all that is in us—which is so tremendous if one could only see it—would guide us. The strength and power that is within us and at our disposal is as great as the strength and power only recently discovered in the infinitely tiny and heretofore insignificant little atom.

We can discover our strength by opening the door to it. We have tremendous inner resources if we would only believe in them and therby believe in ourselves *as we are*. When we stop trying to "control ourselves," we will soon discover that our actions will in no way be different, for we always do what we decide to do anyhow. After this discovery, we shall be ready for the next step: to change our decisions. Then we will be more likely and able to decide what is good for both ourselves and others, and be less afraid of the wrong things we may do.

It is this that will give us a new freedom to grow, to learn, to change our minds, to fulfill ourselves without struggle. This alone is peace of mind.

REFERENCES

1. Adler, A., *Social Interest: A Challenge to Mankind.* New York: Capricorn Books, 1964.
2. Adler, A., *Understanding Human Nature.* New York: Fawcett, 1959.
3. Beecher W., Bruck, M.A., Dreikurs, R., Feichtinger, F., Plottke, P., and Sicher, Lydia, Symposium on Guilt Feelings. *Indiv. Psychol. Bull.,* 1950, 8, 3-48.
4. Dinkmeyer, D. and Dreikurs, R., *Encouraging Children to Learn: The Encouragement Process.* Englewood Cliffs, N.J.: Prentice-Hall, 1963.
5. Dreikurs, R., The Function of Emotions. *Christian Register,* 1951, 130, 11-14.
6. Dreikurs, R., The Hidden Reason. Unpubl. ms.
7. Dreikurs, R., The Impact of Equality. *The Humanist,* 1964, 24, 143-146.
8. Dreikurs, R., Psychotherapy as Correction of Faulty Social Values. *J. Indiv. Psychol.,* 1957, 13, 150-158.
9. Worchel, P. and Hillson, J.S., The Self-Concept in the Criminal: An Exploration of Adlerian Theory. *J. Indiv. Psychol.,* 1958, 14, 173-181.

The Life Tasks III. The Fifth Life Task*

In two previous papers we have discussed Adler's three life tasks (13) and a fourth task, coping with oneself (14). In addition, Adler alluded many times to *the fifth life task,* but he never specifically identified it. This life task may go under several names—the spiritual, the existential, the search for meaning, the metaphysical, the metapsychological, and the ontological. Yet with Jahn he wrote a book on religion and Individual Psychology (25). Even more puzzling, in his pioneer efforts, parallel with the Gestalt school, he titles one of his books *What Life Should Mean to You* (6) and still speaks only of *three* life tasks. In *Understanding Human Nature,* he briefly alludes to the fifth task, starting a sentence with "By situation we mean his place in the cosmos. . ." (5, p. 41) and drops the subject. Adler's most explicit reference occurs in *Social Interest,* in which he remarks, "They [the life tasks] arise from the relationship of man to human society, to the cosmic factors, and to the other sex" (4, p. 14) and "human beings, as products of this earth, could subsist and develop in their cosmic relationship only by union with the community, by making both material and spiritual provisions for it" (4, p. 43).

Psychologists traditionally have been loathe to discuss this task, their reluctance deriving partially from the feeling in some quarters that such a topic is more legitimately within the provinces of philosophy and theology. Freud, in contrast with Adler, did not feel that the development of a new *Weltanschauung* was the task of psychoanalysis (21). Yet for many individuals the existential tasks are perhaps the most important they face. As Pope Pius XI writes in *Caritate Christi Compulsi,* "For God or against God, this once more is the alternative that shall decide the destinies of all mankind . . . ." Adler, in a wry observation, quotes Lichtenberg, who observes how many people are willing to fight for their beliefs and how few

---

*Reprinted by permission from THE INDIVIDUAL PSYCHOLOGIST, 1967, 5(1), 16-22.

are willing to live up to them (8, p. 35). Since the individual's relationship to the tasks of existence involve belief, conviction, and behavior, are these postures not also objects of psychological concern? Certainly these topics emerge from the lips of patients in the consultation room with a frequency equal to that devoted to the more mundane life tasks. Moreover, the subjective overlap between the philosophical and psychological aspects of these tasks is often so intimate as to defy separation. Freud offers such an example of interleaving when he hypothesizes that "now that God was a single person, man's relation to him could recover the intimacy and intensity of the child's relation to the father" (17, p. 31).

The recent mercurial growth of the existentialist movement both in Europe and the United States reflects the increasing attention given by psychotherapists to issues previously considered to be philosophical or metaphysical. Many of these existential analysts, particularly those in Vienna, are either Adlerians or former Adlerians, still either wrestling with the problem of "what life should mean to you" or, like Frankl (15), having discovered the meaning.

1. The sub-tasks of the existential task can be subsumed under five headings. The first of these involves the relationship of the individual to God. There is the individual decision, most often made non-consciously, to believe in God or not. Is this totally a religious task, with which psychologists should remain unconcerned? Obviously not. To cite one psychological example, the "cure" of alcoholics through Alcoholics Anonymous (and Alcoholics Anonymous probably "cures" more alcoholics than we psychotherapists do) asks that the individual acknowledge a superior Being. If the individual believes in God, how does he describe this God? Philosophically, as Maimonides (29) does, in his Thirteen Principles of Faith? As "the man upstairs"? As "the concretization of the idea of perfection, greatness and superiority" (8, p. 460)? Pantheistically, as Spinoza does? (37) Is he a god of wrath poised to punish the sinner, or is he a god of love, a benevolent Father?

Having described this God, consciously or non-consciously, how does the individual relate to this God? Does he "seek the Lord where he may be found" (*Isaiah* LIV:6)? Does he call upon him only when he is in trouble, in confirmation of the sentiment that "there are no atheists in fox holes"? Does he bribe God to win favors from Him? Does he meet God in prayer, regularly, and with the Psalmist does he proclaim, "Everyday will I bless Thee, and I will praise Thy name for ever and ever" (Psalm 145)? Is his communication with God through a "leap of faith" (23), or does he maintain an "I and Thou" relationship with God (12)? Or is God merely that Being whom he visits in church on Sunday? And finally, for many people, their total relationship with God consists of an affirmative answer when questioned as to whether they believe in God. In addition to describing God and his relationship to Him, each individual assumes a posture toward those who either do not believe in God or those who do believe in Him but who do not share the same definitions or the same forms of relating to Him. Here, clearly, there is overlap with the social task. Is he tolerant of others, is he a bigot, a missionary or a spreader of the Gospel? Does he attempt to convert others, save them from eternal damnation, persecute them or burn them at the stake?

Of course, there is a segment of the population which does not share a belief in God. What does the atheist substitute for the belief in God, if indeed he feels he must substitute anything? A rational view of the universe? A naturalistic interpretation of life, a "religion without the supernatural"? In his *De Rerum Natura*, Lucretius, an exponent of Epicureanism, foreshadows this latter view (27). A humanistic rather than a deistic posture? Again the spiritual and social tasks overlap. What is the atheist's attitude toward those who do believe in God? Is he contemptuous of them? Does he missionize and attempt to "convert" them? Is he tolerant or intolerant of the believers? Does he "go along" with the majority, even as he retains his own views according to his personal conscience?

Then, there is the agnostic. Not knowing whether there is a God, does he merely dismiss the problem? Does he, not believing, nevertheless "go through the motions," just in case there is a God? Does he, having doubts, devote himself to the search for signs of God? Or is he a positive agnostic, one not sure whether there is a God but who uses the concept of God as a working hypothesis and conducts his life as if there were a God?

2. The second sub-task involves a consideration of what the individual does about religion. Does he embrace it, accept it, identify with it, run from it, rebel against it, or convert to another? Is he ashamed of this identity and does he attempt to

hide it? Is his acceptance of his religion a joining with others in common religious purpose, common prayer, or common activity? Or is it a personal faith? If he rebels against religion and denies its personal necessity, does he adopt a Freudian, Marxist, atheistic, or humanistic stance? Perhaps, for some individuals, any of these may even be transmuted into "religions."

For the majority of the population which identifies with religion, either through formal church affiliation or otherwise, the matter of observance or how the individual perceives his duty to this religion assumes significance.

Is religion a matter of attending church regularly, performing the rituals, with or without feeling? Does the individual discharge his obligation or satisfy his conscience merely by purchasing a new organ or stained-glass window for his church? Does his religion consist of sending his children to Sunday School at the same time that he sleeps late on Sundays? Or is his religion based upon a conscientious (in some individuals, overconscientious) adherence to the principles and practices of his religion? Perhaps he assigns second place to formal practices, elevating to primary importance the acceptance of Christ as a personal Saviour, a joy in the communion with God (e.g., the Chasidim, the Holy Rollers), or some ethical consideration as the Golden Rule, or "Love thy neighbor as thyself" (*Leviticus* XIX: 18)[1] or the prophet Micah's, "It hath been told Thee, O man, what is good and what the Lord doth require of thee: Only to do justly, and to love mercy, and to walk humbly with thy God" (*Micah* VI:8). Does religion involve missionary work, converting others, or seeking to save the souls of the heathen and the nonbeliever?

How does the individual define the goals of religion? "Nearer, my God, to Thee"? The service of God? The love of God? The performance of good deeds? Greater self-perfectibility or holiness? The assurance of a place in the hereafter? Transcendence over self? Or does he leave these definitions to ecclesiastical authorities and merely render obeisance to them?

---

[1]Variants of the Golden Rule appear in the following Hebrew sources: *Testaments of the Twelve Patriarchs, Targum Jonathan, Leviticus* (XIX:34); the writings of Philo Josephus, and Judah the Pious; and in following Christian sources: *Acts* (XV:20), *Romans* (XIII:10); the teachings of the Twelve Apostles; and the Apostolical Constitutions (20, pp. 563-4).

3. The individual's conception of the place of man in the universe and the psychological movement to which this conception leads comprises the third existential sub-task. "O Lord," asks the Psalmist, "what is man that Thou shouldst notice him?" (Psalm 143). A highly developed animal, replies Sargent (36). Pascal views him as "A nothing in comparison with the infinite, an all in comparison with nothingness: A mean between nothing and all" (37). "Created in God's image," we read in *Genesis* I:27. For Adler, ". . . to be a human being means to feel oneself inferior" (2, p. 63). Basically good, maintains Rousseau (33). Basically bad, Freud disagrees, "a polymorphous pervert" (18). Encumbered by "original sin," according to Catholic doctrine. Determined, Freud (18) and Jung (26) explain. Freewilling, creative, striving, becoming, self-actualizing, counter Allport (7), Maimonides (28), Rogers (33), Adler (3), and Goldstein (20). He is capable of change, of cure, of salvation because he is a human being, or he can change only by being a true believer or through the exercise of certain rituals, religious or psychological. While we have only indicated some of the conceptual approaches developed by religion, philosophy and psychology, non-consciously each of us develops an image of man which guides his relationships to himself, to his fellow man, to his God, if he has one, and to the universe.

4. Partly religious, partly philosophical, partly practical is the fourth sub-task to which people address themselves— immortality. In theological and philosophical contexts the various questions concerning the existence of an afterlife, the nature of the soul and its persistence after death, salvation and eternal damnation are central. In a more practical vein, we endeavor to achieve immortality through endowing a university building, through outstanding positive or negative accomplishment, through bearing children (and naming them after us) and inculcating them with our values and traditions.

5. The basic question in the fifth sub-task of life involves the meaning of life. Does life have a meaning inherent in it? Does it have no meaning, or does it possess whatever meaning with which we endow it? The meaning may reside in an abstraction such as "Beauty is truth, truth beauty—that is all ye know on earth, and all ye need to know." Christian theology and Freud emphasize the meaning and purposiveness of death.

The first reminds the devout that ". . .whoever loses it [his life] will save it and live" *(Luke* XVII:33)[2] while Freud, with his fondness for physical and biological analogies, sees the death instinct in man marching him inexorably toward death (16).

Many individuals find the meaning of life in suffering or through suffering. The trials of Job, narrated in the Old Testament saga, represent the classic attempt to uncover the meaning of suffering. The peak development of this viewpoint is the psychological system known as "logotherapy," whose founder, Viktor Frankl, found this meaning while an inmate of Auschwitz and Dachau: "In a last violent protest against the hopelessness of imminent death, I sensed my spirit piercing through the enveloping gloom. I felt it transcend that hopeless, meaningless world, and from somewhere I heard a victorious 'yes' in answer to my question of an ultimate purpose" (15, pp. 63-64). Frankl's views, nevertheless, stand out sharply against those of other existentialists who emphasize the meaninglessness of life and man's attendant existential despair or existential frustration. For Christians, the meaning of life may be found in Christ's suffering, the crucifixion, and resurrection. Variants of this viewpoint involve sacrifice, self-sacrifice, deprivation or self-mortification, the institutional forms of which exist in such religious communities as the Penitentes and the Trappists.

A graphic description of meaning through self-mortification comes to us from a nun who lived in a convent for twenty-eight years and then was given permission to return to the world. She describes an Irish priest killed during World War I who "felt God demanded of him the complete sacrifice always and in everything, of every human pleasure and comfort and the embracing . . . without injuring his health or work . . . of every possible discomfort or pain . . . Certainly this was [mortification] with a vengeance, an 'emptying of self' that would create a capacity into which the grace of God could flow in an impetuous stream." . . . "It is, however, interesting to note that the extraordinary penances of the Saints were not so much the outcome of a desire for their own sanctification as a tremendous urge to help and save and, if possible, atone for the sins and

---

[2]Paraphrases of this expression may also be found in *Matthew* (X:39), *Mark* (VIII:35) and *John* (XII:25).

sufferings of a world which has very largely lost the true idea of God" (10, p. 152).

Diametrically opposed are the advocates of hedonism, who find the meaning of life in the seeking of pleasure. In the third century before the common era, Epicurus held that it was the pursuit of pleasure that gave meaning to life (31). Not any pleasure would give this meaning, since the only "real" pleasures were permanent pleasures, and these permanent pleasures were the intellectual ones. Temporary pleasures, like the pleasures of the body, were to be courted only to the extent that they did not interfere with the intellectual pleasures. In the 18th century, Rousseau also advocated a hedonistic position as he maintained that ". . . the love of well-being is the sole motive of human actions . . ." (34). Later in the same century, our Founding Fathers declared that one of our inalienable rights is "the pursuit of Happiness," a phrase which has been turned about by "girl-crazy" college students into "the happiness of pursuit."

Longfellow's rejection of both suffering and pleasure as the goals of a meaningful life anticipates another meaning of life—finding meaning through self-actualization. In "A Psalm of Life" he sermonizes:

> Not enjoyment, and not sorrow,
> Is our destined end or way
> But to act that each tomorrow
> Finds us farther than today.

Goldstein refers to this process as self-actualization (20). Rogers holds a view similar to that of Goldstein (33). Allport and Adler share the term "becoming" (7;3), Adler writing "I would like to stress that the life of the human soul is not a 'being' but a 'becoming'!" (3, p. ix). The distortion of this process, which many psychologists see as being at the core of the neurotic process, has been called "the will to power," "the striving for superiority" and "the search for glory" (30; 2; 4; 5; 6; 24).

Some individuals find meaning in their lives through overcoming or having overcome. A case in point is Clifford Beers' overcoming his mental illness and his founding of the mental hygiene movement in the United States (11). Similarly, there are those who feel compelled to climb mountains because "they're there." The scientist finds meaning through overcoming disease, through the conquest of space, through unraveling the mysteries of physical existence. In a revealing autobiographical sketch, Adler analyzes how he chose his career—that of a physician dedicated to overcoming death (1). The distorted counterparts of "meaning through overcoming" may be seen in those who find meaning only in getting, taking, possessing, manipulating, controlling, and conquering.

For still other individuals, the opportunity to make a social contribution gives meaning to life. Closely allied is the endowment of life through work. The "withering away" of workers after retirement furnishes an example of loss of interest in life when the opportunity to work is no longer available.

In the 1950's, a popular song delivered the message that "the greatest thing you'll ever learn in life is to love and to be loved in return." This sentiment is echoed by Frankl in the following statement: "Then I grasped the meaning of the greatest secret that human thought and belief have to impart: *The salvation of man is through love and in love*" (15, p. 59). The rhapsodies of our poets and composers to the effect that love is all, that love conquers all, need not be repeated here. Three forms of love may be distinguished here—the love of God, the love of other human beings, and the love of life. "And thou shalt love the Lord Thy God with all thy heart, with all thy soul and with all thy might," we read in *Deuteronomy* VI:5, and for the devout this love and the opportunity to serve Him create meaning. The Golden Rule has already received our attention above. Fromm gives loving its finest exposition from a psychological viewpoint (19).

Love, for Adler, exists as a component of man's social feeling (8). In this way Adler elevates love to the rank of his highest value for mankind—social interest. "It can easily be shown that love and marriage are on the side of cooperation in general, not a cooperation for the welfare of two persons only, but a cooperation also for the welfare of mankind" (6, p. 263). Adler's assignment of centrality to love and cooperation as giving meaning to life echoes Marcus Aurelius' belief that "we are made for cooperation, like feet, like hands, like eyelids, like the rows of the upper and lower teeth" (9).

God-centered behavior lends a meaningful dimension to the lives of many people. We have already alluded to the love of God. Many add to the love of God the increment of service to God. Some, like the followers of Billy Graham, find meaning through the acceptance of Christ as their personal Savior. The contemplation of God furnishes meaning for the cloistered religious. Any personal "encounter" with God, through acceptance, alliance, public worship, individual prayer, or "miracles" may give meaning to existence.

If social embeddedness is the key to a person's feeling at home on Earth, then cosmic embeddedness is its counterpart in the existential realm. Feeling at home in the universe provides "the true meaning of life" for the "citizens of the universe."

The foregoing discussion gives ample evidence that Adlerians should be speaking of *five* life tasks rather than the conventional three. This can be accomplished without doing violence to Adlerian thought. Indeed, we have attempted to point out that Adler recognized the existence of these tasks even though he did not formally include them in his theoretical formulations.

REFERENCES

1. Adler, A., "How I Chose My Career." *Indiv. Psychol. Bull.*, 1947, 6, 9-11.
2. Adler, A. "Individual psychology." In Murchison, Carl (ed.). *Psychologies of 1930.* Worcester, Mass.: Clark Univ. Press, 1930.
3. Adler. A. *The problem child.* New York: Capricorn Books, 1963.
4. Adler, A. *Social interest: a challenge to mankind.* New York: Capricorn Books, 1964.
5. Adler, A. *Understanding human nature.* New York: Fawcett, 1959.
6. Adler, A. *What life should mean to you.* New York: Capricorn Books, 1959.
7. Allport, G. W. *Becoming. New Haven:* Yale Univ. Press, 1955.
8. Ansbacher, H. L. and Ansbacher, Rowena (eds.) *The Individual Psychology of Alfred Adler.* New York: Harper Torchbooks, 1964.
9. Aurelius Antoninus, Marcus. *Meditations.* New York: Dutton, 1940.
10. Baldwin, Monica. *I leap over the wall.* New York: Signet Books, 1957.
11. Beers, C. A *mind that found itself.* New York: Longmans, 1908.
12. Buber, M. *I and Thou.* New York: Scribner, 1958.
13. Dreikurs, R. and Mosak, H. H. "The life tasks I. Adler's three tasks." *Indiv. Psychologist*, 1966, 4(1), 18-22.
14. Dreikurs, R. and Mosak, H. H. "The life tasks II: The fourth life task." *Indiv. Psychologist*, 1967, 4(2), 51-55.
15. Frankl, V. *Man's search for meaning: an introduction to logotherapy.* New York: Simon & Schuster Pocket Books, 1963.
16. Freud, S. *Beyond the pleasure principle.* New York: Bantam Books, 1959.
17. Freud, S. *The future of an illusion.* New York: Liveright, 1953.
18. Freud, S. *Three contributions to the theory of sex.* New York: Nerv. Ment. Dis. Publ. Co., 1920.
19. Fromm, E. *The art of loving.* New York: Harper, 1956.
20. Goldstein, K. *Human nature in the light of psychopathology.* Cambridge: Harvard Univ. Press, 1940.

21. Hall, C. S. *A primer of Freudian psychology.* New York: Mentor Books, 1955.
22. Hertz, J. (ed.). *The Pentateuch and Haftorahs.* London: Soncino Press, 1958.
23. Heschel, A. J. *God in search of man.* New York: Farrar, Straus and Cudahy, 1955.
24. Horney, Karen. *Neurosis and human growth.* New York: Norton, 1950.
25. Janh, E. and Adler, A. *Religion Und Individualpsychologie: eine prinzipelle Auseinandersetzung uber Menschenfuhrung.* Vienna: Rolf Passer, 1933.
26. Jung, C. G. *The integration of personality.* London: Routledge and Kegan Paul, 1940.
27. Lucretius Carus, Titus. *On the nature of things.* Oxford: Clarendon Press, 1946.
28. Maimonides. M. *The Mishneh Torah.* New York: Azriel, 1937.
29. Maimonides, M. *Perush ha-mishnayoth.* New York: Shulsinger, 1951.
30. Oates, W. J. (ed.). *The Stoic and Epicurean philosophers: the complete extant writings of Epicurus, Epictetus, Lucretius, and Marcus Aurelius.* New York: Random House, 1940.
31. Pascal, B. *Pensees: notes on religion and other subjects.* New York: Dutton, 1960.
32. Rogers, C. R. *On becoming a person.* Boston: Houghton Mifflin, 1961.
33. Rousseau, J. J. *Discourse on the origin of inequality among men.* In *The social contract [and] discourses.* New York: Dutton, 1950.
34. Rousseau, J. J. *Emile.* New York: Dutton, 1948.
35. Sargant, W. W. *Battle for the mind.* Baltimore: Penguin Books, 1961.
36. Spinoza, B. de. *Ethics demonstrated in geometrical order and divided into five parts, which treat (1) of God; (2) of the nature and origin of the mind; (3) of the nature and origin of the affects; (4) of human bondage, or the strength of the affects; (5) of the power of the intellect, or of human liberty.* London: Oxford Univ. Press, 1937.

Various Purposes of Symptoms*

In medicine, a symptom is a condition that accompanies or results from a disease and serves as an aid to the diagnosis of such disease. The concept that a symptom may have a purpose is familiar to medicine. For example, the purpose of diarrhea is to expel the irritant from the digestive tract; of pain, to signify that something is wrong; of a cough, to remove foreign material from the trachea.

Alfred Adler made the basic assumption that "We cannot think, feel, will or act without the perception of some goal" (1, p. 3). He considered the following statement an important proposition of Individual Psychology: "Every psychic phenomenon, if it is to give us any understanding of a person, can only be grasped and understood if regarded as a preparation for some goal" (1, p. 4). A psychic symptom, like any other psychic phenomenon, has a purpose and can best be understood if its purpose is understood.

It is sometimes easier to see symptoms as reactive behavior than as purposive. To illustrate, anxiety can be seen as a reaction to a perceived danger; depression, as a reaction to discouragement. However, in cases where such reactions are exaggerated or overly prolonged or inappropriate, this point of view does not give a clue to their understanding.

Freud's point of view was that "A symptom is a sign and a substitute for an instinctual gratification which has remained in abeyance; it is a consequence of the process of repression" (6, p. 20). "Sometimes the symptoms become valuable to the ego because they obtain for it, not certain advantages, but a narcissistic gratification which it would otherwise forego." Thus the obsessional uses his symptoms to feel "better than others because he is specially cleanly or specially conscientious." Freud calls this the epinosic or secondary gain of the neurosis (6, p. 36). Thus, Freud also recognized that symptoms have a value to the patient, but he preferred to see them primarily as

*Reprinted by permission from JOURNAL OF INDIVIDUAL PSYCHOLOGY, 1967, 23 79-87.

compromises with the instincts, and only secondarily as purposive.

In the eyes of the Individual Psychologist, the main significance of the symptom lies in its service to the individual in striving for his goal. Adler, in discussions of clinical examples, frequently mentioned the purpose or "secret intent" in the use of the symptoms. Thus, a symptom is described as the means of securing a triumph, of retiring from danger, of reproaching another, of creating the fiction of a superiority (1, pp. 11-13), of providing an exemption from the demands of reality (1, p. 23); "to force his environment into his service" (1, p. 38); "compelling [others] to concern themselves continuously with him" (1, p. 55).

Adler's views were presented more systematically by the Ansbachers. In one chapter his writings on the function of the neurotic symptoms are organized (2, pp. 263-280). All symptoms are seen as serving as safeguards for self-esteem, or as excuses. One way to accomplish this is through aggression, specifically through: depreciation of others, as in sexual perversion; accusation of others for imagined faults, etc.; and self-accusation and neurotic guilt.

Another way of safeguarding is through "distance" for which four categories are recognized: "moving backward" which includes suicide, agoraphobia, compulsive blushing, migraine, anorexia nervosa, etc.; "standing still" as in psychic impotence, psychogenic asthma, anxiety attacks, compulsions, etc.; "hesitation and back-and-forth" as in all methods of killing time such as procrastination, compulsions, pathological pedantry; and "construction of obstacles," primarily psychosomatic symptoms.

Adler sees the symptom as an expression which is always in accord with the patient's life style, his basic attitudes toward life. Physical symptoms show the same expressiveness. Thus, vomiting may say, "I can't swallow that," abdominal cramps and rumbling in the bowels, "My bowels are in an uproar," and so on. Such organ jargon (2, pp. 222-225, 308-310) frequently provides the clue to the underlying purpose of the symptom.

To return to the above category of aggression, many symptoms can be regarded as offensive weapons. "Neurosis is the weapon of the coward and the weak" (2, p. 269). Thus, one way the Individual Psychologist tries to understand a symptom is to ask himself against whom or what the symptom is directed. For example, the depressed patient expresses his antagonism to the life situation in his negative feelings (3), the paranoid symptoms destroy logic (9), the hyperactive child annoys his mother (5), the frigid woman rejects a man's power to arouse her, the homosexual negates the sexual value of the opposite sex (7), and the emotionally unstable person punishes those who fail to accede to his demands by making a scene.

Returning to the category of distance, it is a truism of Individual Psychology that neurosis is an evasion of life tasks and neurotic symptoms are evasive devices. "The neurotic has always collected some more or less plausible reasons to justify his escape from the challenge of life, but he does not realize what he is doing" (2, p. 332). The neurasthenic, for example, uses his various sensations to announce to himself his incapability of meeting this or that unpleasant situation (4). Symptoms become part of an overall strategy dictated by the dominant goal, fitting into it in many different ways and serving many purposes.

This paper proposes to spell out further the Adlerian concept of the purpose of the symptom by listing various stratagems which have been most commonly found in patients examined by the authors.

SAFETY STRATAGEM

Some symptoms are intended to insure against failure, exposure, or other catastrophes (2, pp. 263-266). The symptom may have the effect of making it impossible for the patient to meet an onerous responsibility, or at least to delay the "moment of truth" (cf. the various methods of safeguarding through distance described above). He may use the symptom to disqualify himself from a race he does not wish to run.

A 37-year-old bachelor suffered from sexual impotence only with a pretty 33-year-old divorcee who wanted to marry him. He never was impotent with prostitutes or in casual affairs. This was the first girl he really considered marrying. However, he felt he could not propose in view of his sexual inadequacy. When he was asked what he would do if the symptom were not present (2, p. 332), he answered, "Why, I'd get married of course." His dreams and early memories revealed an antagonism toward and fear of close relationships with women.

The symptom of mild depression sometimes has the purpose of safeguarding the person from the demands of an occupation or a life situation that requires some action he is unwilling to take or some commitment he is unwilling to make.

A single man of 30 was alternately a successful salesman and a poor one. He would become enthusiastic and work steadily for several months, then become neurasthenic and depressed and spend several weeks frittering his time away. He also complained that he wanted to get married but would not undertake the responsibility of a family because he could not be sure that he would work steadily. A dream revealed the underlying dynamics and showed his fear of commitment to any particular job or relationship. He dreamed that he was on a battlefield and all about him were men fighting with each other. Corpses were strewn about the field and he was lying quietly, pretending to be dead. He felt himself in the midst of a heroic struggle but had no feeling of belonging to any particular side in the conflict. He had no weapons and wondered if he were supposed to be a combatant. He would have liked to have taken part in the struggle, but felt that to move would be to betray himself and invite the attack of others. He waited until night came and crept away to a safer place.

A special instance of the safety stratagem is "buying double insurance." This device is the opposite of the double bind. It is a double unbind. No matter what the outcome, the safety of the individual is secured and therefore he can afford to take a partial chance. Inability to concentrate on school studies often falls in this category. The real problem consists in the fact that the student dares not make a true test of his intellectual capacity. His symptoms insure him against the failure of being of ordinary intellect.

A student is overambitious and demands of himself that he be "on top." He cannot really afford to take the chance that his best efforts may leave him in the average range of his class. At first he makes resolutions to study and indeed fantasies that he will study exceedingly well and do much outside reading on his subject. But somehow he rarely sits down actually to do the necessary work. In a few weeks he is already behind and the chances that he will do exceedingly well are already poor. Now he feels disappointed in himself and even less inclined to study. People who want to be "on top" have no interest in studying hard to achieve only an average passing grade. This is shown in his procrastination, inability to concentrate, and restlessness when he sits down to his books. Throughout this comedy the student maintains his feeling of intellectual superiority. He blames his trouble with studying and his poor grades on bad habits, "nervousness," lack of discipline, dull teachers, and uninteresting courses. He consoles himself with the thought that his is really a bright intellect that is merely unproductive for the moment, that if only he were able to study properly, he would be at the top of the class. If he should happen to get a high grade in spite of the fact that he did not study, that is all to the good. He may even boast, "I never opened a book." If he receives a poor grade, it is not because he is stupid, but because he was "lazy," and in our society most people would prefer to be regarded as lazy rather than stupid (2, p. 391; 8).

The following is another example of the way in which a symptom is used to "buy double insurance." Once a psychiatrist (Rudolf Dreikurs) mentioned in a talk that neurotic symptoms were often used to evade responsibility. After the talk, a member of the audience introduced himself and stated that he suffered from headaches for which no organic cause had ever been found, but that the headaches were not used by him to evade his responsibilities. The man was indeed a successful playwright whose works were well known. "I seldom let my headaches keep me from working," he said. "I will simply go ahead with whatever I have to do in spite of pain." The psychiatrist confessed this case was perhaps an exception. They chatted a few moments longer about plays and authors and the playwright turned to go. As he left, he said, "Just think what I could have done had I not had these headaches. Who knows? People might have compared me with Shakespeare."

HERO-MARTYR-SAINT STRATAGEM

An efficient, capable individual will sometimes complain of distressing symptoms even when no overt stress is apparent. He may create his symptoms in order to demonstrate his strength, just as some with saintly aspirations create temptations in order to demonstrate their virtue by not succumbing, or the aspiring martyr arranges to suffer in order to demonstrate his moral superiority over his tormenters.

A medical student complained that he became panicky and felt faint during conferences and ward rounds. He feared that his supervisors would ask him questions which he would not be able to answer. He did not have such symptoms during written examinations. Furthermore, in his ward work he made a good record. He developed a reputation for skill in drawing blood and was called upon whenever his colleagues could not find a vein. He felt a sense of triumph at these times. He enjoyed examining new patients and was exhilarated by a diagnostic problem He recognized that he was happier when faced with a challenge. He could not understand his emotional symptoms and felt like a coward and weakling for having them.

One can guess that this man found unpleasant any situation in which his superiority was questioned. Furthermore, his way of being superior was to be a hero, to accomplish what others could not. A situation which did not provide him with an obstacle to overcome had no value for him. At the conference and ward rounds, he not only had no chance to act the hero, he was even in danger of being exposed as someone who did not know as much as he should.

What then is the purpose of his symptoms? They supply him with a challenge and an obstacle and therefore, as Adler says, with a chance to enhance himself (2, pp. 275-276). At each conference he again has the chance to be a hero by struggling with and overcoming his spurious weakness.

ATTENTION-SERVICE-LOVE STRATAGEM

The purpose of some symptoms is obviously to get something. Sometimes it is sympathy, sometimes service, but always in this case it is to make oneself the center of the field of action through the symptom. For example, if a mother pays more pleasant attention to the child when he is sick and tends to ignore him when he is not complaining, it becomes most tempting to the child to complain about some body discomfort in order to win the mother's attention. Symptoms used for this purpose work better if they have some dramatic quality which compels the attention of the observer.

A 22-year-old girl was seeing a therapist weekly for an anxiety reaction. For several consecutive Sunday nights she experienced a panic and telephoned her therapist. On one such occasion the therapist asked, "Why is it that you become panicky every Sunday night and don't seem to have this trouble at other times?" "Well," she answered, "I know you're at home on Sunday night." The therapist confronted her with the purpose of her panic; namely, to give her an excuse to call him at a time he was known to be available. The Sunday night panics subsequently stopped.

POWER STRATAGEM: MANIPULATION OF OTHERS

The most direct example of a symptom which has as its purpose to overpower is the temper tantrum (2, p. 227). The small child with temper tantrums kicks, screams and holds his breath until the parents give in, acknowledging his power. The hysteric throws a fit when someone is displeasing her. The mother who wants to hold on to her adult son develops chest discomfort and shortness of breath when be becomes interested in a marriageable girl. The symptom is designed to overpower the others and permit the sufferer to have his own way. In effect, the patient is saying, "If you don't do what I want, I will suffer and *make* you do it." "Tears and complaints—the means which I have called 'water power'—can be an extremely useful weapon for . . . reducing others to a condition of slavery" (2, p. 288).

REVENGE AND RETRIBUTION

There are times when a symptom has the purpose of destructive retaliation against a person or life situation (3, pp. 269-271). Patients who use symptoms for revenge are usually very discouraged people who have lost the hope of dealing with the situation constructively. In taking revenge, they are striking back in anger, willing to do damage because all is lost anyway. Adler gives an example of a depressed woman who dominated her husband and who developed a guilt complex over an affair she had had 25 years before with another man. By confessing to her husband and accusing herself she could continue to torture him (2, p. 272).

A 17-year-old girl, in a state hospital with a diagnosis of emotionally unstable personality and history of rejection and neglect by her parents, was a problem to the hospital staff for two reasons: she impulsively broke windows with the back of her hand, and she mutilated herself by putting sharp foreign objects in her ears and under her skin. She was well treated in the hospital and given considerable attention since the staff appreciated the extent of her early emotional deprivation. But whether she had privileges or not made no difference in her behavior. On visits to her family she behaved the same way. Under questioning she said that she broke windows to "get even." She wanted to get even with her family and a life situation that kept her a patient in a mental hospital. If she wanted something and did not get it, if her mother's visit had irritated her, or if she had for any reason begun to brood on her lot, she became impulsively angry and broke whatever windows she could reach. She injured herself for the same reason.

FACE-SAVING STRATAGEM

Sometimes a symptom has as its purpose to repair damaged self-esteem. The development of a delusional system in the later stages of schizophrenia is often an example of this. Another common example is guilt feelings. When a person has done something he believes is wrong, feeling guilty about his behavior is sometimes his way of salving his own conscience and consoling himself that he is really a well-intentioned person (2, pp. 272-273).

A 3-year-old girl was observed to sneak to the cookie jar, take out a cookie and eat it. She then slapped her hand and said, "Bad girl." Having made "retribution" she then took more cookies, repeating the self-reproach after each one (5).

Other face-saving devices include the development of symptoms which excuse or mitigate a failure (2, pp. 265-266). Thus, a man who lost his job because he dropped and broke a valuable instrument developed a tremor of the hands. He reported that he lost his job because of his "shakes," not because of incompetence.

CREATING EXCITEMENT

Sometimes a symptom has the purpose of creating a furor and agitating others. The symptom may be directed against a particular person the patient wants to annoy or sometimes against a life situation that is boring and uneventful. The excitement may be generated internally or externally. The former is often the purpose of irrational impulses.

A young law student complained of strange impulses to jump down from heights. He would experience these impulses upon crossing bridges or looking down at the ground from windows in tall buildings. He did not believe that he would give in to the impulses but was annoyed by them and was concerned lest they be symptomatic of an approaching mental disorder. The patient could not seem to relate his symptoms to any particular problems. There seemed to be no critical situation in his life. But the symptoms never appeared when he was busy, under stress of work or school, or otherwise occupied. He experienced them only when he had no immediate task to perform, when he was for the moment idle, bored or forced to wait for events. The symptoms were used by him to keep his life interesting and exciting.

Some people find exciting and dramatic the recital of illnesses, operations and doctor's examinations. Hypochondriacal symptoms (which are often somatic pre-occupations) often make life more exciting.

The creation of external excitement is quite clear when the symptom is a fainting spell or perhaps a hysterical fit. Contagious forms of hysterical behavior, such as mass swooning of young female audiences of popular singers, fit into the category.

A man of 40 went to a management consultant with the complaint that he could not organize his business well. He had a wife, a mistress, engaged in casual affairs, ran two businesses, became constantly involved in community projects and seemed willing to give himself to any new challenge that came his way. When a friend became ill with cancer, he contacted specialists in other cities to ask their advice. He took up the cause of better housing for Negroes. He drove his car at excessive speeds. He encouraged his mistress to date other men and became obsessively jealous when she did. Because of his numerous activities he was a poor family man and erratic provider. In spite of his positive accomplishments, he was much more impressed by the atmosphere of confusion and excitement in which he lived. He recounted his exploits gleefully, dramatizing his narrow escapes and his inability to live a stable life. The excitement actually meant more to him than anything else. A narrow escape afforded more pleasure than a constructive achievement. He scarcely solved one problem before he was embroiled in another.

PROOF STRATAGEM

Some symptoms have the purpose of the patient strengthening his position, of proving to himself that his judgments are correct and thus defeating the logic of those who disagree with him. These individuals "run after their slaps in the face" (2, p. 290). The paranoid may deliberately provoke others to behave badly to him in order to gather evidence that others are unfair to him. "Lack of joy in life, the continuous expectation of accidents, ... superstitious fear, ... distrust" and other manifestations of oversensitivity lead to the repetition of unpleasant experiences and the lack of pleasant ones (2, p. 290).

A 14-year-old boy, subject to much deprecatory criticism from his father, was pessimistically convinced of his own inadequacy. He did not believe that psychotherapy could ever help him. He had originally come with a complaint of pain in the left side which was diagnosed as psychogenic. After several months in treatment, he had long since stopped talking about the pain and complained about numerous other symptoms. One day, as he complained about the ineffectiveness of therapy, the therapist pointed out that at least he no longer had the pain in his side. The patient demurred and changed the subject. When he returned the following week, he gleefully reported that the pain in the side had recurred. This was additional proof that psychotherapy could not help him.

KEEPING A SYMPTOM IN RESERVE

Patients who respond favorably to psychotherapy sometimes retain one or two symptoms for no readily apparent reason. They seem to be functioning well, are happy, and report a feeling of progress. They sometimes feel that some particular problem has not yet been worked out and feel that they therefore need more treatment. The reason for such behavior is sometimes that the patient does not dare to become completely well. He prefers to keep a symptom or two in reserve just in case he may need them. In this way he maintains a form of insurance against future difficulties, keeps himself in training by practicing the symptom, and avoids a complete commitment to the idea that he is now completely well and no longer has excuses for holding back in life. As one patient said when he was confronted with the meaning of his behavior, "After all, nobody can ever get *that* well."

SUMMARY

The purposive nature of the symptom is stressed by Individual Psychologists in accordance with their point of view that behavior is goal-directed, and that the functional mental illnesses represent inadequate or socially useless ways of dealing with the demands of life which arouse in the individual fear of failure. The authors have described some purposes of symptoms found with relative frequency among patients in psychotherapy.

REFERENCES

1. ADLER, A. *The practice and theory of Individual Psychology* (1920). Totowa, N. J.: Littlefield, Adams, 1959.
2. ADLER, A. *The Individual Psychology of Alfred Adler.* Edited by H. L. & Rowena R. Ansbacher. New York: Basic Books, 1956.
3. ADLER, K. A. Depression in the light of Adlerian psychology. *J. Indiv. Psychol.*, 1961, 17, 56-67.
4. DREIKURS, R. The problem of neurasthenia. *Int. J. Indiv. Psychol.*, 1936, 2 (3), 14-34.
5. DREIKURS, R. Guilt feelings as an excuse. *Indiv. Psychol. Bull.*, 1950, 8, 12-21.
6. FREUD, S. *Inhibitions, symptoms and anxiety* (1926). London: Hogarth, 1949.

7. KRAUSZ, E. O. Homosexuality as neurosis. *Int. J. Indiv. Psychol.*, 1935,1 (1), 30-40.
8. LINDGREN, H. C. *Psychology of personal and social adjustment.* New York: American Book, 1959.
9. SHULMAN, B. H. An Adlerian view of the Schreber case. *J. Indiv. Psychol.*, 1959, 15, 180-192.

Aggression as a Secondary Phenomenon*

The widespread delight in reading murder mysteries and watching fights, be they boxing or bullfights, is frequently cited as evidence for an innate aggression instinct as postulated by Freud in 1929 (5). Such stories or events would afford, it is held, a vicarious expression of aggression without the responsibility of either killing or fighting oneself. But actual fighting itself, which is found frequently enough in the world, is pointed to as perhaps the main line of evidence for an innate primary aggression instinct.

The purpose of the present paper is to offer alternate explanations for these phenomena, derived from Adlerian theory. While Adler had spoken of an aggression drive as early as 1908, he soon abandoned this concept, replacing it with the concept of a general upward striving which he called variously striving to be a real man, striving for power, superiority, success, and ultimately for perfection and completion—in the mentally healthy person in a socially useful, contributive direction (2, pp. 34-39).

VICARIOUS AGGRESSION

People, of course, differ and ultimately each individual is unique. Thus, although there are undoubtedly some who derive gratification from identification with the powerful, the cruel, or the killer, it is unlikely that too many people would really like to be in his place.

What apparently fascinates many, especially the highly intellectual people who read mystery stories, is the skill with which conclusions are formed from minimal clues. The mental processes involved in detective work bear striking resemblance to those engaged in by the therapist when unraveling the "mysteries" of his patients (3). Unfortunately, few writers of mystery stories possess sufficient imagination to create literary

*Reprinted by permission from JOURNAL OF INDIVIDUAL PSYCHOLOGY, 1967, 23, 232-235.

productions involving subjects other than murders to arouse the reader's interest. Poe's *The Gold Bug* is a notable exception.

The hunting dog, in flushing out his quarry, has more appeal than the sheepherding dog who is merely a technician. Likewise, gory movies and television plots are attractive to children and rather primitive grown-ups because they denote action. Yet those more sophisticated pictures in which the gore is merely an accessory to a legal procedure or is an avenue for expressing some ethical ideas, ultimately have a greater audience of mature people, viewers who want something to think about, some values that are at stake.

The excitation of the esthetic sensibilities may also be involved, in addition to the stimulation of the logical processes. In such instances a fight is not interesting because someone is rendered punch-drunk or a bull is killed. Rather the "dancing" skill of the boxer and certainly the "passes" of the matador are appreciated as beautiful, while the gore is an unpleasant, negligible accessory to the beauty of the pageant which the picadors and toreadors are presenting. In Portugal, for example, the bulls are not even killed but are led out of the arena after the fight. Shall we assume that the Portuguese are not hostile or aggressive, overtly or covertly?

There is also the mere desire that the side with whom one has identified may triumph. The yelling that goes on at all of these events—boxing, bullfights, automobile races—is generally not due to the fact (or the wish) that someone might be hurt. In many instances it represents the desire to see one on whom one has placed one's hope and confidence, and in many cases, one's money, emerge victorious. The truimph of the underdog unleashes the yelling for some. The thrill seeker finds his thrill, and he whose life style requires to be in control derives vicarious satisfaction in seeing how close one can get to danger and death (the ultimate controller) without losing control and falling victim to the enemy.

ACTUAL AGGRESSION

Where does all the fighting in our world start, and why is it so difficult to call a halt to it? What is this hostility and aggression that now threatens to assume primacy even over the sexual drives? Two factors, fear and greed, seem to lie behind it, both directed toward the same two goals—physical survival and psychological survival.

Out of fear for survival and out of the conviction that attack is the safest defense, methods of defense eventually are used in an aggressive manner. There are people who speak of preventive wars, not because they are hostile and aggressive but because their fear for survival calls for the aggressive defense of preventive war. A youngster, asked by his mother why he had hit another boy at the playgroup, explained, "Oh, Mommy, he had such a mean look in his eye. I knew he wanted to hit me, so I hit him back first!"

Although the child is normally protected against the forces of nature, at an early stage he learns to fear and fight the giants in his surroundings, dinosaurs in the form of grown-ups, whom the child for quite some time cannot understand. Yet they have the right to do with him as they see fit without his having a say in it, except for perhaps a cry or scream. Democracy does not intrude in the baby's world. He may legitimately soon come to feel afraid, since he is small, lacks competence, and is incapable of taking care of himself (1, pp. 48-70). Consequently, many children who are considered aggressive are probably so in the meaning of self-assertion.

If fear for physical survival is responsible for many acts of hostility among adults, the fear for one's value system, one's psychological survival, generates as many, if not more, antisocial attitudes in human interaction. Psychological survival concerns the status of the person, and its preservation is at least as important as the survival in life itself. At times it is even superordinate to physical survival as when a person chooses to die for his principles.

Both fears, for physical and psychological survival, are reinforced by greed. If possessions give one status and importance, then the child must be taught to believe in and practice the "have" position as the one which increases one's stature. The self-training in a child along these lines elicits the praise that he is smart and clever, boding well for his future. The misinterpretation takes hold that it might be smarter to get more while doing less. And nothing seems more despicable than to be made a sucker, to be taken advantage of. If one does not get, life is unfair; the individual feels entitled to express his hostility 6), and feels his greed legitimized.

Is one to believe that these acts of hostility can be attributed to a gene-bound trait? Or are they referrable to an acquired conviction that nothing is enough? Children are trained to worship the false ideas of security, importance, status (4) with which society abounds because of the generally prevalent poorly developed social interest. The associated hostility is the consequence of the acquired greed.

CONCLUSION

Summarizing, we would say that vicarious aggression is often the fascination for action and its excitement and beauty, or identification with the victor or underdog. Actual fighting and other forms of hostility are secondary to fear and greed, both directed toward physical and psychological survival and self-assertion. These points are further arguments against the Freudian notion of innate, universal aggression.

From this follows among other possible conclusions that the selling of guns and war toys for children can no longer be rationalized as affording them an opportunity to discharge their aggression. Rather, we must ask ourselves, toward what goals are we training our children?

REFERENCES

1. ADLER, A. *What life should mean to you* (1931). New York: Capricorn Books, 1959.
2. ADLER, A. *The Individual Psychology of Alfred Adler.* Edited by H. L. & Rowena R. Ansbacher. New York: Basic Books, 1956.
3. COLBY, K. M. *The skeptical psychoanalyst.* New York: Ronald, 1958.
4. DREIKURS, R. The correction of faulty social values in psychotherapy. *J. Indiv. Psychol.*, 1957, 13, 150-158.
5. FREUD, S. *Civilization and its discontents* (1929). London: Hogarth, 1946.
6. MOSAK, H. H. The getting type: a parsimonious, social interpretation of the oral character. *J. Indiv. Psychol.*, 1959, 15, 193-196.

Subjective Criteria of Normality*

Ovid's proclamation "I know myself better than any doctor can" is not without merit. The individual's own subjective evaluation of this normality or the lack of it frequently propels him into therapy, compels him to continue, or impels him to terminate. These subjective criteria define his therapeutic goals and expectations (Mosak, 1950; 1952). Since resistance in therapy occurs when the therapist's and the patient's goals are at variance (Dreikurs, 1961), it is essential that the therapist be aware of the patient's goals if he is to deal with this resistance effectively.

The criteria of normality which follow have been compiled from therapeutic interviews with patients.

THE FREQUENCY CRITERION

This criterion is the subjective counterpart of an objective criterion. If many people possess this symptom or perform this act or experience this feeling, it is normal. If few people think, feel or act this way, it is abnormal. To the extent that I behave like the normal people, I too am normal. Where my behavior resembles that of the minority, I am abnormal. For people with this outlook, statistics, the writings of Emily Post and of Alfred Kinsey are the yardsticks for self-appraisal. Individuality and uniqueness are eschewed as signs of abnormality unless the patient has an investment in feeling that he is abnormal. The watchword of such a patient when the normality of an act is challenged is, "Doesn't everybody?"

THE OTHER-AS-REFERENT

The other-as-referent criterion does not rely upon statistical evidence. The "other" is a vaguely defined representation of other people's behavior. It is the way the patient *thinks* people behave in contrast to the frequency criterion's *informing* him how people behave. The patient can consequently modify

---

*Reprinted by permission from PSYCHOTHERAPY: THEORY, RESEARCH AND PRACTICE, 1967, 4(4), 159-161.

133

his standard at will to suit whatever immediate purpose he might have during therapy, a flexibility not available to the user of the frequency criterion. Asked what they wish to accomplish in therapy, patients in this category reply, "I'd like to be like everyone else." Unfortunately, they usually cannot define even to their satisfaction what everyone is really like.

Patients who must be hospitalized often become depressed (or more depressed) because "I must be crazy if they put me in here with crazy people." Conversely, patients in group therapy experience relief in the consensual validation of their behavior. The feeling of increased or restored normality is reflected in the "I never knew other people had feelings like mine," "I always thought I was the only one who had such screwy thoughts," and "Do you mean that you do that too?" remarks commonly encountered in group therapy.

THE THERAPIST-AS-REFERENT

Many patients endow the therapist with the ideal version of normality. The latter becomes the standard for normal behavior, the possessor of the "know how" to be normal, the custodian of "right" behavior. These patients measure the extent of their normality in terms of the discrepancy between their behavior and that of the therapist. The patient may mimic the therapist's speech, ape his mannerisms, perhaps switch to the therapist's brand of cigarette (obviously not Tareyton smokers), and attend the same social, cultural, and athletic events. He occasionally does "research" on his therapist, "looks him up" in various directories, "interviews" friends and colleagues of the therapist, for the more information one possesses about his therapist, the more adequate and certain the guidelines. Fierce defense of the therapist's behavior is aroused when others are critical of the therapist because if the therapist is not "right" or "normal" or perfect, what referent or guideline will the patient then have for his behavior? Occasionally in group therapy we overhear two patients defending their respective therapists in emotion-laden phrases bordering upon the "my therapist is more normal than your therapist."

This patient tells the therapist, "I wish I could carry you around in my pocket" and in one sense he does. Confronted with

134

the necessity to make a decision, he inquires of himself, "I wonder what 'Dr. X' would do in this situation."

THE SELF-AS-REFERENT

One's own normality is taken as an article of faith by the adopter of this criterion. Only should others' behavior coincide with his is their behavior normal. This condition rarely exists, and he shares the view of the Quaker who told his wife, "All the world's mad but me and thee—and sometimes I have my doubts about thee." He does not make inquiry of the therapist about his (the patient's) normality. He *tells* him that he is normal. Should the therapist doubt or disagree with the patient's assessment, then it follows that the therapist does not know his business or the patient accuses, "You're crazy if you think I'm crazy."

THE PRE-MORBID CRITERION

Investigation of this patient's goals and anticipations elicits the response, "I'd like to be the way I used to be." The patient's pre-morbid adjustment, based generally upon the absence of symptoms, is presumed to be the normal state. Since with the exception of such conditions as transient reactions to stress, "the way I used to be" made the patient vulnerable to his present disturbance, this therapeutic goal is usually not consonant with that held by the therapist.

NORMALITY EQUALS CONFORMITY

From the objective viewpoint this criterion is familiarly known as the "school teachers' criterion." If the child behaves, creates no classroom difficulties for the teacher, he is considered normal (Ruch & Warren, 1948). Should he misbehave in class, he might earn a referral to the school psychologist. From the subjective viewpoint the individual's equation of normality and conformity similarly leads to the corollary that abnormality derives from acting out rather than from manifestation of symptoms. This criterion differs from the other-as-referent in that the person is not primarily concerned with how others behave. He must still live up to the standards of right and of good behavior even when others do not. People who have a strong need for moral superiority find this criterion most acceptable. However, they make themselves vulnerable to upset in that they often court martyrdom and "die for their beliefs" because they must do the right thing at all costs. Overconformity additionally advances the feeling that one may be a "sucker," and therefore abnormal, and invites the lament, "I wish I could let myself do what others do." The restoration of self-esteem is apparent even as the individual downgrades himself. "Maybe I'm a sucker but that's the way I am."

NORMALITY EQUALS MEDIOCRITY

The Aristotelian philosophy of "Nothing in excess" is the creed of this patient. His behavior hews to the golden mean. Extremism is considered abnormal. To dress too loudly or too conservatively, to talk too much or too little, to laugh too hard or not at all may be manifestations of abnormality. Thus, in reply to the therapist's probings, his behavior is generally "average." He engages in sex about the average number of times, and he experiences anxiety no more than the average person. The self-description resembles the test-taking attitude of subjects who commit the error of central tendency.

NORMALITY EQUALS BOREDOM

In a "hip" culture certain segments of society perceive the "normal" society as "square." There are no kicks in being normal. And it perhaps must be conceded that the range of behavior through which one can get kicks is greater in the irresponsible, antisocial world than in the "square" society. The hipster, the beatnik, the con man, the drug user take pride in their abnormality. Even the lonely homosexual refers to his subculture as "the gay world." When he enters treatment, he resists becoming "straight." Simultaneous with the pride in being what others might label abnormal, this patient informs us that his behavior is perhaps supernormal.

NORMALITY EQUALS PERFECTION

The expectation or wish of this patient is to achieve the ideal state where he will be totally adequate, capable of meeting and solving any problem, where he will do everything right, where he will never experience low emotional periods, and where everyone will love him. With some patients the godlike striving is limited to restricted areas of behavior, e.g., to be an intellect like Einstein or a saint.

His therapy is full of ups and downs. One day he relates a positive experience, and he is joyously on the path to the top of the mountain; the next day a negative experience plunges the patient into self-recrimination or self-pity. He is still less than perfect and therefore not *yet* completely normal. The danger of an interminable therapy is obviously omnipresent. When therapy enters the termination phase, the patient conjures up new symptoms (or recurrences of old ones) and new problems in order to assure the therapist that "I'm not 100% yet."

PRESENCE OR ABSENCE OF SYMPTOMS

The judgment of this patient revolves about whether he suffers from symptoms or is asymptomatic. It is the same criterion commonly employed to determine whether one is physically sick. If one has symptoms, one is sick; otherwise one is well. Still the judgment is more complex than this simple distinction implies. One can have symptoms and tell oneself that they are transient ("It must have been something I ate. It'll go away tomorrow.") or irrelevant to the general state of health, e.g., a pimple, an abrasion or "a little heartburn." Consequently, notwithstanding the presence of symptoms, the patient is normal and can make the decision not to seek treatment. Having sought psychotherapy, another patient can become "normal" merely by relinquishing his symptoms, terminating his treatment.

REFERENCES

1. DREIKURS, R. The Adlerian approach to therapy. In M. I. Stein (Ed.), *Contemporary psychotherapies.* New York: Free Press of Glencoe, 1961. Pp. 80-94.
2. MOSAK, H. H. Evaluation in psychotherapy: a study of some current measures. Unpublished doctoral dissertation, Univ. of Chicago, 1950.
3. MOSAK, H. H. Problems in the definition and measurement of success in psychotherapy. In W. Wolff and J. A. Precker (Eds.), *Success in psychotherapy.* New York: Grune and Stratton, 1952.
4. RUCH, F. L. & WARREN, N. *Working with psychology.* (3rd ed.) Chicago: Scott, Foresman, 1948.

The Interrelatedness of the Neuroses Through Central Themes*

It is a frequent observation that many neuroses have elements in common. Some clinicians indicate that these common elements are symptoms, without making any attempt to explain why the identical symptoms occur in several neuroses. If we could ascertain how the neuroses were interrelated, we might perhaps also disentangle the knotty problem of symptom shifting in the neuroses, namely, that if we as therapists or life itself intervene in some fashion in a person's neurosis, he will switch symptoms in an almost predictable manner.

The Freudian hypothesizes that several neuroses are interrelated with respect to fixation at, or regression to, certain levels of psychosexual development (1). If two neurotic syndromes are related in this particular fashion, they will have symptoms in common. Thus, the depressive and the alcoholic will have masochistic behavior in common, since they are both related to the oral stage of psychosexual development.

A second explanation defines all neurosis as either anxiety or a defense against anxiety (8). This as well as the first hypothesis assumes that man is essentially a reactor to either internal or external stimuli.

Adlerian psychology conceptualizes neurosis essentially as a creative and active event rather than a reactive one. The observation that two neuroses exhibit common symptoms, in such a system, would be explained by the assumption that the individuals involved chose, albeit unconsciously, identical symptoms—in accordance with their respective life styles.

One of Adler's outstanding abilities, as can be noted in *Problems of Neurosis* (2), was his characterization of people by a central theme. While there are many descriptive elements in any life style, individuals can be described in terms of a central

---

*Reprinted by permission from JOURNAL OF INDIVIDUAL PSYCHOLOGY, 1968, 24, 67-70.

theme. Thus we can say that some people are "getters," some depend upon control, some seek approval, and still others have the need to be superior. Every individual neurosis can be seen in terms of such central themes based upon convictions which, at certain points, hamper the individual in coping with the life tasks (6, 7). These convictions are called by Adlerians "basic mistakes" (3) and by Horney "overdriven strivings" (4).

The determination of the central theme or themes, since more than one may describe the individual, may be made through observation of behavior, through analysis of the content of the subject's communication, through the analysis of speech and gesture, and from many psychological tests. The writer uses early recollections (ERs) as a projective technique extensively (5). For example, the following ERs reveal a "getter":

> ER 1a. My fourth birthday party. I got a fire engine that I was delighted with. We were playing with it, riding each other around. I was very happy.

> ER 1b. I got an electric train for Christmas. I was in bed and my family thought I was asleep, and Dad was running the train Christmas eve. I came in and saw the train and was considerably delighted.

The person who has the need to be always right gives ERs in which either he does the right thing, or someone or something else is wrong. For example:

> ER 2a. One day I was on my way to Sunday School, and I told my friends I would no longer steal candy from the store (which all the kids did) because we were learning the Ten Commandments and one shouldn't steal. They laughed, I said if they did, I'd tell. They went into the store. Someone was watching to see which kids stole, so they didn't take anything.

> ER 2b. My mother was feeding my brother pablum. He spit it up, and she refed it to him. I was horrified by it.

The controller's ERs center about being in control or the fear of not being in control, as follows:

> ER 3a. My baby sister was in the basinette in the bedroom. Mother was taking a group of ladies in to see her, and I went in with them. They were all ogling her, and one of them reached in to touch her. I said, "Don't touch the baby!" They all said, "OK." I was pleased like I was a policeman or something.

> ER 3b. I had my tonsils out. Someone told me to breathe in deeply as they put the cone over my nose. I was frightened and I struggled.

If we examine the life style of the depressive for example, we find generally that the following convictions exist as central themes in varying proportions: I want to get; I want to be good; I want to (be in) control; I am against. While these convictions *exist* in the depressive, they do not *cause* a depression. The individual's patterning of these convictions, the use he makes of them in meeting the life tasks, and the "tests" which life poses for him are the crucial factors. It has often been observed that depressives have obsessive qualities, and that obsessive-compulsives have depressive qualities. If we examine the obsessive-compulsive, we discover that he too will possess four basic convictions, again in varying proportions: I want to be right; I want to (be in) control; I want to avoid feelings; I want excitement. It will be seen that he shares his first and second convictions with the second and third of the depressive. From this the hypothesis can be advanced: Where symptomatic manifestations are similar, certain underlying convictions will be similar.

When we characterize the neuroses in terms of their major convictions, as in Table I, we see their interrelatedness through common convictions or central themes.

With regard to the shifting of symptoms clinicians have observed, e.g., that if the hysterical process is interfered with, the individual generally will exhibit depressive symptoms. In Table I we can locate both the hysteric and the depressive in the "getters" group. Similarly, when one interferes with the depressive's neurosis, we frequently observe him behaving like the "getting" anti-social personality. In a word, the shift is from the "getting nothing" of the depressive to the "getting everything" of the anti-social personality (6). Symptom shifting thus appears to be another mode of behavior in line with the basic convictions, and we can offer our second hypothesis: Neurotic symptoms will shift in accordance with the basic convictions common to a certain neurotic category.

This formulation would also cast some light on what is sometimes called the "neurotic paradox," the tendency for an extreme pendulum-swing in symptomatology, a common observation during psychotherapy. To illustrate, the "aginners"

TABLE 1. INTERRELATIONSHIP OF THE NEUROSES IN TERMS OF CENTRAL THEMES OR BASIC CONVICTIONS

Diagnostic descriptions[a]	Central themes[b]							
	A	B	C	D	E	F	G	H
Paranoid personality	--	x	--	x	x	x	--	--
Emotional instability reaction	--	x	--	--	--	--	--	x
Passive-dependent personality	x	--	--	--	--	--	--	--
Aggressive personality	--	--	--	--	--	x	--	--
Passive-aggressive personality	--	x	--	--	--	x	--	--
Anti-social personality	x	--	--	--	--	x	--	x
Addictions, incl. obesity	x	--	--	--	--	--	--	x
Nymphomania, satyriasis	--	--	x	--	--	--	--	x
Anxiety reaction, esp. panic	--	x	x	x	--	--	--	--
Phobic reaction	--	x	--	--	x	x	--	--
Hysterical reaction	x	--	--	--	--	--	x	--
Obsessive-compulsive reaction	--	x	--	x	--	--	x	x
Hypochondriasis	--	--	--	--	x	--	--	x
Depressive reaction	x	x	--	x	--	x	--	--
Anorexia nervosa	--	--	--	--	--	x	--	--
Diarrhea, constipation	--	x	--	--	--	--	--	--
Ulcer	--	--	x	--	--	--	--	--
Hypertension	--	--	x	--	--	--	--	--
"Weeping" dermatitis	--	--	--	--	x	--	--	--

[a]These follow the classification of Mosak and Shulman who adhere to the categories of nosology of the American Psychiatric Association (7, p.3).

[b]Code to Columns: A = Getters; B = Controllers; C = Drivers; D = To be good, perfect, right; E = Martyrs, victims; F = "Aginners"; G = Feeling avoiders; H = Excitement seekers.

group provides an often observed example. If the passive-aggressive person is encouraged to assert himself on occasion, he will take (and simultaneously nullify) the therapist's advice by telling *everyone* off, behaving like the theme-related partner, the aggressive personality. While the outward behavior changes, the shared underlying conviction remains.

SUMMARY

The various neuroses have been characterized by one or more basic convictions or central themes which will be in accordance with the individuals' life style. From this understanding two hypotheses have been generated to explain the commonality of symptoms between neuroses and the shift in symptoms which occurs when life or therapy intervenes. These hypotheses are:

1. Where symptomatic manifestations are similar, certain underlying convictions will be similar.

2. Neurotic symptoms will shift in accordance with the basic convictions common to the various neuroses.

A table is presented to illustrate the interrelationships of the neuroses in terms of underlying convictions.

REFERENCES

1. ABRAHAM, K. *Selected papers on psychoanalysis*. London: Hogarth, 1927.
2. ADLER, A. *Problems of neurosis*. New York: Harper Torchbooks, 1964.
3. DREIKURS, R. The psychological interview in medicine. *Amer. J. Indiv. Psychol.*, 1952, 10, 99-122.
4. HORNEY, KAREN. *Our inner conflicts*. New York: Norton, 1945.
5. MOSAK, H. H. Early recollections as a projective technique *J. proj. Tech.*, 1958, 22, 302-311. Also, Chicago: Alfred Adler Inst., 1972.
6. MOSAK, H. H. The getting type: a parsimonious social interpretation of the oral character. *J. Indiv. Psychol.*, 1959, 15, 193-198.
7. MOSAK, H. H., & SHULMAN, B. H. *The neuroses: a syllabus*. Chicago: Alfred Adler Inst., 1966.
8. WHITE, R. W. *The abnormal personality*. 3rd ed. New York: Ronald Press, 1964.

Early Recollections:
Evaluation of Some Recent
Research*

In this paper we shall direct our attention to four recent psychoanalytically-oriented research studies by Robert J. Langs and his co-workers (9, 10, 11, 13). Our purpose will be to summarize this work, and view its findings from an Adlerian orientation.

Two methods of psychodiagnosis have been most closely identified with the name of Adler: the analysis of the family constellation or birth order, or what Murphy (19) calls "positional psychology"; and the interpretation of early recollections (ERs) which Munroe appropriately recognized as "the first approach toward the projective methodology now so widely used" (18, p. 428n), a theme upon which the author has previously elaborated (15).

What has consistently distinguished Adlerian from Freudian theory concerning ERs, and this is equally true of dream interpretation, is the temporal orientation. Freudian psychology, with its archaeological excursions into the past, conceptualizes the ER as a screen memory, covering up a more highly emotionally charged, repressed incident (5). Adlerian psychology relates ERs to a current apperceptive posture, part of the individual life style (1, 2, 3, 15). In Freudian terms, the Adlerian approach would deal with the manifest content of the ER, the Freudian approach, with the latent content. Consequently, Freudians would be interested in the repressive mechanism through the ER, while Adlerians are interested in the here-and-now individual.

A second distinction originates in the opposing models of man of the two systems—the atomistic versus the holistic. The former, Freudian, model necessitates relating psychoanalytic research to the tripartite topology of id-ego-superego. It requires fractionating the ER into component parts and then

*Reprinted by permission from JOURNAL OF INDIVIDUAL PSYCHOLOGY, 1969, 25, 56-63.

describing and counting these (20). With its emphasis on the individual as "indivisible," the Adlerian model conceptualizes the ER as a creation of the individual rather than as a compromise formation between competing, antagonistic psychic substructures. With this approach the ER is studied in its totality as a conveyer of a message reflecting the individual's life style. Yet, the holistic position does not preclude directing the interpreter's attention to the details of the recollection. On the contrary, as Adler wrote:

> We can begin wherever we choose: every expression will lead us in the same direction—towards the one motive, the one melody, around which the personality is built . . . Any mistake we might make in considering one expression too hastily can be checked and corrected by a thousand other expressions. We cannot finally decide the meaning of one expression until we can see its part in the whole; but every expression is saying the same thing (2, p. 71).

SCORING METHOD

The first paper by Langs *et al.*, on "A Method for Clinical and Theoretical Study of Earliest Memories" (13) has a dual purpose: it focuses on *A Manual for the Scoring of Earliest Memories* (12); and it presents a pilot study "as a vehicle for the description of the Manual" (13, p. 525). A discussion of the differences in the above approaches forms the introduction, followed by a review of the experimental approaches to ERs. It is pointed out that since screen memories are best understood in the context of the psychoanalytic therapy setting, they are less feasible for systematic study than are "revealing memories." This term is used as a synonym for manifest content: "What was revealed [in previous studies] included important aspects of the individual's personality, perception of the world, and his ways of dealing with this world," for which concept reference is made to Adler (13, p. 523). While Langs professes throughout a psychoanalytic preference, the studies covered here are limited to manifest content.

The pilot study utilizes the Manual as a scoring scheme to determine whether the ERs of a group of 10 women hysterics differed from those of a matched group of paranoid schizophrenics. The memories were scored independently by three scorers without knowledge of the patients aside from their sex. Through conferences a consensus was reached on all items scored, which scores were then used in the study. Unanimous agreement before conference among all three scorers averaged 77.1%.

The findings are that the ERs of hysteric women tended "to be grossly traumatic with themes of punishment and illness common" (13, p. 531); to be action oriented; and to evidence concern with body parts, clothing, and appearance, rejection, and moral issues. The most striking difference from paranoid schizophrenic women was that the latter exhibited lack of interaction between persons. Their memory-content tended toward the ideational rather than actionful, and was thematically centered about happy occasions. But the number of patients in each group was small (N = 10), and the frequency of almost all content items even smaller.

The researchers concluded that "such manifest material is psychologically important and useful" and that the data obtained "are related to clinical diagnosis in a gross manner" (13, p. 531). These conclusions would be in support of the Adlerian position, and away from the emphasis on screen memories. However, we cannot accept them because they are based on very few cases, and most comparisons are not statistically significant.

Since the primary goal of this study was to test out the scoring method, what can be said for its value? Adlerian content analysis of ERs has been scant, and this constitutes a serious shortcoming in the understanding both of ERs and of the people who produce them. Would the categories of an Adlerian manual differ from the one of Langs, and if so, how? The difficulty in any such categorization is that in satisfying the requirements of objective research, one risks losing the phenomenology of the individual, his biased apperception, which constitutes so much of the life style, or "cognitive style" (see below). Whereas the Manual does include items of mood, sensory modalities, and feeling tone, it is not clear how these are used in the tables given. For instance, the theme "happy occasions" is used to include birthdays. If a birthday party has been recalled as embarrassing, or otherwise unpleasant, is it still listed under "happy occasions"? And if not, under what category would it be listed? More work will have to be done before such important nuances of ERs can be accurately recorded, as Langs would agree. They say, from the psychoanalytic point of view, "certainly, without associative comments, the idiosyncratic aspects of the memory, such as the special significance of a given person, cannot be understood" (9, p. 389).

PREDICTIVE STUDY

Langs' second paper (9) extends ER research into the area of prediction—from first memory to personality. Excluding studies which are devoted to description, classification, and validity, research has generally centered about postdiction. A study by McCarter, Tomkins, and Schiffman (14) found that performance of the Tomkins-Horn Picture Arrangement Test was to a considerable degree successfully predicted from ERs; and Mosak (16) described the use of ERs to predict the relationship of the patient to the therapist, but his method has never been subjected to experimental or formal clinical test. Thus Langs' study is something of a pioneer effort in formal prediction from ERs.

The conceptual framework for his study recognizes the ERs are a "concentrated expression of cognitive style" (9, p. 379). In Langs' psychoanalytic terminology this includes, "the precipitates of drives; superego promptings; and ego functioning, particularly defensive operations and modes of adaptation; and the person's view of reality and the self" (9, p. 379). This comprehensive list would seem to cover the whole way of an individual's functioning from the Freudian frame of reference, but otherwise has little in common with the Adlerian concept of life style.

ERs from 48 men were scored, as in the first research of Langs. For the 60 items selected for study, two major groupings were made; population counts (10 items), direct counts of the persons present in the memory in respect to sex, age, family status, etc.; and complex and thematic items (50 items) such as roles, perceptions of the environment, etc. Each S was scored for the presence or absence of each item. Each S's personality assessment consisted of a rating on 76 personality variables selected from personal interview, Rorschach, Thematic Apperception Test, Wechsler-Bellevue, and autobiography. Predictions of the personality correlates of the ER scores were significantly more often correct than expected by chance alone.

In a subsequent exploratory study, *post hoc* correlations between all 60 memory variables and the 76 personality variables were made, as well as intercorrelations among the memory variables. These correlations were frequently greater than expected by chance. Specific findings are given in relation to 22 ER themes. Altogether there were 773 predictions and 4,560 intercorrelations, indicating the scope of Langs' study.

The findings are undeniably positive, as we would have anticipated from the basic assumption regarding revealing memories. Thus, in spite of differences in terminology and interpretation, there is much which will be of great interest to Adlerians who have never applied such a quantitative approach. For example, Langs found a positive relationship between the "traumatic grouping" of ER themes of illness, damage, and conflict and low self-esteem, poor attitudes toward work and responsibility, homosexual trends, manipulative attitudes, acting out, and projection as prominent defenses (9, p. 380). This finding would certainly be meaningful for Adlerians who use most—if not all—of these descriptive terms, and are familiar with this general personality syndrome.

Again, Langs found that ERs with content of anal derivatives correlate with "demandingness and hostility, thrift, and the use of isolation and intellectualization as defenses" (9, p. 388). The category of anal derivatives is explained as including references to cleanliness, dirt, thrift, and money. Accepting these contents of ERs as themes which can often be observed, but rejecting the interpretive cover-term, we should find this correlation of interest to Adlerians, and not surprising.

A few predictions are based on exclusively psychoanalytic interpretations, e.g., "vehicles were also considered in their phallic symbolic aspects" (9, p. 384), an assumption which Mosak and Todd (17) found untenable. But Langs does state that "the main thesis of this report lies not in the specific findings, which must be subjected to confirmation, but in the general hypothesis [which appears strongly confirmed] that the manifest content of the first memory is predictive of, and has a broad relationship to, personality" (9, p. 389). This is sufficiently supportive of Adlerian position.

CHARACTEROLOGIC DIAGNOSIS

Langs' third study (10), the briefest of the four, takes its place as one of several attempts by investigators of diverse orientations to correlate ERs and clinical diagnoses. Thus his references could have included several additional studies (4, 6, 7, 8). Langs compares ER scores of four diagnostic groups—obsessive-compulsive (N = 12), inhibited obsessive-compulsive (N = 14), hysteric (N = 9), and narcissistic (N = 13), all males. He finds confirmation for his hypothesis that ER scores are reflective of characterologic disgnosis, although of 28 chi-squares only 8 are significant at the .05 level or better.

The most significant results were that ERs of obsessive-compulsives showed a paucity of people, and low degree of activity for the S and others. Inhibited obsessive-compulsives showed significant traumatic and destructive content. Although we would not concur with the statement, "Structurally, character refers to facets of the relationship between id, superego and ego elements and their crystallization in a relatively permanent style of adaptation and identity," we regard as supportive of our position the conclusion that ERs are 'reflective and predictive of current functioning and personality" (10, p. 320).

LSD-25 EFFECTS

In his most recent paper Langs (11) investigates a hypothesis which Adlerians accept as an article of faith—the stability of ERs—inasmuch as ERs reflect the individual's life style which is also held to be relatively stable. Only when the life style is altered, as for example in psychotherapy, are ERs assumed to change (15). The stability of ERs under ordinary conditions has been reported by Winthrop (21). But Langs' interest here is in stability or change under LSD-25. His S's were the same 48 males of the previous study, 28 of whom were given the drug, and 20, a placebo.

149

Langs' main hypothesis was that the drug will have a regressive effect upon the report of the ERs, an effect distinguishable from that of a placebo. Two supplementary hypotheses were (a) that regressive changes occur only in certain S's, related to personality; and (b) that the changes will be related to a strong drug effect.

The first finding was that 60% of the drug S's and only 40% of the placebo S's had stable single ERs. Entirely new ERs were given by 20% drug and 30% placebo S's, while new ERs with mention of former ERs were given by the remaining 20% drug and 30% placebo S's. If this low stability comes as a surprise to Adlerians, it should be pointed out that it may, to an unknown extent, have been induced by the experimental instructions. When the S's returned for the stability test the following day they were specifically told "to disregard the recall of the previous day and to reply directly to the present inquiry" (11, p. 172). These instructions may well have suggested the report of new ERs.

The hypotheses regarding regressive ER changes were considered confirmed. S's who regressively changed their ER under LSD tended to be schizoid. LSD only constricts or does not affect ERs of "impulsive, rigid, guarded, and inhibited obsessive persons who mostly show a minimal reaction to the drug" (11, p. 184). In the placebo S's, ER changes showed no relationship to personality make-up, "do not tend to be regressive and seem, instead, to reflect a search for readily available, alternate recollections" (11, p. 184).

What these findings could mean to Adlerians is not clear. To them the issue would be whether the *message* conveyed, and not the ER itself, is changed. To clarify this issue would take more careful study of Langs' data, or possibly further studies. Furthermore, although this investigation addresses itself to ERs, it is equally noteworthy for the questions it raises with respect to the effects of LSD, but these are outside the scope of this review.

SUMMARY

The studies of Langs *et al.* represent the first large-scale precise research on ERs. They constitute an important contribution and demonstrate convincingly that such topics as ER length themselves to quantitative investigation. Although the approach of this research is psychoanalytic, this does not influence its methods or findings. In his discussions Langs interprets ERs as "derivative of latent content" (9, p. 390). But his data, nevertheless, consist exclusively of manifest content, and his results show simply that "such memories are reflective and predictive of current functioning and personality" (10, p. 320). Such results can be welcomed equally by Adlerians and others who are nonpsychoanalytically oriented. The hypotheses explored in these studies, taken in themselves, are those to which Adlerians in some instances have been attending, and in others should be attending now that Langs and his co-workers have shown the way. A major weakness of Langs' studies lies with the limited data collected so far.

REFERENCES

1. ADLER, A. *Problems of neurosis* (1929). New York: Harper Torchbooks, 1964. Chapt. 8. Also, slightly edited, as: The significance of early recollections. *Int. J. Indiv. Psychol.*, 1937, 3, 283-287.
2. ADLER, A. *What life should mean to you* (1931). New York: Capricorn, 1958. Chapt. 4.
3. ANSBACHER, H. L. Adler's place today in the psychology of memory. *Indiv. Psychol. Bull.*, 1947, 6, 32-40. Also *J. Pers.*, 1947, 15, 197-207.
4. EISENSTEIN, V. W., & RYERSON, ROWENA. Psychodynamic significance of the first conscious memory. *Bull. Menninger Clin.*, 1951, 15, 213-220.
5. FREUD, S. Screen memories. In *Collected Papers.* Vol. 5. London: Hogarth, 1950. Pp. 47-69.
6. FRIEDMAN, J., & SCHIFFMAN, H. Early recollections of schizophrenic and depressed patients. *J. Indiv. Psychol.*, 1962, 18, 57-61.
7. FRIEDMANN, ALICE. Early childhood memories of mental patients. *J. Child Psychiat.*, 1952, 2, 266-269.
8. JACKSON, MARILYN, & SECHREST, L. Early recollections in four neurotic diagnostic categories. *J. Indiv. Psychol.*, 1962, 18, 52-56.
9. LANGS, R. J. Earliest memories and personality. *Arch. gen. Psychiat.*, 1965, 12, 379-390.
10. LANGS, R. J. First memories and characterologic disgnosis. *J. nerv. ment. Dis.*, 1965, 141, 318-320.
11. LANGS, R. J. Stability of earliest memories under LSD-25 and placebo. *J. nerv. ment. Dis.*, 1967, 144, 171-184.
12. LANGS, R., & REISER, M. *A manual for the scoring of earliest memories, revised.* New York: Albert Einstein Coll. Med., 1960.
13. LANGS, R. J., ROTHENBERG, M. B., FISHMAN, J. R., & REISER, M. F. A method for clinical and theoretical study of the earliest memory. *Arch. gen. Psychiat.*, 1960, 3, 523-534.
14. McCARTER, R. E., TOMKINS, S. S., & SCHIFFMAN, H. M. Early recollections as predictors of the Tomkins-Horn Picture Arrangement Test performance. *J. Indiv. Psychol.*, 1961, 17, 177-180.

15. MOSAK, H. H. Early recollections as a projective technique. *J. proj. Tech.*, 1958, 22, 302-311. Also in Lindzey, G., & Hall, C. S. (Eds.), *Theories of personality; primary sources and research.* New York: Wiley, 1965. Pp. 105-113. Also Chicago: Alfred Adler Inst., 1972.
16. MOSAK, H. H. Predicting the relationship to the therapist from early recollections. *J. Indiv. Psychol.*, 1965, 21, 77-81.
17. MOSAK, H. H., & TODD, F. J. Selective perception in the interpretation of symbols. *J. abnorm. soc. Psychol.*, 1952, 47, 255-256.
18. MUNROE, RUTH. *Schools of psychoanalytic thought.* New York: Dryden, 1955.
19. MURPHY, G. *Personality: a biosocial approach to origins and structure.* New York: Harper, 1947.
20. WALDFOGEL, S. The frequency and affective character of childhood memories. *Psychol. Monogr.*, 1948, 62, No. 4 (Whole No. 291).
21. WINTHROP, H. Written descriptions of earliest memories: repeat reliability and other findings. *Psychol. Rep.*, 1954, 4, 320.

A Full Time Internship in Private Practice*

Harold H. Mosak[1]

The request by a University of Chicago student for the establishment of a full time internship in private practice was received enthusiastically by this Adlerian therapist. As attractive as the proposal was, several problems immediately presented themselves, and still others emerged as the first year of the program progressed. First, there was the question of whether the university (in this case my *alma mater)* would accept the internship for credit. Since the members of our practice enjoy the good opinion of the university faculty, we encountered no problems in this regard. The Director of Clinical Training at the university and I exchanged letters, on his part stating the university's formal requirements, and from our side informing him what we had to offer a prospective intern. After sending me some references concerning the student, the appointment of the intern was made and accepted.

What did we have to offer a prospective intern? The answer to this question requires an understanding of the structure of our practice. The practice is a group practice consisting of approximately a dozen therapists—psychiatrists, psychologists, social workers, a psychodramatist, and a priest. The selection of a therapist for our practice is based upon our assessment of his competence or the likelihood of his acquiring competence through additional training or experience rather than upon the type of academic background or degree he possesses. This is consonant with the description of Adlerian psychology as a psychology of use rather than a psychology of possession (Adler,

[1]The author is engaged in private practice in Chicago and is past president of the American Society of Adlerian Psychology. He has taught for 20 years at Roosevelt University and is a consultant at V. A. hospitals in the Chicago area as well as at St. Joseph Hospital.

*Reprinted by permission from THE CLINICAL PSYCHOLOGIST Official Publication of American Psychological Assn., 1970, 14(1), 5-7.

1964). All patients are routinely seen in multiple psychotherapy. While the intern had the opportunity to observe and participate in individual group therapy, he additionally participated in multiple psychotherapy, family therapy, and psychodrama. We afforded him the opportunity to sharpen his interviewing techniques, his diagnostic skills in observation, testing, and life style analysis, and to collect case history information. We also stressed the acquisition of skills in the communication of assessment information via oral and written report. Although all of the members of the practice are Adlerian in orientation, several of us have had training in Freudian-oriented psychology, client-centered therapy, and Meyerian psychobiology.

As with any private practice, we must occasionally hospitalize patients, and we are fortunate in having several members of our staff who hold appointments on the staff of the mental health unit of a general hospital. The unit, headed by one of our staff members, is a milieu unit, and the intern devoted a portion of his time to in-patient activities with patients generally more disturbed than these encountered in our office practice. Orientation to the hospital, its administration procedures—admitting, discharge, and commitment procedures—and to the ancillary therapies it provides constituted another part of the training program. The hospital also conducts a Day Care and out-patient program, broadening the training experiences further.

Since the clinical psychologist in private practice is confronted with such problems as crisis and emergency intervention, dealing with patient problems over the telephone, the determination of the seriousness of a threat of suicide, and being on call 24 hours a day, the intern was introduced very early to the criteria and techniques for coping with these problems. Multiple interviews, supervisory interviews, and the "cry for help" to a supervisor ameliorated the intern's anxieties by offering him support and guidance in the making of decisions.

Academic training and practice teaching were possible through the Alfred Adler Institute, a training institute for Adlerians, and supplementary experience in family counseling could be provided through the Family Education Association of Chicago which conducts family counseling centers in the Chicago metropolitan area.

Two unexpected and unplanned developments occurred. As a result of his experience with us, the intern wrote two professional papers, acquainting himself with the APA *Publications Manual* in the process, and discovered a topic for his doctoral dissertation.

Some of the problems emanating from the establishment of an internship in private practice are:

1. Space—Most clinicians in private practice rent only enough space to conduct their practices. Where does one make working space for the intern?

2. Patients—If an intern is accepted, the clinician will be obliged to have a surplus of patients. Otherwise the clinican's income will be reduced as he sits idle that part of the time when the intern is seeing the supervisor's patients. The latter situation may constitute a blessing in that the clinician may catch up on his reading, research, and administration.

3. Activities—Our practice is fortunate in that it can provide varied forms of training experiences. Most clinicians, however, would find it difficult to expose interns to a great variety of experiences. Polster (1967) would solve this problem with a part-time internship in private practice which would supplement an internship in an institution. Another solution might be sharing of a single intern by several clinicians who might be able to contribute to different parts of the intern's training. An accompanying benefit of such a rotating internship is that several clinicians, rather than one, would furnish patients for the intern. Moreover, the intern's tendency to imitate the model of a single supervisor would be rendered more difficult. Such a plan would require careful planning and cooperation among the clinicians involved.

4. Identification of the intern—In clinics and institutions assignment of a patient to a therapist who is not a "doctor" meets readier acceptance than in private practice. In our practice less complaint is voiced since several of our journeyman therapists are "misters." The question of whether the intern should be identified as an intern raises many concerns, including ethical ones. We have

155

resolved the question through imitating established medical practice, i.e., if the patient asks, we tell him.

5. Fees—Where to set the fee charged for the intern's services raises some tricky questions which can be rationalized in many ways. While the intern's services are less valuable than those of a more experienced clinician, a clinician's fees reflect more factors than what he considers his worth to be—the type of clientele he chooses to work with, his geographical location, his professional degree, his rent and other overhead, his inferiority (or superiority) feelings, and more subtle factors. An intern practicing with upper class patients in Beverly Hills might conceivably charge more than an advanced clinician in Mississippi. Some clinicians with whom I have discussed the matter of fees feel that the intern's fee should be the standard office fee, and that the difference between the fee charged the patient and the salary paid the intern could be utilized to reimburse the supervisor for the income lost through supervision. They argue further that in offices where uniform fees are not maintained, patients maneuver to be seen by either the "expensive" and therefore "superior" therapist or by the "inexpensive" therapist in order to minimize their therapeutic expenditures.

6. Supervision—Supervision requires time, a precious commodity for the clinician in private practice. Moreover, every hour of supervision time, since it is non-income producing, decreases the supervisor's income since he would ordinarily be seeing patients during that time. The supervisor finds himself weighing the amount of supervision time he can afford to give against the resulting decline in his income, a somewhat difficult decision. We have resolved this conflict by providing some supervision time outside of my regular office hours, a practice which might meet with the disapproval of some clinician's wives.

The major media through which supervision is conducted are multiple psychotherapy, "sitting in" with the intern, and supervisory hours, the first two of which permit observation of the intern *in situ* rather than relying upon the intern's report with the attendant possibilities of retrospective falsification and selective emphasis and omission. Weekly case seminars, "no-holds-barred" seminars where the discussants may discuss any topics they wish, and accompanying the senior members of our practice to other institutions where the latter serve as consultants round out the supervision program.

While the preceding description might contraindicate the possibility of establishing internships in other than unique practices such as ours, my optimism remains undiminished. Certainly several psychologists in one area could band together to provide the various experiences which a single practitioner might be unable to provide. With the assistance of local, regional, and national psychological groups such as Divisions 12 and 27 and Psychologists in Private Practice, such programs could be formalized and implemented. The need is great since the majority of universities provide no preparation for private practice and in many quarters it is discouraged. Accompanying the improvement in the quality of services offered to the public would be accretions to the supervisor's knowledge and awareness. Our intern this year has forced me to become gratifyingly aware of what I know—and painfully aware of what I still don't.

REFERENCES

1. Adler, A. *Social interest: A challenge to mankind* (1938). New York: Capricorn, 1964.
2. Polster, E. Internship in private practice. *The Clinical Psychologist*, 1967, 20, 144-146.

Robin Gushurst[2]

The previous paper described an internship in private practice from the point of view of the supervisor. The present paper conveys my reactions, that of the student intern. I considered myself a most willing participant in a novel program which was designed to fulfill the major APA requirements for a clinical internship (American Psychological Association, 1950; 1958). Not only were these criteria fulfilled, but because of the structure of the private practice involved, there were sufficient additional advantages to argue strongly for the future use of similar programs.

The private practice consisted of several highly qualified clinicians who had worked together in Chicago for many years—five psychiatrists, three psychiatric social workers, two psychologists (one of whom was certified by ABEPP), a priest, and a psychodramatist. The members shared a group of offices and a common psychological orientation (Adlerian); and each of them was involved in additional professional activities in which I was permitted to participate. Since two of the psychiatrists supervised the care of hospitalized patients at St. Joseph Hospital in Chicago, I was able to include experience with the institutional treatment of both in-patients and out-patients. Similarly, since the psychodramatist was a practicing therapist at St. Joseph, my experience included participation in psychodrama with the entire ward of hospitalized in-patients. The diplomate psychologist in the practice was a group therapy consultant at Veterans Research Hospital, and I was therefore able to attend his weekly seminar there. Finally, since another of the psychiatrists was a consultant for the Chicago Family Education Association, I was able to attend special demonstrations of child guidance and family counselling. Thus, the diverse activities of the various members of the private practice were able to provide a breadth of experience equal to, and perhaps beyond that of most traditional training facilities. At the same time, quality supervision was insured by making the ABEPP psychologist responsible to the University of Chicago for progress reports at various intervals.

---

[2]At the time of this writing, the author was a doctoral student in clinical psychology at the University of Chicago and engaged in writing a doctoral dissertation on the projective interpretation of early recollections. He is currently on the faculty of Mary Washington College and is engaged in private practice.

My own background was that of a doctoral candidate in clinical psychology at the University of Chicago. I had a special interest in Adlerian psychology, had completed my required diagnostic and theoretical courses, finished my clerkship experience, and passed my preliminary examinations. The university faculty, being flexible and broad minded, permitted the internship on an experimental basis, hoping it would prove successful and thereby provide a new avenue for high quality student experience and training.

For both institutional and private practice activities, I was trained in the usual areas of diagnostic testing, report writing, interviewing and psychotherapy. My testing activites were concerned with the administration, scoring, interpretation and reporting of the Rorschach, MMPI, WAIS,WISC, TAT, CAT, Bender Gestalt (for both adults and children), and Memory for Design, all of which were supervised and constructively criticized. I was also permitted at various times to report my findings on these tests directly to the patient involved, in the course of a therapy session, and thereby received immediate feedback from the patient. Report writing was done for the purpose of communication both with other agencies, such as schools or hospitals, and other therapists; and I was therefore taught to adjust my content and style both to the nature of my own purpose and the character of my audience. Interviewing was approached in light of the dual aims of establishing a good therapeutic relationship, and collecting information for the location of central problems and formulation of a diagnostic picture.

Psychotherapy was taught in its four major varieties—individual, group, family, and multiple therapy. Individual therapy began initially by allowing me to participate in individual sessions with my principal supervisor; later, I was given patients of my own, whom I saw for several sessions alone, and then met for "double interviews" with my supervisor; the two of us would then conduct a "multiple therapy" session—to review what the patient had learned, resolve problems, further the ongoing therapy, or decide on a change in treatment, depending, in each case, on the nature of the problems involved (Dreikurs, *et al.*, 1952). Group therapy was taught through observation of some of the on-going groups in the office, and by having me function as a co-therapist in a group with my principal supervisor. Questions of technique and various therapeutic phenomena were discussed later, at either supervisory conferences, the VA seminar, or at odd-lot intervals, such as lunch or a coffee break. Toward the end of the program, I was allowed to start a group of my own with adolescents. Finally, family therapy was introduced by having me observe both my principal supervisor and some of the office psychiatrists, and also by having me attend special demonstrations at the Family Education Association. Later, I was asked to counsel one or two families alone, but continued to work in close consultation with my supervisors. Further, for all of these activities—testing, report writing, interviewing, and therapy—there was a list of recommended readings which I was expected to pursue during my unstructured time.

Concurrent with all of these activities, there was additional training in several didactic and case-presentation seminars. For one, there was a weekly seminar dealing with the meaning of various behaviors, both verbal and non-verbal, and what could be anticipated in conjunction with such behaviors. It also covered such topics as the interpretation of early recollections, signs of organic pathology, how to move from diagnostic formulations to therapeutic discussion, areas of possible and needed research, etc. A paper emerged from this, which I wrote in conjunction with my supervisor, and which is now being submitted for publication. Second, there was my supervisor's group therapy seminar at Veterans Research Hospital, which covered such topics as, how to constitute a group, how to begin a group, typical group problems, dramatic and action techniques, etc. Third, there were weekly case presentations in which the senior psychiatrist of the group gave demonstrations of both diagnostic and therapeutic interviews, which were then followed by group discussion. Finally there were occasional training sessions for the nurses at St. Joseph Hospital, and psychodrama sessions for the staff, both of which I attended whenever possible.

The opportunities for psychological research, in comparison with those available at most training institutions, were somewhat limited, for there were no laboratories with instrumentation, recording facilities and electronic computers. But at the same time, had I chosen to do research, my supervisors were not only well acquainted with research procedures, but were willing to make available both their own office records and those patients who would be suitable and agreeable to the research. Furthermore, research questions were discussed at some of the didactic seminars, and I was able to gather ideas for my required doctoral research.

As I said earlier, I feel that my internship adequately met the APA criteria. It may nevertheless be noted, however, that the formal APA statement on private practice internships reads as follows:

The Committee believes that the probability of adequate supervision by the private practitioner is so small at the present time that it would not consider it desirable to list such work as potentially meeting the standards of a clinical practicum. The profession of medicine, for example, does not approve the practice of medical internship in the offices of private practitioners because of lack of variety and intensity of experience and supervision (APA, 1950, p. 607.)

The APA objections focus on two points—the variety and intensity of experience and the adequacy of supervision—both of which were more than sufficiently provided for in the described program. The APA criteria, therefore, should not *a priori* exclude private practice internships in general, but should only exclude those where the criteria can not be adequately fulfilled. In fact, the APA (1950) itself takes note of this point by saying: ". . .the type of agency is not as important for purposes of practicum training as is the character and quality of the work done in it (p. 609). It should also be noted that the above statement, which has unfortunately not been reconsidered since its publication in 1950, refers to "the present time"; and needless to say, a good bit of therapeutic water has flowed under the statutory foundations in the past eighteen years.

Since internships are always completed in conjunction with university programs, it could be considered the responsibility of the university to evaluate the eligible private practices in its area, provided it chose to use these practices as alternative sources of student training. The university could then be made responsible to the APA, as part of its APA certification requirement, for the assurance of adequate internship training, whether it be in a local training institution, or a private practice. In essence, this was the procedure used in the internship

161

described above—though in this case, the procedure was non-formalized, and assisted by the fact that the practitioners in question were both well known and well respected by the university faculty. There is, however, no obvious reason why such a procedure could not be used more widely, in the service of expanded training opportunities and greater use of the available clinical experience. It would also be possible, it seems, to consider the alternative of a part-time private practice internship that was completed in conjunction with a part-time institutional internship—a possibility which might compensate for the limitations of a private practice that was unable to fulfill all the APA requirements by itself.

REFERENCES

1. American Psychological Association. Committee on Training in Clinical Psychology. Standards for practicum training in Clinical Psychology. Standards for practicum training in clinical psychology: Tentative recommendations. *American Psychologist*, 1950, 5, 594-609.
2. American Psychological Association. Education and Training Board. Criteria for evaluating training program in clinical or in counseling psychology. *American Psychologist*, 1958, 13, 59-60.
3. Dreikurs, R., Mosak, H. H., & Shulman, B. H. Patient-therapist relationship in multiple psychotherapy: Its advantages for the patient. *Psychiatric Quarterly*, 1952, 26, 590-596.
4. Dreikurs, R., Shulman, B. H. & Mosak, H. H., Patient-therapist relationship in multiple psychotherapy: Its advantages to the therapist. *Psychiatric Quarterly*, 1952, 26, 219-227.

Strategies for Behavior Change in Schools: Consultation Strategies a Personal Account*

Three years ago I was invited to serve as a consultant for a Title III project in Rockford, Illinois, 80 miles west of Chicago. This project, called the Teacher Development Center (TDC), was not a laboratory school. In a laboratory school it is assumed that teachers are well-trained, and the laboratory school will merely afford them an opportunity to try out some new teaching methods, some new technologies, some new machines, some new books on children. At the Teacher Development Center, our assumption was that teachers were not necessarily well-trained but that they could become well-trained. Teachers from the Rockford school system volunteered to spend one year at our school learning about classrooms and about children, and at the end of the one year period they returned to their regular schools within the Rockford system. In addition, each year principals from various schools in Rockford also attended the TDC and learned or relearned about children.

When I was asked to take this position, I discussed it with some of my friends who were engaged in school counseling. I do not have a background in education or in school counseling; I am a psychotherapist. Consequently, I was not quite sure what people did in this area. As I discussed it with them, they informed me that the school counselor or the consultant for school counseling had a rather limited role in schools. Usually behavior problems in the school were collected all week, and then the consultant came to the school, met with children and with the teachers and told the teachers what to do. Frequently he taught the teacher how to understand the child, but left the teacher not knowing what to do about it.

It was in this way somewhat reminiscent of the old story of two men walking down the street in Chicago. They had not seen

*Reprinted by permission from THE COUNSELING PSYCHOLOGIST, 1971, 3(1), 58-2.

each other in a long time. One greeted the other and said, "Gee, I haven't seen you in a *long* time!" His friend replied, "Well, I've been in Freudian analysis four times a week. I'm so busy that I just haven't had any time to get around and see friends." The first exclaimed, "That's interesting! You're the first person I've known who's been in Freudian analysis. Is it all as great as they say?" "Great? It's remarkable. The insights! The things I've learned about myself! You should know how many things I've learned about myself that I just never knew before." To which the other man answered, "I'm very happy for you, but there's one thing that's always bothered me as I've read about Freudian analysis. If Van Gogh had been analyzed, would he have cut off his ear and sent it to a prostitute?" Whereupon the first explained, "Oh, he still would have done that, but at least he would have known the reason why!"

Often this is about all the school consultant has to offer the teacher—insight. Not having been trained primarily in either education or school counseling, I was not encumbered by these limited role definitions. I could create my own role as I saw fit. I decided to help create a school atmosphere where children were happy, where children actually liked school.[1] This has always constituted a problem for me. When my two college-age children came home from school when they were youngsters, they sang, "Hi Ho, Hi Ho; It's off to school we go. We learn some junk and then we flunk. Hi Ho, Hi Ho." My youngest came home last year singing the same song with new words in keeping with the times: "Hi Ho, Hi Ho; It's off to school we go. With razor blades and hand grenades. Hi Ho, Hi Ho." I thought that this was not the kind of anti-intellectual atmosphere I would like to see in schools. My daughter, who is now in teachers' college, visited the TDC school one afternoon. She found four first graders sitting around about half an hour after school had let out. My daughter introduced herself and said, "School's out. What are you still doing here?" And the four girls said, "We love it here."

We wanted a school where each child could have a feeling of worth. In accordance with Adlerian psychology, we wanted a school where children were encouraged rather than discouraged

---

[1]Subsequent to the presentation of this paper, the children of the TDC were featured in an article in Life magazine, April 24, 1970.

(1, 2, 3, 4, 6, 15). There is an old cliche that "seeing is believing." At our school (and Rosenthal's work (13) confirms this), we feel that "believing is seeing (11)." When we believe in children, we see dramatic changes in them. We therefore tried to create a climate where every child has a feeling of value and of being valued. We wanted a school where the tug of war between children and teachers did not exist and where failure was a dirty word. Since it was immediately apparent that this was a very ambitious program, we adopted the advice of George Miller, who has indicated that there will never be enough therapists to deal with all the problems of society, and therefore, we must give psychology away to the people (12). Following this line of thought, we set up programs to train administrators, teachers, parents and children first to adopt responsibility for themselves. For, when a child misbehaves in class or underachieves, the teacher is apt to say, "It's the child's fault. There must be something wrong with him. Let's send him to the principal for discipline or to the school psychologist for diagnosis." Similarly, from the child's point of view, his failure, his unhappiness are the teacher's fault. And, if the teacher is unhappy with the child, she can always send a note to the parents and make it the parents' fault. "Why does your child daydream in class?" How should the parents know the answer, and does the teacher expect the parents to come to school, sit behind the child, and poke him every time he daydreams?

We also wanted to make sure that these people— administrators, teachers, the janitor—were trained to be therapeutic. This does not suggest that everyone become a therapist. It is meant in the sense that Bernice Grunwald has also referred to (11). There is much too much talk; there is much too much effort made to understand and much of this understanding never leads to action. I have been trained to believe, since I am a so-called "insight therapist," that changes are not made until you have insight. After 25 years, I regard this as so much nonsense. An encouraging word can be ever so much more effective than insight on many occasions. Insight is not always a prerequisite for change.

We attempted to implement change in the TDC through the following methods:

1. Formal teaching. The teachers were taught about behavioral goals (5), encouragement (4), logical consequences

(6), and other Adlerian classroom techniques (6). Supplementing the work at the TDC, Dreikurs and Grunwald taught courses at Rockford College.

2. "Thoughts for Teachers." We issued at intervals a paper with a sentence or paragraph which invited teachers to think about teaching. Unfortunately, in the past, prospective teachers were not encouraged to think but merely to accept uncritically the word of their professors. A typical "Thought for Teachers" reads, "Before you write on Johnny's report card, 'Johnny does not always live up to his potential,' ask yourself, 'Do you?'" We rarely find that phrase on report cards today.

3. Observation. The consultant visits with teachers in their classrooms, and the teachers are asked to observe and relate what is going on in their rooms at the moment. Sometimes we make interesting observations, like that of the little boy whose first grade teacher and I agreed was "a little prince." The following week, the teacher came to see me and said, "I never realized it until we talked about it last week, but just now as I was coming through the gym, I observed my class there. The gym teacher was saying, 'I want everyone to make himself as big as possible.' And all the kids stood up on their toes and raised their arms and made appropriate noises. Then the gym teacher instructed, 'I would like everyone now to make himself as small as possible.' All of the kids crouched except the little prince who said, 'Teacher, I can't do that.'" Princes can't make themselves small.

4. Creating a classroom climate. In some classrooms, children were given the opportunity to choose the decor, to decide whether to keep animals or tend plants or not, and to choose the seating arrangement. In other classrooms, teachers experimented with various seating arrangements in an effort to discover which arrangements were best in keeping with their educational objectives. Since the focus of the school was upon cooperation rather than upon competition, progress charts were removed from walls. Group projects were initiated. Papers were graded in terms of what the pupil got right rather than red-penciled with what he had done wrong.

5. Tapes. When a teacher felt she had a problem with a child, one of the approaches we used was to interview the teacher and the child together with a view to inviting them to

cooperate on tackling the problem. These interviews were tape-recorded and filed so that others teachers with similar problem situations could listen to the tape and determine whether any of the recordings were applicable to their problems.

6. Class discussions. We also taught teachers about class discussions, a procedure utilized by Adlerians for over forty years (2, 9, 10, 15). We conducted several forms of discussion in the TDC. First, there were discussions for teachers. Some of these centered around "mental hygiene" topics—"I'll go crazy in one more day" or "Monday, Tuesday, Wednesday, and Thursday are fine, but I can never get through Friday." Much to our delight we discovered that teachers could speak about these topics freely. Other teacher discussions revolved around exchanging experiences and techniques. For instance, in one discussion, a teacher told the group how she solved the problem of little boys who were always roaming out of their seats. She merely smiled and said, "Johnny, if you get out of your seat, I'm going to come over there and kiss you." After that she had no trouble.

A second kind of discussion we had was with parents. Teachers were instructed in the conduct of parent-teacher conferences, and we strove to make these conferences mutually helpful rather than recriminative, as too often occurs. Since we also feel that the school is an integral part of the community, we instituted parent discussions where parents could discuss the problems they encountered relative to school. The teacher receives the child at 8:30 in the morning. By that time the child has been "prepared" by a mother who has been pushing, nagging, threatening—"You'll be late to school. Brush your teeth, hurry up, get dressed, the school bus is coming, eat your breakfast, don't forget your books, stop fighting with your sister, and how do you expect to last until noon if you don't drink your orange juice?" To counteract this, we made "ladies" out of a number of Rockford mothers. We told them to take a cup of coffee and a newspaper into the bedroom, lock the bedroom door, and not to emerge until the children were off to school. The children arrived at school at just the same time they ordinarily did. Mothers were not harassed, and we didn't get children at 8:30 who had already spent 30 or 45 minutes fighting with their parents.

Our third kind of discussion was a *regularly scheduled* classroom discussion with children. To illustrate the kind of atmosphere we had, several of these discussions will be described. The first was a problem-solving one. Some children were complaining in one classroom that on cold days the patrol boys permitted their friends to come into the school but would not permit anyone else to enter. The usual question arose about what to do about it. It's unfair; we shouldn't play favorites in school. Then someone advised, "Go talk to the patrol boys," advice which was quickly countered with the question of who was going to "bell the cat." At this point, we discussed the United States Constitution and informed them that there was an answer to their problem in the Constitution. The following week they were circulating a petition for peaceful redress of grievances, and it was acted upon by the administration.

The discussion also lent itself to teaching. In one class the opening and the closing of the session was conducted in French. In another class we discussed love (One wintry day a boy approached me on the playground, pinned a pin on my coat, and informed me that I had to wear it if I worked at the TDC. It read, "I am loved.").

Sometimes the discussions centered about ambitions, things that scare us, why we should stay off the railroad tracks, boy-girl relations, the war, and the community. A classroom leader of discussions might expect almost any topic to be introduced. And the children felt understood and accepted. As one sixth grader told me, "I'm in the sixth grade and this is the first time that anyone asked me how *I* felt."

We came to school one day and there was a poster in the corridor announcing, "Kindness is in. Punishment is out!" It had come from one of the sixth grades. It seems that they had decided to have a class election, and since they were learning civics, they were conducting it with campaign speeches, slogans and platforms. Two boys, one more popular than the other, were running for office. The less popular boy was basing his campaign on the above slogan. His program was, "Each one teach one!" He felt that every person had a *responsibility* for every other person, and since people have many kinds of abilities and information which other people don't have, it is the *responsibility* of every child to teach any other child who knows less than he. The more popular boy ran on the traditional platform of "If Charles doesn't do what he's supposed to do, we punish him in order to motivate him to do more or better." The second boy won, perhaps because he was more popular rather than because of his platform, because when he made his inauguration speech, he proclaimed that one of the marks of a good leader was to know when he was wrong. "I ran on the wrong platform so after this, 'Kindness is in. Punishment is out.' and we operate on an 'Each one teach one' basis."

In another instance, we had a teacher who was very conscientious—a very, very good teacher. Only she did not know it. In class discussion I proposed, "I'm Dr. Frankenstein. I have a big pot, and I'm going to make the ideal teacher. Now you tell me what to put into this pot." "She has to know subject matter," and "She should have a smile on her face," and "She has to be willing to listen to children's problems," and "She mustn't be mean." One girl objected to the last requirement with "She should be a little bit mean. That's just to keep the boys in line." Whereupon another girl corrected her, "If she were the ideal teacher, she wouldn't have to keep anybody in line." The final ingredient was thrown into the pot, at which time I asked the teacher to put her head down on the desk, and I said, "Let's talk about Mrs. J. How does Mrs. J. compare to the ideal teacher we just created?" One child confirmed that she really knew the subject matter. Another girl described having gone to Mrs. J. with a problem the previous week, and Mrs. J. listened, and before they were through, everything was fine, "and I felt good and I knew what to do about the problem." We went around the circle with the children continuing to award Mrs. J. "good grades," and then one girl remonstrated, "Hey, what are we talking about? This is nonsense. Dr. Mosak, if you created the ideal teacher the way we just said, it wouldn't measure up to Mrs. J." I quickly dismissed the children because the teacher was racked with sobs. After that she was still a very, very good teacher—but a relaxed one.

Finally, there was the discussion which started with "Dr. Mosak, is it true that the TDC will go out of existence next June?" I replied that I did not know. I only knew that our federal funds ran out the following June, and that if we did not receive local funds, the TDC would be terminated. There was an immediate outcry. "How can they let a school like this die?" "That would be crazy. This is the best school ever." When these sentiments had run their course, one boy raised his hand and offered a suggestion. "Let's all bring our pennies and nickels to school and we'll raise the money to keep it going." I didn't know whether to laugh or cry as I told them that the federal government provided almost $200,000 annually for the school's operation. But he was not about to be deterred by this bit of information. "You don't understand, Dr. Mosak. I didn't mean just this class. I meant the whole school." Almost tearfully, I suggested that even with such group effort, their fund raising would still fall short of the amount needed. Upon hearing this, a girl said, "I still think we ought to do it, because if the adults see us bringing our pennies and nickels, they'll see how important this school is to us, and they might give their dollars."[2] I knew our three-year effort had not been in vain.

There are those who may say that programs like this are overambitious, that we are idealistic, that they can't work or they won't work. I can only say that one program can work, has worked, does work. For those who do not get started with such programs because of the enormity of the task or because they feel that it takes a generation to reform education, I would in closing quote the words of Rabbi Tarfon, written in the *Ethics of the Fathers* about 2000 years ago. He used to say, "It is not thy duty to finish the work, but thou art not at liberty to neglect it."

---

[2]Two weeks after this class discussion the Board of Education of the Rockford schools voted to continue the TDC with provision of local funds.

REFERENCES

1. Adler, A. *The education of children* (1930). London: Allen and Unwin, 1957.
2. Adler, A. *The problem child.* New York: Capricorn Books, 1963.
3. Adler, A. & associates. *Guiding the child* (1930). London: Allen and Unwin, 1949.
4. Dinkmeyer, D. & Dreikurs, R. *Encouraging children to learn: The encouragement process.* Englewood Cliffs, N.J.: Prentice-Hall, 1963.
5. Dreikurs, R. *The challenge of parenthood* (1948). New York: Hawthorn Books, 1958.
6. Dreikurs, R. *Psychology in the classroom* (1957). New York: Harper and Row, 1968.
7. Dreikurs, R., & Grey, L. *Logical consequences: A new approach to discipline.* New York: Hawthorn Books, 1968.
8. Dreikurs, R. & Soltz, Vicki. *Children: The challenge.* New York: Hawthorn Books, 1964.
9. Grunwald, Bernice. The application of Adlerian principles in a classroom. *American Journal of Individual Psychology,* 1954, 11, 131-141.
10. Grunwald, Bernice. Group procedures in the classroom. *Alfred Adler. His influence on psychology today.* Park Ridge, N.J.: Noyes Press, 1973.
11. Grunwald, Bernice. Is the teacher a psychotherapist? In R. Dreikurs (Ed.) *Education, guidance, psychodynamics.* Chicago: Alfred Adler Institute, 1966. Pp. 1-6.
12. Merton, R.K. The self-fulfilling prophecy. *Antioch Review,* 1948, 8, 193-220.
13. Miller, G. On turning psychology over to the unwashed. *Psychology Today,* 1967, 3(7), 53-54.
14. Rosenthal, R. Self-fulfilling prophecy. *Psychology Today.* 1968, 2(4), 44-51.
15. Spiel, O. *Discipline without punishment.* London: Faber and Faber, 1962.

What Patients Say and What They Mean*

Despite the skepticism, in some quarters, regarding the accuracy and utility of "verbal reports" (1), clinicians have found such statements extremely valuable for the comprehension of the individual person (2-4). As one form of expressive movement, such statements offer clues to both immediate goals and underlying personality; consequently, they are fruitful sources of both diagnostic and therapeutic information. The present paper has therefore assembled a number of such statements together with our guesses about their meaning for different types of patients. We have made no attempt to be either comprehensive or exhaustive, nor have we sought to select the most frequent, outstanding or important patient statements. The statements we have collected are simply those that came to mind when we sat down to think about the problem. Consequently, if the reader should think of statements and explanations that we have failed to indicate, his statements and guesses may easily be as accurate and helpful as our own. Our aim has been to stimulate further thought in this area, and to alert other clinicians to some of the recurrent patterns that we have discovered in our own experience. To facilitate this aim, we have categorized our statements into three broad areas: presenting problems, obstacles to change, and transactions with the therapist.

PRESENTING PROBLEMS

In the first category, patients will sometimes say, "I have conflict"—which is usually explained as feeling "pulled in two directions at the same time." The patient will often present this as his main problem, handing it to the therapist for resolution. Equally often, however, the patient does not really want the dilemma solved, and will present a "yes-but" as soon as the therapist urges him in one direction or the other (5, 6). He

*Reprinted by permission from AMERICAN JOURNAL OF PSYCHOTHERAPY, 1971, 25(3), 428-436.

statement, in other words, contains the hidden intention, "I'm not going to go anywhere," and the "conflict" is his method of immobilizing himself. The reasons for such immobilization vary from patient to patient, but they tend to fall into one or the other of two major categories: protection from a loss, or retention of a gain.

An example of the first case is the ambitious but discouraged artist, a man unwilling to test himself. Such a person might say: "If I pursue my art, I won't be able to make enough to eat; but if I take a job, I won't have any time left to pursue my art." The result is that he stays home and never puts his ability to the test. An example of the second case is the insatiable "getter," a man who wants to have his cake and eat it too. Such a person might say: "If I give up my mistress, she'll be broken-hearted and may kill herself; but if I get divorced and marry my mistress, my wife will be hurt and the kids won't have a father." The result, of course, is that he remains undecided and keeps them both. In either case the patient creates a double bind for himself and the therapist.

A second presenting problem, perhaps more frequent than ever before, is the statement: "I guess you'd say I'm a dependent person." It is tempting to speculate about the influence of psychologic theory in this case, for it is now common to speak of "unsatisfied dependency needs" as some encompassing, fundamental deficiency that originates and perpetuates all manner of psychologic disturbances; in fact, several schools of therapy speak publicly of fulfilling these needs to insure therapeutic progress (7, 8). From an adlerian perspective, however, "dependency" is a life movement in which the individual places others in his service (9). Convinced of his own inadequacy and consequent exemption from responsibility, the "dependent person" concentrates on evoking and maintaining the assistance of others whom he sees as stronger and therefore obligated to help him. In this sense, it is quite convenient for the dependent person to think of himself as the victim of "unsatified dependency needs." He is then able to justify his lack of courage, his irresponsibility, and his demands on others, in terms of some historical parental failure in which his innate human needs were neglected. Thus, the above statement is usually not only an excuse (phrased as a confession of self-knowledge), but frequently an attempt to secure from the

173

therapist the same kind of service the patient has obtained from others. After all, as long as he is a "dependent person," how can he be expected to assume responsibility for his own therapeutic progress?

Another way of declaring impotence is contained in the statement, "I can't seem to let go of myself"—and here the patient is generally referring to his feelings and his inability to live spontaneously. In reality, the manner of stating the problem conceals the patient's investment in keeping himself "held in"—keeping himself safe, in control, free of blunders and exposure. This kind of statement is frequent among controllers and perfectionists (10), people who want to keep their best profile forward. They finally come to treatment when the task of sustaining their image begins to sap their energy and impoverish their enjoyment of life.

Of a slightly different order is the statement of a depressed patient, who may say, "I'm a burden to everyone." In most cases of this kind, the patient is probably telling the truth: his family and friends are probably quite tired of his complaints, lack of energy, and miserable appearance. But the patient is not willing to change his behavior, so he does the next best thing—he joins the forces of good and displays his own deepest regrets. He may do wrong and be a burden to others, but at least he knows it and feels terrible about it. His statement, in other words, serves the same purpose as "guilt feelings": it pleads for acquittal by virtue of remorse (11).

Introspective patients will often complain, "I watch myself all the time." They feel divided into two parts—an acting self and a watching self. They cannot seem to get their minds off themselves and onto the world outside. But while they find this activity uncomfortable and burdensome, they have good reasons for continuing it, and have spent considerable effort in developing it to a fine art. On the one hand, their perpetual self observation is simply the most efficient way of pursuing their high ideals (12). On the other hand, it is a convenient "side show" that keeps them so busy they have no time or energy for the life tasks. They play "cops and robbers" with themselves, one part running, one part chasing, gaining time by losing time (6).

OBSTACLES TO CHANGE

A second group of patient statements seems to be concerned with the task of reorientation and personality change. For example, there is the patient who says, generally with a grim appearance and a heavy sigh, "Well, I'll just have to force myself." Several things may be going on here, perhaps all of them at the same time. For one thing, the patient is clearly making a bid for sympathy. His sigh communicates his profound misery and says to the therapist, "Look how hard life is for me; I have to force myself to do the simplest things." It is also a preparation for a "cop-out." With a task so very, very difficult, who can blame him if he is unable to handle it successfully? It is not as if the patient could get up and do it by simply deciding to do it. Not at all! He has to force himself to do it. There is thus an opportunity for the patient to be heroic as well: for if he is able to accomplish such a monumental task, it will really amount to something. In this way he converts tasks which others consider ordinary into heroic endeavors.

Furthermore, the whole structure of the patient's statement indicates that he views himself as if he were divided into two warring elements—a "good" part that wants to do the task, and a "bad" part, a "block," that for some reason holds back (10). In this way, if the good part fails to force the bad part to cooperate, it is not as if the person just did not want to complete the task at hand. Not at all! His good part just was not strong enough. He cannot be condemned totally; he is not really a rebel who does not want to cooperate with life. He is simply a person who lacks "will power" and needs moral sustenance; and in this way he is able to conceal from both himself and others his real intention of refusing to participate unless life meets his hidden conditions.

This same person, when asked how he is doing on a certain task, will often reply, "Well, I'm certainly trying." And he will then proceed to give instances of how hard he has tried: not instances of success, but instances of effort that just did not, for some reason, work out. His statement is therefore an expression of good intentions, designed to get the therapist off his back.

Similar to this in sound, but quite different in practice, is the statement, "I'll try." This too can be a form of good intentions, but is more frequently expressed by the inadequate and

175

discouraged person who does not believe in his own potency and therefore implicitly adds to the above statement, "but I won't succeed." He wants to please the therapist, and he does want to get better; but he never makes positive statements because they only set him up for the inevitable failure. He therefore protects himself by never anticipating success; and consequently, he never tries hard enough or correctly enough to actually succeed at anything.

A somewhat unusual but not infrequent line, often used by the intellectualizer, goes something like: "Ok, I agree with you; I won't change unless I really want to change. So how can I want to want to?" A beginning therapist can sometimes be stymied by such a statement, because it is not easy to answer—unless, of course, the therapist recognizes its purpose. In essence, it alters the course of discussion, introducing a philosophical question and eliminating the problem of a personal decision.

Another way of resisting change is to call one's behavior a "habit," usually in the form, "I just can't help it; it's a habit with me." In saying this, the patient prefers to view himself as a conditioned reflex, a machine that has already been programmed by inappropriate child rearing and therefore has no ability or responsibility to change. He declares, in fact, his intention not to examine the problem and feels relieved by labeling it irremediable. In order to perceive himself as a victim of his habits, he must remain oblivious of his knowledge that people change habits throughout their life span.

As a variation of this approach, a patient will sometimes call a particular behavior a "bad habit." Here the patient maintains the same unyielding attitude, but he indicates good intentions at the same time: he is not willing to change, but at least he shares the therapist's (or society's) criticism of his behavior. For example, a patient may realize that his fiery temper is a "vicious habit," but how can he change such a thing? The best he can do is apologize afterwards, often with considerable remorse. Secretly, however, he has no intention of changing his temper, because it is so effective for intimidating others and enabling him to get his own way.

On the other hand, just as some patients profess their good intentions regarding change, others profess their bad ones. For instance, some patients will say, when asked why they do not tudy or work at their job, "I guess I'm just lazy." In some cases his statement will come from an "inadequate personality"—a person who, by displaying deficiency, has excused himself from the obligation of making efforts. He blames everything on his bad" and "defeatist" attitude. He knows full well that such an attitude is undesirable, but he would rather be publicly frowned upon than expected to accept responsibilities. In other cases, such a statement will conceal very high ambitions which the person has no hopes of reaching; and rather than be known as a coward who is afraid to try, he will accept the reputation of an uninspired loafer—and may even develop this attitude into a supposedly superior way of life, as do some of the contemporary hippies and beatniks.

As a slightly different variety of this genre, the discouraged teenager, when confronted with his failure in school and asked what he wants to do about it, will often exclaim, usually in a loud angry voice, "I don't care! I'd rather go to Alaska and be a ditch digger." He acts, in other words, much like the fox in Aesop's fable (5). When the fox leaped for a cluster of delectable grapes and discovered that he could not reach them, he consoled himself with the thought, "Well, who cares? They're sour anyway." The movement is an attempt to maintain what Horney (12) calls "the pride system"—one's sense of self-esteem. It relieves the sense of failure by shifting emphasis to a different set of values; and the loud petulant voice is an essential part, because the shift has to be dramatic and persuasive in order to obtain the needed relief.

TRANSACTIONS WITH THE THERAPIST

A third and final group of statements seems to center around the patient-therapist transaction. Some of these transactions are very obvious, but others are not so obvious. For example, when the patient seeks to hurt or humiliate the therapist, his "attack behavior" is usually fairly transparent. Praise, however, is sometimes much less apparent and often much more significant. For example, whenever the therapist makes an interpretation, the patient may let him know how great it is—sometimes in a mild way, like, "Of course! I'd never thought of that. You always hit the nail right on the head." At other times the patient may exclaim, in a very obvious and dramatic way,

177

"Magnificent! That's it, that's *really* it!" Some patients will even keep score, or report on how they thought all week about what the therapist said, marveling all the while.

Flattery of this kind can be very deceptive, and in some cases is designed to sabotage therapeutic progress. It is sometimes a device used to conceal the patient's lack of initiative and improvement. As long as the therapist is bedazzled by the patient's applause, he may forget to examine what the patient is actually doing to change things. Berne (6) illustrates this point with his story about the Bulgarian peasant who praises her doctor so lavishly he fails to notice that her arthritic leg, instead of improving, has remained the same for years. Another danger is that the therapist may become unconsciously addicted to such praise; and to maintain it he may avoid saying things the patient does not like. In this case, the patient becomes the covert boss of the treatment, and the therapist becomes an unwitting servant.

A third possibility is that the patient will begin therapy by appearing very impressed and satisfied; he will set the therapist up on a pedestal and practically worship him. However, as therapy begins to deepen, the patient may begin to resist, and his praise will begin to decline. Whenever the therapist fails to come through with a brilliant observation, or whenever he says or does something the patient does not like, the patient will indicate his disapproval and attack the therapist for letting him down. Such a strategy is very frequent among "scalp collectors"—patients who achieve a sense of triumph through defeating their therapists, and often go from one doctor to another, collecting trophies. They elevate the therapist initially in order to knock him down later. As a warning against such behavior, there is a famous joke about the American in Paris who was approached by a stranger in the men's room. *"Mon Dieu,"* the stranger said, "What magnificent genitalia! I've never in my life seen any so large and healthy. Couldn't I hold them for just a second? They're so superb and beautiful!" The American did not know what to think, but not seeing any great harm in it, looked around hastily and said, "Ok, just for a second, and then get out of here." The stranger then closed his hand tightly around the man's testicles and said calmly, "And now, sir, give me your wallet."

In a second kind of transaction that occurs frequently, certain questions are addressed to the therapist, for any number of different reasons. For example, there is the very common one: "Well, what would you do if you were in my place?" That question is sometimes genuine and simply reflects the patient's desire for a different point of view. At other times, however, it is a disguised invitation to begin a round of "Why don't you . . .," "Yes . . . but." For each alternative the therapist suggests, the patient finds several more or less plausible reasons why it will not work.

"Am I making sense to you?" is also a query that can be either legitimate or deceptive. In the former case, it can be made by a patient who feels quite confused and is not sure he is making sense. It is then a "reality check" and can be much needed by the person who is making it. On other occasions, especially during an initial interview, a patient may ask this question after he has made, sometimes quite consciously, a number of befuddling statements. His hidden intention is to find out if his therapist is bright and clever. The confusion presents the therapist with a puzzle; and if he can put it together, he passes the test and wins a client. A third purpose of this question is to provoke further inquiry—an indirect way of getting the therapist to be solicitous and draw the patient out. It is used by timid people who want constant support and encouragement.

In this last case, the question is more rhetorical than real, and the same is true for the question, "Why did this have to happen to me?" The patient does not really want an answer; he simply hopes to elicit sympathy and understanding. He takes the position of the innocent victim, singled out to be abused by life and other people, hurt and helpless. The role he has played—in either provoking or failing to stay clear of trouble—usually goes unrecognized and unexamined. The investment of energy is found in suffering and complaints, not in foresight or problem solving. Sometimes, however, the patient really has been singled out—for instance, as the victim of a natural disaster, a death in the family, or an incapacitating illness. In these cases, the statement is in many ways justified by the circumstances; but the patient's attitude not only gives meaning to these circumstances, but shapes his response to them (5, 13). The choice of attitude is basically a simple one, though not always an easy one to make. One can either accept adversity and work to improve it; or one can shake an angry fist at life and fate, crying out like King Lear, "I am a man more sinned against than sinning." And when patients choose the latter they choose to magnify their rage and suffering, as a kind of impotent and self-destructive revenge.

"Have you ever seen anyone like me before?" or, as heard more frequently, "I'll bet you've never seen anyone as crazy as me, Doc!" are both forms of boasting. The patient is revealing his subjective sense of specialness—a specialness on the unproductive side of life, one of the many secondary gains of illness. And because the patient's "pride system" is so deeply involved, when the therapist seeks to assure him that he is indeed like certain other people, he will either remain unconvinced, or become noticeably disappointed. He may even become worse in order to reinforce his claim and persuade the therapist that he is wrong.

At other times, these two statements carry the implication that the patient is an especially *difficult* case—so different and extraordinary that no textbook or theoretical framework will do him justice. The therapist is therefore obliged to be a "super doctor," capable of transcending the limitations of knowledge and experience, to the point of almost mystic empathy and intuition. And should the therapist fail to meet these requirements, then he simply is not good enough, and the patient can not only retain his sense of superiority, but can cherish a moment of triumph as well. An exception to these general cases can be seen in patients who use the first version to mean something like, "Am I normal, Doc?" or "Is this a sickness?" In these cases, the patient means what he says and is quite concerned with his health or non-health. He wants an expert to check him out and give him a diagnosis. He is the kind of person who will read statistics describing the "average man" or the "sexually adequate male," and fill out *Reader's Digest* questionnaires on "good husbands," "good fathers," and the like (14). He always has to know exactly where he stands—like the mythical Calvinist who is always searching for evidence to confirm his predestination.

A somewhat different sort of statement is sometimes used by a patient to introduce his forthcoming thoughts or actions. For example, the patient may say, "Do you really want the truth?" In some cases the patient is simply asking permission to go further. He wants to be good and do the right thing, and he uses this statement so that he will not be blamed if any of his statements appear inappropriate or provoke disfavor. For other patients this innocent phrase conceals a desire to criticize and even injure, especially as it occurs in group therapy. Under the guise of being "constructive," such patients can severely attack and injure. And should their victim protest, they will protect themselves with the reply, "Well, you wanted me to be honest, didn't you?" In yet another case, this statement will come from a con-man, a sociopathic liar, who will use any device available to evade, distort, beguile, and manipulate. His "telling the truth" is simply an attractive lure to entangle the unsuspecting and gullible therapist.

"Well, if you really have to know . . ." comes from "reluctant dragons"—patients who avoid initiative and thereby force the therapist to pressure them. The therapist is then a "bad guy" for pressuring; and the patient, in yielding to the pressure, is able to demonstrate what a good patient he is, how very much he is willing to do for the sake of treatment. At other times the patient may be willing to give the requested information, but does not want it to look that way, because he does not know how it will be received. With his statement, he makes it appear *as if* the therapist is pressuring him, and the responsibility is therefore not his own, should the information be poorly received.

"In answer to your question . . ." has several purposes, one of which is merely a stall for time. It is fairly common among patients who want to do just the right thing. They want it made absolutely clear that they are being good patients, to the letter of the law. Other users of this statement are "passive-aggressive," and when they do not like a particular question, their answers are so complete and meticulous that it will take them forever to make their point. Their anger is indirect and concealed, like that of the child, who, when told, "Throw all your clothes in the washer," includes his shoes. Under the pretense of "following directions" they manage to provoke and retaliate.

SUMMARY

As one form of expressive movement, patient statements offer clues to both underlying personality and immediate goals. They are therefore fruitful sources of diagnostic and therapeutic information. We have attemped to demonstrate this by presenting and analyzing a number of such statements—not with the aim of completeness or the conviction that our guesses are the correct ones, but with the goal of alerting others to the pregnancy of such statements and stimulating further investigation.

REFERENCES

1. Skinner, B. F. *Science and Human Behavior.* Macmillan, New York, 1953.
2. Allport, G. W. *The Use of Personal Documents in Psychological Research.* Social Science Research Council, New York, 1942.
3. Adler, A. *The Case of Mrs. A.* Alfred Adler Institute, Chicago, 1967.
4. Ansbacher, H. L. and Ansbacher, R. R. Eds. *The Individual Psychology of Alfred Adler.* Harper Torchbooks, New York, 1964.
5. Feldman, S. S. *Mannerisms of Speech and Gestures of Everyday Life.* International Universities Press, New York, 1959.
6. Berne, E. *Games People Play.* Grove Press, New York, 1964.
7. Whitaker, C. A., Warkentin, J., and Malone, T. P. The Involvement of the Professional Therapist. In *Case Studies in Counseling and Psychotherapy,* Burton, A., Ed. Prentice-Hall, Englewood Cliffs, N.J., 1954.
8. Searles, H. F. The Evolution of the Mother Transference in Psychotherapy with the Schizophrenic Patient. In *Psychotherapy of the Psychoses,* Burton, A., Ed. Basic Books, New York, 1961.
9. Mosak, H. H. The Getting Type: A Parsimonious Social Interpretation of the Oral Character. *J. Indiv. Psychol.,* 15:193, 1959.
10. ————. The Controller: A Social Interpretation of the Anal Character. *Alfred Adler: His Influence on Psychology Today.* Noyes Press, Park Ridge. N.J., 1973.
11. Beecher, W. Guilt Feelings: Masters of our Fate or our Servants? *Indiv. Psychol. Bull.,* 8:22, 1950.
12. Horney, K. *Neurosis and Human Growth.* Norton, New York, 1950.
13. Frankl, V. E. *The Doctor and the Soul.* Knopf, New York, 1965.
14. Mosak, H. H. Subjective Criteria of Normality. *Psychotherapy,* 4: 159, 1967.

Lifestyle*

AN INDIVIDUAL'S LIFESTYLE *(Lebensstil),* his "style of acting, thinking and perceiving," constitutes a cognitive framework within which he selects the specific operations which enable him to cope with life tasks. (1) It expresses the central theme through which his behavior can be understood. (8) While he may not be completely aware of his lifestyle, he acts congruently within this apperceptive scheme, and we can deduce his lifestyle through observing his verbal and nonverbal behavior. (9) The lifestyle forms a unifying principle, a *gestalt,* to which behavior is bound in accordance with the individual "law of movement." Through this framework, developed early and remaining fairly constant throughout life, an individual interprets, controls, and predicts experience. (2)

Since the lifestyle is a subjective view of self in relationship to life, conclusions arrived at through "biased apperception" contain fictional elements. The individual, however, may persist in assuming that only under the conditions held in the lifestyle can he adequately cope with life tasks and find his place in life. When life puts him to the test, he frequently finds himself mistaken. He may then resort to behavior which he presumes will facilitate the evasion of life tasks, provide an excuse for that evasion, and protect his self-esteem. Both constructive and nonconstructive behavior can emanate from the lifestyle convictions, (6) and we cannot predict which behavior will coincide with a given lifestyle. We can speak only of more or less *probable* selections of behavior.

Probable behaviors associated with commonly observed lifestyles may be described as follows:

1. The "getter" exploits and manipulates life and others by actively or passively putting others into his service. He tends to view life as unfair for denying him that to which he feels entitled. He may employ charm, shyness,

---

*Reprinted by permission from TECHNIQUES FOR BEHAVIOR CHANGE edited by Arthur Nikelly. Springfield. Ill.: Charles C. Thomas, 1971.

temper, or intimidation as methods of operation. He is insatiable in his getting. (7)

2. The "driver" is the man in motion. His overconscientiousness and his dedication to his goals rarely permit him to rest. He acts *as if* he wants to have "it" (whatever it may be) completed on the day he dies. Underneath he nurses a fear that he is "nothing," and his overt, overambitious behavior is counterphobic.

3. The "controller" is either a person who wishes to control life or one who wishes to ensure that life will not control him. (3) He generally dislikes surprises, controls his spontaneity, and hides his feelings since all of these may lessen his control. As substitutes he favors intellectualization, rightness, orderliness, and neatness. With his godlike striving for perfection, he depreciates others.

4. The person who needs to be right elevates himself over others whom he arranges to perceive as being wrong. He scrupulously avoids error. Should he be caught in error, he rationalizes that others are even more wrong than he. He treats right and wrong as if they were the only important issues in a situation and cannot tolerate ambiguity or an absence of guidelines.

5. The person who needs to be superior may refuse to enter a life arena where he will not be seen as the "center" or the "best." He may devote himself to socially nonconstructive endeavors—achieving the record for number of days of underground burial. If he cannot attain superiority through being first or best, he often settles for being last or worst (4).

6. The person who needs to be liked feels required to please everyone all the time. Particularly sensitive to criticism, he feels crushed when he does not receive universal and constant approval. He trains himself to read other people carefully in order to discover what might please them and shifts from position to position in an attempt to please. He sees the evaluations of others as the yardsticks of his worth.

7. The person who needs to be "good" prefers to live by higher moral standards than his contemporaries. Sometimes these standards are higher than God's, since he acts as if God will forgive trespasses that he, himself,

cannot. This goodness may serve as an instrument for moral superiority so that he may not only elevate himself over others but may actually discourage the "inferior" person, a frequent device of the "model child" (4) or the alcoholic's wife.

8. The person who opposed everything life demands or expects of him rarely possesses a positive program in which he stands *for* something. He only knows he is against the wishes or policies of others. He may behave passively, not openly opposing but merely circumventing the demands of others. "Mother deafness" is not uncommon in children this type.

9. Everything befalls the "victim," sometimes called the *schlimazel.* (3, 10). Innocently or actively he pursues the vocation of "disaster chaser." Associated characteristics may be a feeling of nobility, self-pity, resignation, or proneness to accident. Secondarily, he may seek the sympathy or pity of others.

10. The "martyr" is, in some respects, similar to the "victim." The "martyr" also suffers, but whereas the "victim" merely "dies," the "martyr" dies for a cause or for principle. His goal is the attainment of nobility, and his vocation is that of "injustice collector." Some martyrs advertise their suffering to an unconcerned audience, thus accusing them of further injustice; others enhance their nobility by silently enduring and suffering.

11. The "baby" finds his place in life through charm, cuteness, and the exploitation of others. Often his voice is high pitched, and the intonation and meter of his speech is childlike. Often he has been the baby in his family constellation, but this is not a necessary condition.

12. The inadequate person acts as if he cannot do anything right. Through his default, he indentures others as his servants. He may be clumsy or awkward; he may limit his activities to those few where he is certain he will succeed; he may fail whenever responsibility is given him. Since his behavior proclaims his inferiority, he is the paradigm of the inferiority complex.

13. The person who avoids feelings may fear his own spontaneity which might move him in directions for which he

has not preplanned. He holds the conviction that man is a rational being and that reason can solve all problems He lacks social presence and feels comfortable only in those situations where intellectual expression is prized. His most valued techniques are logic, rationalization, intellectualization, and "talking a good game."

14. The "excitement seeker" despises routine and repetitive activities, seeks novel experiences, and revels in commotion. When life becomes dull, he stimulates or provokes it in order to create excitement. He requires the presence of other people and often places himself in league with others on whom he can rely to assist him in search for excitement. Some excitement seekers, however, do not involve others and find excitement through fears rumination, or masturbation.

Since the individual is holistic, his lifestyle may be assessed at any point—through either past or current behavior—and through a variety of behavioral manifestations, gestures, language, early recollections, or life narrative. Some Adlerians who do a formal analysis of a client's lifestyle collect information concerning his family constellation—birth order, sibling relationships, achievements and deficiencies, parent-child relationships, parental relationships, and family climate. To understand his current outlook and goals the client's early recollections are interpreted. The goal of this diagnostic activity is to elicit the *pattern* of living—the lifestyle.

REFERENCES

1. Adler, A.: *The Individual Psychology of Alfred Adler.* Edited by H. L. and Rowena R. Ansbacher. New York, Basic Books, 1956, pp. 172-202.
2. Ansbacher, H.: Lifestyle: A historical and systematic review. *J Indivi Psychol,* 23:191-212, 1967.
3. Berne, E.: *Games People Play.* New York, Grove Press, 1964, pp. 113-114.
4. Dreikurs, R.: *The Challenge of Parenthood.* New York, Hawthorn Books 1948, pp. 187-281.
5. Mosak, H. H.: The Controller: A Social Interpretation of the Anal Character H. H. Mosak (Ed.): *Alfred Adler: His Influence on Psychology Today.* Park Ridge, N.J.: Noyes Press, 1973.
6. Mosak, H. H.: Early recollections as a projective technique. *J Project Techn* 22:302-311, 1958.
7. Mosak, H. H.: The getting type: A parsimonious social interpretation of the oral character. *J Individ Psychol,* 15:193-196, 1959.

8. Mosak, H. H.: The interrelatedness of the neuroses through central themes. *J. Individ Psychol,* 24: 67-70, 1968.
9. Mosak, H. H., and Gushurst, R.: What patients say and what they mean. *Amer. J. Psychother.,* 1971, 25(3), 428-436.
10. Rosten, L.: *The Joys of Yiddish.* New York, McGraw Hill, 1968, pp. 347-348.

Some Therapeutic Uses of Psychologic Testing*

Many clinicians view psychologic testing in a negative light. They feel that testing concentrates on pathology, is frequently unreliable in its results, tends to stereotype, and emphasizes the static rather than the evolving nature of human beings. Indeed, some schools of psychotherapy, particularly the client-centered and existential, adamantly reject the use of psychologic testing, considering it inimical to psychologic growth (1, 2). Other schools of therapy, such as the psychoanalytic and its modern variants, consider testing to be helpful to the therapist, but remain extremely hesitant about revealing to the patient the results of such testing (3, 4). From our perspective, while there is definite merit in these views, psychologic testing can nevertheless be extremely beneficial, and therapeutic, when used in the proper way. The following remarks will present a number of such uses and benefits, all of which, within the conditions described, have been used with considerable success over an extended period of time.

THE THERAPEUTIC COMMUNICATION OF TEST RESULTS

In conveying test results to a patient, several aspects must be conscientiously considered. For one, the style of communication should be simple, direct, and easily comprehensible. Technical concepts should be translated into everyday, common-sense terminology, and psychologic jargon should be scrupulously avoided. For example, instead of saying, "this patient uses the defenses of rationalization and projection," the psychologist can say, "when this person feels in danger of 'looking bad,' he tends to make excuses and blame others." Furthermore, the presented information should be personally relevant, should be related as much as possible to the patient's immediate life-concerns, and should be sufficiently idiographic to permit a

*Reprinted by permission from AMERICAN JOURNAL OF PSYCHOTHERAPY, 1972, 26(4), 539-546.

specific agreement or disagreement. The general aim should be to evoke in the individual patient the feeling that he is understood.

Secondly, the therapist's attitude is extremely important. The test results should be seen as a place to begin, as an early attempt at understanding. The resort to dogma and infallibility should have no place, for in cases of disagreement, the individual's personal assessment should be taken as a major criterion of accuracy: questionable findings should be held in abeyance, awaiting the testimony of further evidence. Most importantly, the test results should be presented in a nonjudgmental fashion: just as the physician can report the presence of syphilis without revealing his personal evaluation of its usual origin, the psychologist can just as easily describe the many varieties of psychologic disturbance without condemning or disapproval. And if the therapist cannot, for some reason, make a dispassionate statement, then he should refrain from making any statement at all.

The individual should be prepared for a testing report. He should be informed about the nature and purpose of the testing, and the report should be presented only if he specifically indicates that he is interested in hearing it. The individual's expectations should also be discussed, for adverse reactions can often be anticipated and prevented if the individual's hopes and fears are made explicit and dealt with prior to the report.

During the report, the therapist should remain sensitive to the individual's immediate reactions, and should respond to these reactions in a therapeutic manner. The fact that a report has been started should not be viewed as an obligation to continue, regardless of the patient's response. If a patient becomes upset, his upset should be dealt with immediately, just as the therapist would respond to any other intercurrent disturbance. Indeed, it is sometimes necessary to abandon or postpone the whole project after a single sentence.

Finally, it is necessary to observe certain general cautions which can either be anticipated on the basis of general clinical experience, or in view of the test results themselves. For example, it is usually pointless to provide psychologic information to someone in the midst of a psychotic episode, for he is in no position, intellectually or emotionally, to receive or use such information. The same can usually be said for cases of severe depression and various states of intoxication, drug withdrawal, or physical exhaustion. Similarly, the psychologic conditions that are referred to as "borderline psychotic"—regarding schizoid and cyclothymic personalities—remain quite vulnerable to information that can shake their tenuous sense of worth and precipitate great anxiety. In all of these cases dynamic interpretations should either be avoided completely or made with considerable caution and sensitivity.

In addition, in many cases the patient is not so much threatened by a testing report as provided with an instrument to further his battle with the world. For example, the person who always feels abused—the "injustice collector"—will tend to feel abused by a report of his problems: he will feel accused and criticized; and in return he will blame the therapist and may even leave therapy, consoled by a sense of righteous indignation. Similarly, the person who always has to be "right" will often quibble with every word, insist on perfect accuracy, and explain at length how the test results are mistaken. On the other hand, some patients will literally embrace a report of pathology, for they hope to use such a report to get other people—a wife or husband, an employer or relative—to relax their demands: the demonstration of "craziness" is used as a certificate for exemption.

For all of these cases, it becomes essential for the therapist to anticipate the patient's probable reaction to the report, and to prepare an appropriate strategy to handle it (5). In this respect, it is fortunate that test results often provide the best kind of assistance: they frequently make possible both an estimate of an individual's "ego strength"—namely, his ability to tolerate information that may lower his self-esteem or contradict certain aspects of his self-image—and indicate his primary methods for dealing with life.

THE ESTABLISHMENT OF A THERAPEUTIC RELATIONSHIP

Psychologic testing can be used very fruitfully as an introduction to the therapeutic process. This is often conducted most effectively in a "double interview" where the major therapist presents his findings to a second therapist who serves as a consultant. The cards are placed on the table: the therapist says what he thinks, and the patient is encouraged to respond with a similar openness, especially if he shows signs of disagreement or irritation (6, 7).

This approach has a number of advantages. For one, it commences the relationship on an honest footing. It prevents the patient from thinking that the therapist knows more than he will reveal—that he is withholding information or secretly harboring a condemning judgment. It therefore avoids the anger that frequently accompanies the mystery surrounding psychologic treatment.

Secondly, this approach often engenders in the patient a large measure of confidence in the therapist. The testing itself tends to indicate that the therapist is trained, conscientious, and scientific: he does not guess at the problem, he studies it. And to the extent that the patient places confidence in science, or in the diagnostic procedures that are common to most medical treatment, his faith in these methods may extend to psychologic testing as well. Furthermore, if the therapist, in the eyes of the patient, is generally accurate in his assessment, his skill will be openly and sometimes dramatically demonstrated; and the patient may then feel much more willing to risk his confidence. This effect is especially common when the therapist uses the Rorschach, for patients are frequently surprised and impressed that so much precise and relevant information can be extracted from a few statements about rocks and animals. This effect is also quite helpful with patients who doubt the utility of psychology in general, for nothing dispels skepticism like a clear display of competence.

Thirdly, a testing report can be used in a number of ways to encourage a patient and arouse hope for the future. For one, the mere gesture of providing feedback indicates a genuine belief in the patient's strength—in his ability to comprehend and tolerate information that may, in some respects, be unfavorable or unpleasant. And conveying this belief frequently has the effect of bringing into being its desired object: it becomes a self-fulfilling prophesy that elevates the patient's sense of confidence and self-worth. The same is true whenever the therapist shows respect for the patient's comments or disagreements: by putting his findings aside, in deference to the judgment of the patient, the therapist demonstrates his recognition of the patient's intelligence and self-knowledge. It is also encouraging, in general, for the patient to feel understood: it re-establishes communication and belonging, calling to an end that lonely twilight of confusion and inarticulate fears.

THE ACCELERATION OF THERAPEUTIC PROGRESS

In many forms of therapy the movement is slow and cautious. The patient begins without knowing how to "do" therapy, without a clear idea of the therapist's goals or expectations, and without much confidence in either himself or the therapist. On the other hand, when therapy begins with a report of psychologic testing, the issues are immediately clear and specific. If the patient disagrees with the report, he may feel disgusted, disappointed, or discouraged; but he will at least know where he stands. He can then decide whether or not he wants to drop therapy completely, find a new therapist, or try to convince his present therapist of his mistaken ideas. He will at least have avoided the extended, costly, belabored, and sometimes fruitless search for his "deep-seated problems." On the positive side, if he should agree with the findings, he will not only feel understood and have some idea of his therapist's general orientation and competence, but he will also have a very concrete place to begin—some problems on which to focus his attention and energy.

Secondly, confronting a patient with his problems frequently "opens him up." If he feels understood, he often wants to be even more understood, and will often bring forth problems which the testing only intimated or may have missed completely. This effect is probably, at least in part, related to the therapist's demonstration of understanding and competence: he can now be trusted with difficult and intimate problems. But also, once the patient's problems have been brought into the open and treated with genuine candor and empathy, their secrecy, shame, and incoherence is removed. They can then be discussed with more emotion, but no less objectivity, than having boils or wetting the bed. This is especially true for sexual problems, most of which are cloaked with layers of humiliation and self-hatred.

192

Finally, the testing report can be used immediately and effectively to stimulate self-awareness: the problems it identifies can be presented, not only in words, but in concrete behavior. By carefully observing the patient, both during the report and in the discussion that usually accompanies or follows it, the therapist can frequently move directly from a statement in the report to a parallel example taken from the patient's immediate behavior. For example, the patient who presents, according to the testing, the life style of a "critic," will often illustrate his typical life-posture by commencing an attack on the validity of the testing. On the other hand, the person who always has to please will often agree with anything the testing says, even if two different statements have been made deliberately contradictory! By calling attention to such parallels, the therapist can use the testing to illuminate immediate behavior, placing certain patterns before the patient with a clarity and directness that is difficult to deny or refute (8).

RESOLVING THERAPEUTIC PROBLEMS

A number of specific therapeutic problems can be handled very effectively with the aid of psychologic testing. One of these concerns "reluctant dragons"—patients who have come for treatment under duress and will acknowledge no problems. With some of these patients it is possible to make a "deal": if psychologic testing, done by a third party who has no stake in the outcome of the testing, reveals no problems, the therapist will call the relatives, employer, or spouse and urge them to desist; if, however, the testing reveals some genuine problems, the therapist will expect the patient to begin treatment in earnest. The "deal" is acceptable to most patients not only because the therapist maintains his neutrality in the struggle between the patient and his opponents, but also because the therapist demonstrates his central concern with the patient's personal welfare: he will help in the way that seems most beneficial, regardless of what the patient's adversaries may say or do. Whether the patient ultimately follows through with his side of the "deal"—to the point of genuine involvement—is of course dependent upon both the persuasiveness of the therapist and the willingness of the patient to work on personal problems. The "deal," however, provides an entry: it gets the patient hooked long enough for the therapist to exercise his skill.

In a similar case, the therapist is sometimes confronted with the mildly paranoid patient who does not trust people or psychology in general. With some of these individuals it is helpful to offer a "completely objective" form of testing, such as the computerized MMPI. The patient's answers to certain questions will be "untouched by human hands": they will be mailed directly to a computer and the therapist will never see them. The computer will not know the patient or the therapist, and its analysis will be completely "scientific," based upon a comparison of the patient's answers with those of other patients, numerous and nameless. This approach seems acceptable to some people because of their faith in science, the modern witch doctor. They may not trust people or subjective impressions; but if computers can place a man safely on the moon, they can also be trusted to plumb the depths of human personality.

Some patients do not listen to the therapist: the brief intervals when the therapist is speaking provide opportunities to relax, catch one's breath, and think of what to say next. The therapist becomes increasingly frustrated, for he feels like a third party at the scene of a duet—the patient talking to himself. The solution is to reverse the roles: a "double interview" is set up, one therapist presenting the results of psychologic testing, and the other therapist taking notes and making comments. The patient, forced to be somewhat of an outsider, has an opportunity to "overhear" a conversation about himself; and most people, in a situation of this kind, respond with tremendous curiosity and attention: what are these people saying about me?

Other patients, particularly those who have been hospitalized, sometimes feel that nothing is being done for them. This reaction is especially common among patients who feel that therapy is "just talk" that does not get anywhere. One method for dealing with this syndrome is to begin psychologic testing—especially in a medical setting, where "treatment" often consists of blood tests, X-rays, urine analyses, and so forth. The purpose is not to placate the patient, but to respond to his subjective definition of "treatment" in a way that is both helpful in the long run and immediately therapeutic.

194

During the course of treatment a disagreement will sometimes arise between the patient and therapist. In most cases such disagreements are resolved and progress continues. At other times a disagreement can become so strong that it not only prevents further progress but threatens dissolution of the therapeutic relationship. When this occurs, it is often helpful to suspend the usual procedures and appeal to a third party who is uninvolved in the conflict and can use psychologic testing to shed light on the problem. If the testing vindicates the therapist, the patient's respect for the therapist will sometimes be enhanced, and the therapeutic relationship can then be reestablished on a new footing. On the other hand, if the testing vindicates the patient, at the expense of the therapist, it will sometimes be necessary or fruitful to transfer the patient to a new therapist. But in either case, and regardless of the arrangements that are made subsequent to the testing, therapy is usually permitted to continue, and the patient is assured that his welfare remains the foremost consideration.

Another kind of "impasse" occurs when the patient reaches a plateau on which further progress is blocked by an indeterminate problem or the patient simply appears incapable of presenting new material, despite a mutual feeling that additional problems definitely exist. In a case of this kind, psychologic testing can be used either to discover the hidden "block," to reveal completely new problems, or to present new aspects to the old problems. It often serves, in other words, like a shot of adrenaline: it stimulates movement.

At other times the patient begins to move on his own, in directions unanticipated by the therapist. For example, a previously passive patient may begin to act out sexually, or an adolescent may begin to take drugs. In some cases, the therapist may be able, through conversation, to determine the reasons for such behavior; but in other cases he may remain uncertain and confused. Psychologic testing can assist at this point—and basically at any point where the therapist is baffled—by revealing, or at least suggesting, the underlying motivations. Also, by resorting to testing at a time like this, the therapist not only acknowledges his human limitations, but demonstrates a concerned and professional way of handling his limitations—which, from the standpoint of imitation, provides the patient with a realistic and constructive role model.

Two common patient reactions can be fruitfully dealt with through the use of psychologic testing. The first of these is a discouragement reaction. As therapy progresses, the patient seems to learn more and more about how "mixed up" he is; for every solution he discovers a dozen problems. As a result, he begins to feel worse and worse, until he begins to dread coming at all. When this occurs, testing can be used to identify the patient's assets—the areas where he functions well, the many skills he has mastered, the attitudes which stand him in good stead. Even his shortcomings can be presented in a positive light: for example, self-criticism can be seen as a readiness to seek self-improvement, or sensitivity as a capacity to perceive and respond to the feelings of others. For some patients, this procedure can have dramatic effects: it can introduce them to new aspects of themselves, things they never considered or valued. For others, it simply helps to offset the predominantly "negative" focus on problems and mistakes.

The other common patient reaction is more frequently a "presenting complaint," but it also occurs during the course of therapy. The patient is afraid he is "going crazy"—and the mere fear, of course, tends to increase anxiety and its many side effects, thereby intensifying the basic fear. Testing can be used here to differentiate between an anxiety reaction and something more profound, such as an incipient psychosis. In either case, whether the results confirm a psychotic process or not, the patient is usually relieved to know; for just as fear breeds on ignorance, hope and self-possession arise from knowledge, especially when the patient credits the knowledge as "scientific."

Finally, testing can be used prior to termination of therapy, both to identify the problems which still remain and to highlight those that are improved or solved. As one example of this, adlerian therapists have used early recollections in this way for a number of years (9). In this sense, testing facilitates closure: it helps to summarize the experience, giving it perspective and unity. It also tends to engender a sense of achievement even when many of the initial problems remain unresolved: for knowing where one stands, in light of where one used to be, is not only reassuring, in the sense of feeling "located," but also offers a road to the future, and a sense of hope that is based on clearly perceived progress.

SUMMARY

As indicated above, it is neither fruitful nor necessary to make a sharp distinction between diagnosis and treatment, confining psychologic testing to the former. When properly presented, psychologic testing can be used with considerable success at either the start of therapy to establish a firm therapeutic relationship; during the course of therapy to accelerate progress or resolve specific intercurrent problems; or at the end of therapy to identify gains and solidify a sense of accomplishment.

REFERENCES

. Rogers, C. *Client-Centered Therapy*. Houghton Mifflin, Boston, 1951.
. May, R., Angel, E., and Ellenberger, H. F. *Existence*. Basic Books, New York, 1958.
. Fromm-Reichmann, F. *Principles of Intensive Psychotherapy*. University of Chicago Press, Chicago, 1950.
. Appelbaum, S. A. Psychological Testing for the Psychotherapist. *Dynamische Psychiatre*, 2:158, 1969.
. Mosak, H. H. Predicting the Relationship to the Therapist from Early Recollections. *J. Indiv. Psychol.*, 21:77, 1965.
. Dreikurs, R., Shulman, B. H., and Mosak, H. H. Patient-Therapist Relationship in Multiple Psychotherapy. I. Its Advantages to the Therapist. *Psychiat. Quart.*, 26:219, 1952.
. Dreikurs, R., Mosak, H. H., and Shulman, B. H. Patient-Therapist Relationship in Multiple Psychotherapy. II. Its Advantages to the Patient. *Psychiat. Quart.*, 26:590, 1952.
. Sangiuliano, I. Transactional History-Taking. *J. Contemp. Psychother.*, 2:33, 1969.
. Mosak, H. H. Early Recollections as a Projective Technique. *J. Proj. Tech.*, 22:302, 1958.

Life Style Assessment: A Demonstration Focused on Family Constellation[1,2,*]

The phrase, life style, is currently used in many way which Adler never intended. As Adler used it, life style refers t the "unity in each individual—in his thinking, feeling, acting in his so-called conscious and unconscious, in every expressio of his personality. This unity we call the style of life of the in dividual" (3, p. 175). While we agree with this definition of lif style, we prefer one somewhat more limited, namely, a person' central convictions which, to oversimplify, describe how h views himself in relation to his view of life.

We formally assess a life style by interviewing the perso regarding his family constellation and his early recollections, a Adler had emphasized the importance of birth order positio and early recollections (3, p. 328). The family constellation par was described first by Dreikurs (4) and then by Shulman (7) the early recollections part has been described by this autho (5). In an actual case we give equal importance to the two part: In the present demonstration early recollections are merel touched upon during the last few minutes, while the emphasi is on the investigation of the family constellation. Dreikurs out lines the significance of this procedure in the following:

The family constellation is a sociogram of the group at home during the person's formativ years. This investigation reveals his field of early experiences, the circumstances unde which he developed his personal perspectives and biases, his concepts and convictior about himself and others, his fundamental attitudes, and his own approaches to life, whic are the basis for his character, his personality (4, p. 109).

---

[1]The tape of the demonstration at the Fourth Brief Psychotherapy Conferenc Chicago, March 25, 1972, was not available to the author. The demonstration reported he instead, was conducted the following day before the audience at a workshop of the Alfr Adler Institute, Chicago.

[2]Introductory statement and comments addressed to the audience are in large type; th interview proper is in small type.

*Reprinted by permission fro.n JOURNAL OF INDIVIDUAL PSYCHOLOGY, 1972, 2 232-247.

Some comments are in order regarding variations from our usual clinical procedure. At a demonstration such as the present, time is limited. Therefore, *(a)* we could not complete the assessment nor write the summary we ordinarily undertake in clinical practice, *(b)* we interpreted for the client as we proceeded whereas in actual practice the interpretive summary is postponed until data collection is complete, *(c)* the result is not necessarily a model of good interviewing. We also wish to mention that at a demonstration we use a blackboard to enter the main facts obtained through the interview as we go along, so that the audience may keep these before their eyes.

At the present session the client was a high school student, Ann, whom I had never met before, and about whom I did not have any information. Her high school counselor, who attended the workshop, had invited her to serve as a subject for this demonstration before an audience, and she had agreed.

At the beginning of the interview we established that Ann was 17 years old, one of five children, with an older sister, Debbie, age 19; a younger brother, Sam, age 13; and a pair of twins, Marty and Mary, age 10. One can start formulating hypotheses immediately. Thus I said, looking at this information, my best guess at this point is that Debbie, Ann and Sam form one subgroup and the twins, a second subgroup.

DR. M.: How do you feel about this, Ann?
ANN: It's right.
DR. M.: To confirm this, let me ask, who played with whom?
ANN: I played with Debbie. Sam usually played by himself, and Marty and Mary played together.

Here Ann may be suggesting that my guess of a two-group family was wrong, that it was actually a three-group family, 2-1-2. We shall keep this in mind and see which it might be. To help ascertain I shall ask:

DR. M.: Who fought with each other?
ANN: Debbie and I fought constantly, and Sam and Debbie fought constantly.
DR. M.: And who else fought?
ANN: The twins fought.

"Sam and Debbie fought constantly" would suggest that they are in the same subgroup. At this point I could ascertain more information about the subgroups, but I shall not go into that. These questions, and most of those which I shall ask can be found in the Dreikurs paper to which I have referred (4).

Regarding subgroups, psychologists have a difficult time with families beyond three children. They can more or less accurately describe an oldest, a middle, or a youngest child; but the fourth child is not described and the fifth certainly not. However, by dividing families into subgroups of children, it is possible to determine the psychological position of each child within the family. Sometimes, just on the basis of what we have so far here on the blackboard we can already begin to formulate some hypotheses, some alternatives.

DR. M.: What kind of child was Debbie when you were growing up?
ANN: She was *very* studious all the time . . . Well, from my point of view, she was a goody-goody . . . It's hard to talk about your own sister.
DR. M.: Especially if you have to say such nice things about her.
ANN: No, she was *very* reliable and *very* responsible . . . and *very* talkative.
DR. M.: Did she get into trouble at school for that?
ANN: Occasionally.
DR. M.: So, while she was a goody-goody, she still got into trouble occasionally. She wasn't quite perfect. What else was she like?
ANN: Well, she *always* tried to please my parents. And she was *very* sensitive. You know like she cried very easily . . . that's about all.
DR. M.: I'm going to invite you, Ann, to look at all of this on the blackboard. If you had one word to describe your sister, what word would you use? Let me give you an incomplete sentence. She was . . .
ANN: Responsible, I guess.
DR. M.: That's a good word.
ANN: I can't do it in *one* word.
DR. M.: I can. Would you like to hear my one word?
ANN: Yes.
DR. M.: She was *very* . . . (*Audience laughter.*) How does that sound?
ANN: *Very* good. (*Ann and audience laughter.*)

She was not just *very* studious, but *very* studious *all* the time. She *always* tried to please the parents. Even though Ann does not use the word "very" each time, she uses it quite consistently. Even when she doesn't use it, she still describes her sister as a "very," and a "very" is *always* something positive.

Very responsible, good-goody, *very* studious, *always* wanting to please, and so forth. It must have been a hard act to follow.

Now, one thing Adlerians observe is that when you have two children in competition (and when two children are this close in age, they generally are in competition), they operate as "teeter-totter twins." Where one succeeds, the other fails or does not even get into that area. He just decides, "The heck with it; it's really not worth it. I'm going to do something else." They carve up the territory because every child in every family, you *(to audience)*, Ann, and I, is striving for significance. We want to count; we want to belong; we want to have the feeling that people take notice of us, that we are part of it. We don't always use the best methods for gaining significance, but even sometimes with the poorest methods, people do take notice of us, as any teacher will testify. If that is the case, we can already begin to make some predictions in terms of probabilities with respect to Ann.

> DR. M.: Since Debbie was "very," and "hardly ever," let's find out, Ann, what kind of kid you were.
> ANN: "Hardly ever" and not "very." *(Ann and audience laughter.)* I wasn't studious, and I wasn't a goody-goody. Well I was actually . . .
> DR. M.: Very reliable? *(Traits with which she described Debbie.)*
> ANN: No, I wasn't.
> DR. M.: Very responsible?
> ANN: No.
> DR. M.: Very talkative?
> ANN: No.
> DR. M.: Always tried to please parents?

If you could see Ann as I can see her from this position, you would have seen the glimmer of a recognition reflex when I mentioned "always tried to please parents." And you are going to discover that she does not try to please them very much— although she wants to.

> DR. M.: Right?
> ANN: Right!
> DR. M.: Very sensitive? Cry easily?
> ANN: Yeah!

Sibling competition is one of the major factors leading to differences between children. Similarities occur in the area of the family values. A family value is one which *both* parents hold in common, and every child must take a stand, positive or negative, with respect to that particular value or behavior. You can well imagine because of the potency of the parents that most of the children will adopt positive attitudes to the parental values. If it's a family where both parents stress being good in school, all the children will do *something* about being good in school. They'll either be very good or very poor. Where the family values are not involved, the child may not take a stand at all. Consequently, one can suspect that both parents have some kind of stand in common on sensitivity, and Ann is now nodding her head, and consequently each child has to make up his mind whether he is going to be sensitive or not. It is not determined by the competition, because in terms of the competition, whatever Debbie does, Ann does the opposite.

> DR. M.: Anything you want to add to just the "minuses"?
> ANN: I was athletic, whereas Debbie didn't even bother with sports.
> DR. M.: You were athletic and therefore Debbie was minus.
> ANN: I think I was more interested—well maybe I was more generally creative than she was as a child.

You notice here the intensity of the competition. She does not merely say, I was athletic or I was creative. I was *more* creative, I was *more* athletic, which means that she grew up with one eye on her sister, watched how well her sister was doing and then compared herself to that. Since her sister was so "very," she had to feel inferior in most respects. Ann lives life *comparatively*.

> DR. M.: What was Sam like?
> ANN: If you want to compare him between Debbie and me, he was more like Debbie. He was a good student, but at the same time he was athletic and enjoyed sports like my parents did.
> DR. M.: Both parents did? So you see we have another family value. Both parents enjoyed sports and every child is going to take a positive or negative stand on it.
> ANN: He's athletic, *very* responsible for a kid his age, too, and likeable. That's about all.

That makes a good start. If you look at Sam, you will notice that he has many of the same characteristics that Debbie had, with one major exception. He's not "very." He's likeable, he's athletic, and he's a good student, but he's not "very." Only one time does she use the word "very" with respect to him. One reason that Sam could become these things is that Ann had already become discouraged and had defaulted. Therefore, he could become those things which she was not. Since Ann was a poor student, it was easy for him to become a good student, but, of course, as he became a good student, Ann found herself in the middle of a pincers movement—the two "good" ones, and herself in the middle. Not "very" good, not "very" accomplished, between two good kids! The squeeze was on. Now she said previously that Sam and Debbie fought, not Sam and she, but Sam and Debbie. And you can see the competition there, too, because Sam wanted to do the same things Debbie was doing, except she had a six-year head start. She could even like her six-year younger brother as long as he knew his place. If he occasionally decided to compete, she shoved him down.

DR. M.: What kind of boy was Sam?
ANN: Well, he was the kind of boy that I suppose any father would like.

"The kind of boy any father would like." You see that Sam had a place merely by being a boy, so that while he competed, he didn't *have* to compete. But he wasn't merely content to take the place he could have had easily. He figured that you can't have enough of a good thing, so he would see if he could also intrude on Ann's territory a bit. She has not told us this yet, but she will *(Ann nods and bursts out laughing in confirmation.)* I sometimes tell my interns that someday I hope to get good enough at this so that I won't even need the subject. *(Audience laughter.)*

If *any* father would like a boy like this, then her father would like a boy like this. So, Sam must have been his favorite, at least his favorite in the older group. Perhaps when Marty arrived her father transferred his preference to the younger boy; but at least in the older group, we would guess that Sam was father's favorite.

Now, you have Debbie who was "very," and she must have been everybody's favorite—teacher's, parents'. I suspect when teachers got Ann after Debbie, the first day they said, "Gee, I hope you're like your sister."

DR. M.: Did they?
ANN: Occasionally.

Teachers, incidentally, think that this is an encouraging remark *(audience laughter)* and they probably said to Sam, "I hope you're not like your sister, Ann." You can imagine what Ann must have felt like, growing up. Unless she had grandparents or an uncle or aunt or a favorite teacher, it must have been, "Why does everyone love everyone else but me?" *(Ann nods.)*

DR. M.: Tell me a little bit about Marty.
ANN: He's very likeable.
DR. M.: Does anybody know what the next word is going to be?
ANN: It's not going to be "very." *(Audience laughter.)*
DR. M.: Don't let us intimidate you, please, Ann. If you want to use it, okay.
ANN: He's amusing.
DR. M.: To whom?
ANN: To me, I like him. I think he's just a typical little kid with a big imagination.
DR. M.: He's something like you?
ANN: Yes, he is in a way.
DR. M.: And what about Mary?
ANN: Mary is a replica of my mother, sort of.

Now, without asking a question about her mother, you're going to find out what her mother was like.

DR. M.: What was Mary like?
ANN: She's very domestic, but she's intelligent. *(Audience laughter.)*
DR. M.: And your mother is not?
ANN: Well, I don't want to go . . . well, they're both domestic, yet they're both intelligent at the same time.
DR. M.: Are you trying to say or indicate that these two don't ordinarily go together?
ANN: Not ordinarily. I was just . . . you know, you asked me what Mary was like and she's . . .
DR. M.: Are you a candidate for Women's Lib?
ANN: Yes!
DR. M.: I thought so.
ANN: Well, I was just trying to straighten you out that Mary . . . she tries to act like a mother. Like any ten-year-old girl, she tries to assume the tasks that my mother assumes. It's obvious to me.
DR. M.: Is there much competition between her and Marty?
ANN: No, not really.

DR. M.: Yet you said they fight.
ANN: Yes, they do fight, but . . .
DR. M.: Go on, tell us how it is.
ANN: Well, I don't know. It seems like Mary has her own . . . well my parents expect one thing of Mary and one thing of Marty. I think the twins realize this and they don't cross in each other's territory, so to speak.
DR. M.: Except, apparently when they do, and then they fight.
ANN: Then they fight.

If you look at the blackboard, you will see something interesting. You might not catch it if you did not write it down. Every person but one is "very" in something. Some more than others. If you look at the positive traits that Ann has described—studious, responsible, reliable, etc.—everybody has at least one "very," except Ann. She's the only "un-very" child in this family, except that she is not, because her parents probably regard her as "very" much of a problem.

ANN: *Very* true. *(Ann and audience laughter.)*

That is apparently the only way in which Ann makes sure that the family or school community take notice of her. She can't be "very" studious "all" the time; she can't please "all" the time; she's had "very" little training in responsibility. She figures that at least through—and I will use the word broadly because I have no more knowledge than you—some kind of "misbehavior," they take notice of her. They know she's there. I would also suspect that through her own "very" she keeps her parents and teachers busier than the other four kids together. Now, her hairdo is hiding her recognition reflex. *(Audience laughter.)*

DR. M.: I know you have given us these descriptions as best you could, but let's round out the picture a bit. Who was the most intelligent, and who the least intelligent?[3]
ANN: Sam, I think, was most intelligent, and Mary, the least.
DR. M.: I'll tell you what I'm going to do. Ordinarily I would ask you to rate all five of you. But because of the limited blackboard space, and since the twins are not in your group, I am going to restrict the rating to the older three who make up one group. Now

---

[3]All the "most" and "least" questions, as well as other pairwise questions, were asked separately, but we combined them here for more compact presentation.—Ed. note.

then, the most intelligent is Sam, and the least intelligent is?
ANN: Well, me.
DR. M.: You say that almost proudly.
ANN: Well, no.
DR. M.: Who got the best grades in grade school, and who the poorest?
ANN: Debbie got the best grades. Yours truly got the poorest.
DR. M.: What were your favorite subjects in grade school?
ANN: Art, gym, and English.
DR. M.: And you didn't like?
ANN: Math, science, and social studies.

Yesterday, at the Brief Psychotherapy Conference, I discussed with some of you the meaning of achievement or underachievement in school subjects. Unfortunately I don't have time to go through all subjects today, but let me take math as an example. Math is a problem-solving activity. To do math or arithmetic isn't, like spelling, a matter of just putting it in your head and when the teacher says, "Okay, spell 'dog,'" grinding it out for the teacher. You must be able to use past experience to solve the current problem. You have to use your brain as a filter. You have to know what solutions seem to be on the right track (even if eventually they are not) and to discard immediately those which you know aren't going to work at all.

Adler had noted, "Arithmetic demands the greatest degree of independence. In arithmetic, apart from the multiplication table, there is no security: everything depends on free and independent combinations" (2, p. 10). The child who does poorly in math, assuming he's had reasonably good instruction, is not self-reliant. Faced with a problem, he says, "I'll never figure that out. Gee, I hope someone will help me. Maybe somebody will get me out of this jam, or maybe fate will do it, but I don't trust my own abilities to do it." So, apparently Ann had already made up her mind very early that all the capability in the family lay with her siblings and there was none left over for her.

DR. M.: Who's the most industrious, and who the least?
ANN: Debbie, the most; me, the least.
DR. M.: Who's the "goodest", and who rebelled openly?
ANN: Debbie was the "goodest," and I was the rebel.
DR. M.: Proudly?
ANN: Yep!
DR. M.: Who was the covert rebel, never fought openly, just did what he wanted?

ANN: Sam.
DR. M.: Who demanded his own way, and who got it?
ANN: I demanded it, and Debbie got it.
DR. M.: And Sam?
ANN: Sam got his way also.

After all, if you're the kind of boy that any father would like, you get your way. Besides which he was the baby of the older group. And that isn't going to hurt your chances of getting your own way. If you look at these two things in combination—who demanded and who got his way—you know the answer to the next question. Who felt sorry for himself? And the answer, of course, has to be Ann. She demanded most and got least. Or perhaps, she felt she got nothing. *(Ann nods.)*

DR. M.: Who has a temper?
ANN: I do.

There are only two major reasons for temper. One reason is to announce to the world, "I want to have my own way. You better do it or I'm going to intimidate you." In the words of Adler, "Children make use of outburst of temper to conquer by terrifying" (1, p. 59). Such a child throws himself on the floor, bangs and kicks, turns purple, hoping that you'll come across. The other reason is righteous indignation. "I'm the custodian of the right, and how dare you do something as wrong as that?" From Ann's answers it would seem that her temper was in the service of enforcing her own way. "I'm going to do what I want; I'm going to get what I want, and nobody's going to tell me how to do, what to do, when to do, and if they don't like it, too bad."

ANN: Exactly!

Even though she says, "Exactly," I should like to take a stab also at the second reason for temper. "This family may have its set of values, but I have my set of values, and my ethic is higher than theirs. Therefore, if they don't come across, they are wrong. Those old fogies over thirty don't understand, etc." She already told you she is a candidate for Women's Lib so she has her own ethic there, and I am quite sure that what started out as "I want my own way," as she got older, was tied in with "and I'm right, besides." And because she is right, nobody can tell her anything. Is that the problem?

ANN: It seems to be.
DR. M.: Who's considerate of others, and who's inconsiderate?
ANN: Debbie is considerate, and I guess I am inconsiderate.
DR. M.: Who is most sensitive, and who is least sensitive?
ANN: I'm probably the most sensitive, and Sam the least sensitive.
DR. M.: I think we have forgotten to tell them something. Were you a tomboy?
ANN: Yes.

Ann was the tomboy. She was the tomboy for several reasons. One is, it was the opposite of what her folks wanted. Ann is what I call a "reverse puppet." With a regular puppet, if you pull the right string, the right hand goes up; but with a reverse puppet, the left hand goes up. It doesn't stop you from being a puppet. Yet many kids think, "Look how free I am when I am defiant." But actually they are still puppets. The person who is free decides for himself; he does not just do the opposite. If he does, he is still a puppet; he is merely wired wrong, i.e., his left hand goes up instead of his right. You can well imagine that at one level Ann was a tomboy because this is what she should not have been according to her parents. For another reason, it was easier to compete with Sam than with Debbie. At least in competing with Sam she had a chance. With Debbie, there was no chance. So she tried to tackle him on his home grounds, and of course this was reinforced by the fact that the parents were athletic and fostered or encouraged athletic behavior. So it was not a total disaster. She was doing something her parents wanted, and maybe, just maybe, her parents would be pleased with her if she were athletic. She almost *had* to be a tomboy. Let's get back to the ratings.

DR. M.: Who had the most friends and who the fewest?
ANN: Sam probably had the most friends, Debbie the fewest.
DR. M.: This is the first area we find where you did better than Debbie. Except for one thing. Do you want to tell the audience? According to your family, you didn't have the *right* friends?
ANN: Exactly, exactly. *(Audience laughter.)*

Even where she did find some significance, where she did out-distance her sister, it still did not gain her what she really wanted, namely the feeling of belonging. Even though she had more friends and outdid her sister, they really were not the

208

friends a girl like her ought to have, as far as her parents thought.

> DR. M.: Who was the most shy, and who the least shy?
> ANN: Maybe Sam was most shy. I was least shy.
> DR. M.: Who was most neat and who was least neat?
> ANN: Debbie was the neatest, and I was least neat.

There are many more of these ratings but time will not permit me to continue with them; yet each one we have so far, seems to follow in the same pattern. You can almost predict the sequence. As you have seen, as I say these things, Ann says, "exactly." I am going to have to, at this time, move on to her parents.

> DR. M.: How old is your father, and your mother?
> ANN: My Dad is 46; my mother is 42.
> DR. M.: So you had relatively young parents. Now, when you were growing up, let's say during your grade school period, what was your father like?
> ANN: Well, my Dad was the type of person that expected a great deal from everyone, including all of his children.

She tells us here that her father was a discouraging individual in the guise of an encouraging individual. He was the type of man who had such high standards that people had to push and push to achieve them, and probably feeling that they could not achieve them, they became more or less discouraged.

> ANN: He is a business man, *very* industrious, *very* responsible. *(Audience laughter.)* He tried to be understanding.

"He tried to be . . ." Ann just said about her father. Now, in therapy, in counseling, you hear people say, "I tried," "I'm gonna try," "I will try," etc., especially when you ask them to do something. "I try" or "I will try" has an implicit ending to that sentence. The ending is, "but I don't have the feeling that I will succeed." And when a person starts trying without expecting any success, he usually makes his anticipations come true. He does not succeed. So Ann feels that her father did not succeed in understanding. He merely "tried" to be understanding. Perhaps, father himself, despite his tremendous ambition and varied successes, was discouraged like the rest.

Dr. M.: Did your father have many friends? Was he respected in the community?

ANN: Yes, both.

DR. M.: We know he favored Sam, but was Sam his *very* favorite?

ANN: I don't think he made it that obvious. I don't think he did that to the rest of us kids. He's *very* fair. *(Ann and audience laughter.)*

DR. M.: Yes, he had to be *very* fair.

ANN: He *tried* to be fair. *(Audience laughter.)*

DR. M.: And he didn't succeed at that, either.

In a recent paper, Dr. Gushurst and myself (6) described these phrases that patients use, and what they really mean. Most of us are not tuned in. I would suspect that most people in this room if they heard "he tried," would write it down on their sheet dutifully without realizing what it really means. He did not expect to succeed, and probably did not succeed.

DR. M.: Okay, he tried to be fair and therefore, he never expressed favoritism.

ANN: He seemed to . . . Well, he was a strong person. At least he wanted to live up to the reputation that he was strong, so he concealed any emotion that he might have. He did not allow things to faze him, because he had to be the strong individual. By the same token he also believed that his was the role of the father of the house. His authority should not be questioned.

Here you see a strong masculine value. This is not a family value unless shared by mother. I don't know yet. With such a strong, masculine value, you can imagine the pressure on Sam and Marty. The girls, at least, to some extent, escaped this. However, now Ann is ready to give father his comeuppance.

DR. M.: Women are just as strong as men, aren't they? *(Ann nods.)* What was mother like?

ANN: Mother *tries* to be understanding. *(Audience laughter.)* Okay, she isn't either. She's pretty weak, weaker than my father. In fact, she's everything that he is not. They fit together perfectly for that reason.

DR. M.: A sort of master-slave, superior-inferior relationship?

ANN: No, I don't want to get that across.

DR. M.: A dominant-submissive kind of relationship?

ANN: No, I think it's more of a what she doesn't have, he fills in, and what he doesn't have, she fills in. I think she fills in for the emotional part of the relationship.

DR. M.: Yes, I buy that, but what about the strong-weak bit? You know if father married a strong woman, they would "kill each other."

ANN: No, she's *not* strong.

DR. M.: So, on that basis, they have a sort of covenant—he's the head of the house, and she knows the proper responses to make so they don't run into trouble.

ANN: Probably.

DR. M.: But other than that you see them as rather complementary? What he has, fills in for what she doesn't have; and what she has, fills in for what he doesn't have?

ANN: If she's a slave, I think she enjoys being one. She's happy.

DR. M.: Tell me some of the things that she is.

ANN: She's creative.

DR. M.: That sounds like somebody else in the family.

ANN: She's very emotional.

DR. M.: Like somebody else in the family. And it isn't Mary. You mean you grew up weak like mother? Is that what you've been thinking the whole time? That you're creative and sensitive and in other ways like mother, instead of the strong, "I can do anything I want and people better listen to me," father? I am going to ask you to look out into the audience a minute, Ann, because I'm going to ask them a question. I don't know the answer but we're going to have to take our chances. Willing to risk it?

ANN: Sure!

DR. M.: *(To audience.)* I want you to give an honest answer. I don't want you to please me nor Ann. How many of you feel that creativity and sensitivity are negative traits? Not one. How many think that they are positive traits? All. Well, they are neither intrinsically positive nor negative. Either can be *used* negatively. Of course, one can use, as many delinquents do, his creativity to make all kinds of mischief. As Dr. Dreikurs has said, "Neurosis is a testimony to man's ingenuity." *(Audience laughter.)* What do *you* think?

ANN: I think I realize that creativity and sensitivity aren't bad things to have; it's probably just my way of looking at it. It's the thing I associate with my mother's weakness and inability to cope with my father, or my inability to adjust in school.

DR. M.: You know, Ann, those people in the audience are creative and sensitive, but since they don't know your mother, they don't worry about it. They just enjoy being creative and sensitive. But you associate it with your mother's weakness and don't want any part of it. May I suggest what you might do with that vote you got out there? How you might interpret it? There's an old Hungarian proverb: If one person tells you you are drunk, laugh it off. If two people tell you, give it some serious thought. But if three people tell you, you better go home. *(Audience laughter.)* Now there are at least three people out there who say that your creativity and your sensitivity can be used as *positive* traits. You might want to think about it. *(Ann smiles and nods.)* What's the nature of the

relationship between your parents? I know we discussed that just a little while ago in terms of complementarity.
ANN: Well, basically they both have great ambitions, materialistic ambitions. They want to make money. They *are* making money They enjoy eating out. They enjoy playing golf.

Ann is now telling the family values. *They* enjoy. Not *he* enjoys, but *she* does not; not that *he* would prefer, but *she* would not prefer. *They* are materialistic, etc. These are the family values.

ANN: They are united in what they are supposed to accomplish. I don't know, I guess their relationship is . . . it's mutual what they want, and I think money is a big factor, even bigger than happiness, sometimes.
DR. M.: Who's mother's favorite?
ANN: I think I am.
DR. M.: Why?
ANN: Maybe it's because she recognizes that I have some of the same traits that she has. Creativity and sensitivity.
DR. M.: In other words, we two people who have nothing going for us have to stick together.
ANN: *(Reflectively.)* Maybe. I never thought of it that way.
DR. M.: I hope you will because it's a myth. It's just as much a myth as the belief that Zeus is sitting atop Mt. Olympus. It's something you believe but it just isn't so. We'll have to stop here with respect to your family. I would like to use my last few minutes getting your early recollections.

From all the things which a person can remember from his early childhood, each of us remembers about a half dozen incidents. It is not important whether these things actually happened or happened the way the person says they happened. What is important is that the individual says and feels that he remembers them. A person engages in this selective process and believes that these things are so because they describe how the individual right now views himself in relationship to life.

DR. M.: I want you to think back as far as you can. What is the first incident you remember? Something about which you can say, "One thing I remember . . ."
ANN: I remember my First Communion.
DR. M.: Okay, please tell us about your First Communion.
ANN: It was about 7 o'clock in the morning and we all had to get up real early to get down to the church on time.
DR. M.: And, what's going on? Supposing you are making a motion

picture right now of what's going on at 7:30 in the morning on the day of your First Communion.

ANN: I remember I was half asleep and my mother was pulling curlers out of my hair, telling me what I had to do and what I had to say, and all that kind of stuff.

DR. M.: And you were feeling . . .

ANN: I was feeling tired and I was scared, too.

DR. M.: Scared of what?

ANN: Of walking down the aisle in front of all those people.

DR. M.: And . . . and you were just lying in bed and mother was pulling curlers out of your hair?

ANN: It was like everyone was making a big fuss over me and I was supposed to feel something and I didn't feel anything.

Here you see, first of all, her role in life. She is the person they do it to. Secondly, she tells you their standards are quite different from her standards. They are making a big fuss, and she feels, "I'll be darned, I don't know what everybody is excited about, because I sure am not." Third, you see her own reflection of her own lack of self-reliance. "I'll have to walk down that aisle, and I'm scared."

DR. M.: What is the next thing you remember?

ANN: I don't remember anything specifically, but I just remember soon after I made my communion, I joined a speed skating club. One day I cracked my head open, because I slid into the wall.

DR. M.: How did that happen?

ANN: I was racing. I was about ten years old, and it was up in Minneapolis. Somehow I just cracked my head open, and I remember that my Dad was real upset about it, and I probably felt sort of guilty, you know, for him for letting this happen to me.

DR. M.: How did he let it? I'm not quite clear. How did he let it happen to you?

ANN: I was going to get into that. When I got home, my mother was aghast that my father had . . . She blamed the fact that I cracked my head open on him.

DR. M.: But how was he responsible for it?

ANN: Because he had encouraged me to go out for speed skating. He had taken me up there against my mother's wishes.

DR. M.: In the first part of the recollection what are you trying to do? What do you do on a speed-skating team? What's the whole goal?

ANN: To get there first.

To get there first, to get ahead, to win. Even when she tries, it does not happen. I can't go into any more recollections with her, but you see, she sees herself as a victim of life. She is also a victim, as is mother, of father's encouragement or neglect, or something or another. She is the victim; whether she tries to get ahead, or to be first, or to succeed, all she is going to get for her troubles is a split head. Actually, what she is saying is she is discouraged. Why try if you can't win? Since she is working with a counselor now, her counselor will have to encourage her. At this moment she does not believe in herself.

DR. M.: We can see, Ann, why you would not believe in yourself, growing up the way you did. I guess if I grew up in that spot, I would feel pretty much the way you feel. The question is, is it necessary *now?* Or do you want to stop being a "reverse puppet" and decide what *you* want to do in life? Not, "what *they* want me to do which I will not do." That's the issue you and you counselor will have to work out together. Is there anything you would like to add, ask, or comment on?

ANN: I think you are just remarkable, I mean the way you can ... *(Audience laughter and applause.)*

DR. M.: Thank you, you are very kind. Other than that . . .

ANN: I guess I didn't realize that I was the victim of, what I was suffering from. I think I can accept myself a lot easier now.

DR. M.: You are suffering from the ignorance that you are a good, competent person. You *are* competent, you *are* good, but you are too busy looking at Debbie and your mother, and judging youself negatively, instead of deciding what *you* want to do. Did you feel comfortable up here. Ann?

ANN: Well, no, to be perfectly honest, I didn't.

DR. M.: Why?

ANN: I just feel self-conscious in front of all these people.

DR. M.: But this thing itself did not make you uncomfortable or nervous or anything like that?

ANN: No, I enjoyed it.

DR. M.: We didn't step on your toes in any way?

ANN: No!

DR. M.: Thank you very much for coming.

REFERENCES

1. ADLER, A. *Problems of neurosis* (1929). New York: Harper Torchbooks, 1964.
2. ADLER, A. *The problem child* (1930). New York: Putnam Capricorn Books, 1963.
3. ADLER, A. *The Individual Psychology of Alfred Adler.* Ed. by H. L. & Rowena R. Ansbacher. New York: Basic Books, 1956.
4. DREIKURS, R. The psychological interview in medicine. *Amer. J. Indiv. Psychol.,* 1952-53, 10, 99-122. Also in *Psychodynamics, psychotherapy, and counseling.* Chicago, Ill.: Alfred Adler Inst. Chicago, 1967. Pp. 125-152.
5. MOSAK, H. H. Early recollections as a projective technique. *J. proj. Tech.,* 1958, 22, 302-311. Also in G. Lindzey & C. S. Hall (Eds.), *Theories of personality: primary sources and research.* New York: Wiley, 1965. Pp. 105-113.

6. MOSAK, H. H., & GUSHURST, R. S. What patients say and what they mean. *Amer. J. Psychother.*, 1971, 25, 428-436.
7. SHULMAN, B. H. The family constellation in personality diagnosis. *J. Indiv. Psychol.*, 1962, 18, 35-47.

The Controller—A Social
Interpretation of the
Anal Character*

The possibility of translating a psychoanalytic character description based upon libido into social terms has been demonstrated in a previous paper on the "oral character" (13). Similarly the "anal character" may be described in social terms as the controlling personality.

When one thinks about controlling, generally our first associations center about the active forms of controlling. We perhaps think about mastery or dominance or the manipulation of the environment. While the controlling individual certainly engages in such activities, there are controllers who do not endeavor to control actively; they are merely unwilling to permit life and others to control them.

CONTROL THROUGH USE OF THE INTELLECT

The active forms of control vary from individual to individual depending upon their perceptions, and ultimately their convictions as to what will give them a place. Some controllers, having learned that "knowledge is power," rely upon intellect. Have a party, and they are off in a corner leading a discussion, a discussion about some topic they know well. If you become engaged in the discussion, they resort to intellectualization to advertise their superiority and to defeat you. This can be accomplished in two ways, first by definition of terms, what one newspaper columnist calls "antics with semantics." Ask a person whether he has ever been in love and he answers, "Yes," "No," "Many times," "I thought I was but it was only puppy love." The controller meets your question with the response, "What is love?"

*Reprinted by permission from ALFRED ADLER: HIS INFLUENCE ON PSYCHOLOGY TODAY, edited by Harold H. Mosak. Park Ridge, N.J.: Noyes Press, 1973.

The second method is talking beside the point. An old joke illustrates this maneuver well. "Should olives be eaten with the fingers?" "No, the fingers should be eaten separately." One receives the impression that the controller understands your communication quite well although his answer seems to negate such comprehension.

CONTROLLING THROUGH RIGHT

Other controllers place their faith in the right. When coupled with reliance upon intellect, these opinionated and argumentative people inform you, as one joke has it, "I'm not always right but I'm *never* wrong." Controlling through being right generally involves creating an orderly world where the credo for living is "Everything in its place and a place for everything." These people are organized, methodical, and orderly. Punctuality is exalted. Since a person who wants to be right must know his duty and then do it, the controller customarily practices over-conscientiousness. In the words of the television commercials, the good housewife controls dirt. She does it from morning to night. Parenthetically, the overconscientious controller, as hard as he may work, never permits himself to complete all of his tasks. If he should, there would be nothing left to control tomorrow. He is always behind schedule and consequently he must push himself to do more, work faster, and not take time off. He is always busy catching up. If his alarm clock fails to go off one morning, he is not merely fifteen minutes behind in his schedule. It is catastrophic; his entire day lies in ruins. Routine and schedules appeal to the controller. He brags about eating the same lunch every day at the same restaurant for the past twenty years. Frequently, although there are exceptions, as Adler takes care to explain in *The Case of Mrs. A* (1), the controller is overconcerned with his appearance, being super-neatly groomed, immaculately dressed, scrupulously clean, and having every hair in place. After all, if "cleanliness is next to godliness," is it not only right that one should keep oneself clean?

The insistence upon being and doing right creates dilemmas, subjective conflict, and malaise, for not to be right is to be wrong, and to be wrong leads to drastic consequences. Therefore where his assurance of being right is not guaranteed,

217

he must assume a posture of caution. As one of my patients remarked, "Nothing ventured, nothing lost." Another patient lamented, "They'll engrave on my tombstone, 'She never did any thing wrong . . . because she never did anything.'" Chronic doubt afflicts the controller. Sometimes he doesn't know what the right is; how can he then do it? Sometimes he is confronted with the choice between two rights, e.g. between personal interest and social interest. Worse yet, he may feel required to choose between two evils, and then his movement is paralyzed indeed, for the "lesser of two evils" does not fall within the realm of possible solutions for the person who has to be right. If only there were guidelines for everything so that one could always know what was right. He cannot tolerate ambiguity. This hesitating attitude toward life, marked by pronounced overcautiousness, is seen in exaggerated form in the neurotic controller, the obsessive-compulsive, who not only feels compelled to do the right thing but attaches the direst consequences to his failure to execute it, e.g. "I must say this three times or someone will die." While subjectively the controller exhibits doubt, ambivalence, and indecisiveness (in terms of movement, these are all one step forward and one step backward; the net effect is to remain in the same place) (5), he does not realize that he creates these feelings in order not to make a decision because in doing so, he might be wrong. The goal of perfection is, of course, transparent.

THE "RULING TYPE"

A third group of controllers are what Adler called "the ruling type" (4, 8, 9), many of whom develop attributes of leadership and some of ruthlessness, and others of non-amenability to authority. They speak with authority and perform with apparent confidence. There are parents and teachers who command children, "Do it because I tell you to." To reinforce authority and control, they resort to intimidation, threat, and violence. The teacher threatens, "If you don't do this, you'll go to the principal's office." The mother threatens, "Eat your spinach or no dessert for you." The university student admonishes the administration, "Acquiesce to our demands or we'll take over the university." The militant black encourages others to carry guns in their confrontations with the honkie. The child throws himself on the floor, holds his breath, or yells, screams and kicks in the hope that his parents will succumb. If parents can resist this form of control, the child can still conquer them utilizing the light artillery of "I don't love you" or the heavy artillery of "that just proves that you don't love me." The controlling wife, having been raised in a culture and by an educational system which emphasizes reward and punishment as motivating forces (11), uses sex as a motivater. We might also observe that the redhead is born with a license to intimidate, and if you're fortunate enough to be Irish, you are entitled to have an Irish temper.

Threat, violence, intimidation, temper, tyranny are repugnant to many individuals, controllers and otherwise. The controller who feels compelled to do the right thing finds these methods especially repulsive. Opposed to these methods, some people control through the use of money. "Money talks." It buys things. "Everyone has a price." Through generosity one may acquire the positive regard of others. Moreover, it may make them obligated to you. Others may rely instead upon charm and try to wind people around their fingers. Youngest children and girls often have a head start in training for such a role.

So-called passive methods constitute another resource for the ruling controller. Consider the shy child who hides behind his mother and makes you coax him out. Or the Victorian lady who fainted when she wished to control the situation. Or the wife, in imitation of her Victorian counterpart, who turns on the tears and makes her husband succumb. These devices are popularly considered to be signs of weakness, delicate nerves, a hypersensitive nature. Adlerians, interpreting these and all other behavior in terms of movement, consider them oppositely. Adler calls this utilization of crying, "water power" (3, 8). Weakness is nevertheless not excluded from the armamentarium of control. Some examples are the Goal IV child (10), the woman who has headaches at bedtime and the patients who use various forms of symptoms. An interesting use of weakness characterizes those who lose control, using active or passive means, in order to preserve control. People who fly off the handle, have emotional "fits," and behave with emotional instability lose control in order to gain control.

As any actor knows, the voice constitutes another vehicle for control. Speak in a low tone, and people either will bend forward, the better to hear you, or will lose interest in listening.

Speak rapidly or slowly and you may grab your listener by the lapels. Speak seductively and you enchant. Thunder and you intimidate. Speak monotonously and you *arrange* to bore.

In the ruling type the crucial issue is to make others behave in the manner one desires. "I made you" represents the essence of control. We can observe it in a children's playground game. One child obtains the attention of another child, points in the direction behind the other child's back, and exclaims, "Look!" The second child turns and sees nothing there whereupon the first child chants tauntingly, "Ha, ha! I made you look! I made you look! I made you buy a penny book!" Similar observations can be made among adults. For example, when a man gets a girl to do what he wants, he is said to have "made" her. Thus, where the getting personality is "on the take," the controlling personality is "on the make." His emphasis upon who can make whom do what leads to the perception of others as potential antagonists and the ruling controller must constantly be vigilant, perhaps even suspicious, since others are potential adversaries. Because he perceives the world as populated by enemies, his feeling of hostility toward the world is appropriate from his frame of reference. His posture, based upon his self image and his evaluation of the environment, is one of defensiveness in the face of the hostility from others. Only the external observer regards his assumption of hostility from others as the controller's own projection. One can understand that the controller who chooses psychosis makes his choice for paranoid symptomatology where he suspects life, and where people and forces are conspiring to do things to him or to make him do things which he is not inclined to do. His delusions of reference, influence, and persecution provide reinforcement for his stance.

Psychotic, neurotic, or normal, the controller does not find the world a resort area in which he can relax. To the contrary, the world is a jungle, survival of the fittest is its law, and if it's a dog-eat-dog world, he must prepare himself to be the dog who does the eating. But he must keep one eye open while sleeping lest someone snatch his bone or attack him. Incidentally, the controller does have periods of insomnia (7) since conditions must be just right in order for him to sleep. "I just can't sleep except in my own bed," he sometimes tells us.

Since people are frequently unpredictable and unmanageable, the controller tends to shift his concerns to ideas and objects. We have already spoken of his tendency to accumulate ideas but he also accumulates possessions. He is frequently a collector, often a hoarder, and since he believes, as the comedians put it, "Rich or poor, what difference does it make as long as you have money?", he may decide to acquire, hoard, and not expend money. When the check comes to the restaurant table, he has an impediment in his reach.

RESISTANCE TO BEING CONTROLLED

In contrast to the person who actively controls is the individual who does not permit life to control him. He may be constantly late and make others wait for him. Swimming disconcerts him, and a trip to the dentist is life's most terrifying experience—next to flying. He is further recognizable through his three major fears, the three situations which would deprive him of control. First, he fears the loss of physical control—blindness, paralysis, etc. Second his fear is of loss of psychological control. He fears his "ego-alien impulses," "blowing his cool," or losing his mind. However, even if he could succeed in controlling mind and body, there is one element in life to which he must eventually relinquish control—the great controller, Death.

To avoid being controlled such people adopt several methods of operation. They circumnavigate the demands of others. Mothers lament about their children, "One word from me, and he does just as he pleases." Some controllers become overconscientious, a not uncommon phenomenon in controllers in general, and defeat others' control by observing their demands literally. To illustrate, a child comes home covered with mud, and his mother despairingly tells him to undress and to deposit all of his clothes in the washing machine. The child complies. Several minutes later hearing a thumping in the machine, she opens the lid and discovers the child's shoes swirling about amidst the clothes. When she asks the child why he placed his shoes in the machine, he retorts, "You said *all* my clothes."

Some, and this is notably true among adolescents, become "reverse puppets." When one pulls the right string of an ordinary puppet, his right leg raises up. When one pulls the right string of the "reverse puppet," his left leg elevates. The "reverse puppet" adolescent treats a demand from others, especially his parents, as a signal to do the opposite. He identifies himself as emancipated and independent, unaware that his freedom is illusory, that he is just as much a puppet as the more conventional puppet.

The more the controller attempts to avoid being controlled, the more he runs into it. One of my obsessive-compulsive patients, "deathly" afraid of death, reads the newspaper, turning each page gingerly and scanning it rapidly to assure himself that there was no mention of death on the following page. In this way he never missed an article which alluded to death. This relationship between avoiding being controlled and thus courting it was known at least as far back as King Solomon's time. A Talmudic story relates, "There were once two servants of Solomon, Elihoref and Ahyah, scribes of the King. One day Solomon observed that the Angel of Death was sad. 'Why are you sad?' he asked. 'Because,' he answered him, 'I have been ordered to take these two servants of yours who sit here.' Whereupon to save them from death, Solomon sent them to the district of Luz. When, however, they reached there, they died. The next day, Solomon observed that the Angel of Death was in cheerful spirits. 'Why,' he said to him, 'art thou cheerful?' 'Because,' he replied, 'you sent them to the very place where I was to slay them!' " [1] A modern version of the story may be found in the frontispiece to John O'Hara's *Appointment in Samarra*.

The diagnostician will discover that women who resist being controlled hate wearing girdles. If they must wear them "to hold up their stockings," they still dislike the feeling of being controlled.

When the controller feels incapable, or as Adlerians would see it, he is unwilling to meet the life tasks, his fear of loss of control mounts. Then he may give way to a panic reaction or he may create hypochondriacal concerns in order to impress himself with the dangers of loss of control. He may develop phobic behavior, and a recent article by Leifer discusses the relationship of phobias to feelings of lack of mastery (12). Or he may create a sideshow—instead of controlling life, he diverts

[1] This excerpt from the Talmud Succah, p. 53a, is the translation of Rabbi Irving Rosenbaum of Chicago.

his attention to controlling himself. He deprives himself of his spontaniety because emotions can get out of control. He creates "ego-alien impulses" and then spends his time and energies controlling himself. Since these "ego-alien impulses" are viewed as demonic, certainly he is not responsible for them. He has thoughts which must be controlled, and he creates elaborate rituals for controlling his behavior. Dreikurs [2] recounts the legend of the wizard who knew the entire art of black magic. His king, wishing to learn these secrets, summoned the wizard to his court, and offered him up to half of his kingdom if the wizard would induct him into the secrets of black magic. The wizard, wishing to earn the king's reward, exacted only one condition—"If you wish to learn black magic, you must never think about crocodiles." And so the king never learned because every time he told himself, "I must not think about crocodiles," he violated the wizard's prohibition.

To permit this fictitious battle with the "ego-alien impulses" the controller must create two antagonistic, competing systems roughly corresponding to a "good-me" and a "bad-me" and make of himself a battleground upon which the angels wrestle with the demons. In his verbal communications we hear him declaring, "I have to force myself" or "How can I make myself?", reflective of a "good-me" with the best of intentions and the "bad-me" which gives the "good-me" a hard time. However, the combatants must be endowed with equal strength. Otherwise one set of "forces" will prevail, and the battle for control will terminate. With the sideshow stopped, he would be compelled to address himself to the solution of the life tasks which he has been avoiding. One of my obsessive-compulsive patients who had not worked in years and who had retreated from social relations felt that Truman was good and Castro was bad. Without warning, the name "Castro" would intrude into his thinking, and he would counteract this intrusion by repetitively uttering, "Truman, Truman, Truman." When he then relaxed, he would, to his dismay, find his mind thinking, "Castro, Castro, Castro," and the process would continue. And thus we have the obsessive-compulsive locked in an unending heroic fight to the finish to determine who is stronger—me or me? One can appreciate how heroic when you consider that in

---

Personal communication.

contrast to other neuroses whose symptoms come and go, the obsessive-compulsive syndrome is a twenty-four hour a day neurosis.

In the psychotic categories the controller, as already noted selects paranoid symptomatology and wrestles with his delusional demons. Among the psychophysiological reactions impotence and frigidity are common. The controller's impotence manifests itself in the effort to maintain an erection or in premature ejaculation. The controller's frigidity expresses itself in the ability to be aroused and the inability to achieve orgasm since the latter is often perceived as a loss of control or a loss of consciousness or as being transported to ecstatic heights where control surrenders to passion. Most prevalent among the psychophysiologic reactions of the controller is colitis, partly because the bowel is a most appropriate organ for expressing in organ dialect the problems with control and partly because seeing the world as hostile territory and being hostile himself, as a colleague indelicately but graphically describes it, "He shits on the life which he feels shits on him." Other neuroses to which the controller is "vulnerable" are discussed in a previous paper (14).

Whether the controlling personality controls or resists being controlled, he sporadically must permit life to get out of control. He arranges the consequences in such a way as to confirm the dangers of loss of control and thus reinforces the conviction that one must always be in control.

Teleologically, what is the controller up to? The Babylonian Talmud, in discussing the various names of God, gives one of these names as "the all-capable, the all-wise, and the perfect.' And this is the secret goal of the controller—to be omnipotent, omniscient, and perfect (2). Only then would he feel certain of having a place. The goal becomes transparent in the neurotic controller, the obsessive-compulsive, who usurps God's prerogatives over life and death in such compulsive thoughts as, "If I don't count to three, someone will die." Since he can never achieve this lofty goal, he is doomed to failure. He is "full of shit" but this is a metaphor for his self-image, not a cause of his behavior. The godlike aspirations have already been explained according to Adlerian theory as compensatory for the individual's inferiority feelings (2).

THE GOALS OF THE CONTROLLER

To leave it at this would not nearly do justice to insight into the person's goals. Since behavior occurs in a social context, let us examine the social functioning of the controller. At the same time that he exalts himself, he depreciates others and treats them badly. People are malevolent, enemies; only he is good. Yet if we look closely, we can observe that he uses his goodness to defeat. A parent nags his child all evening to do his homework but the child has other plans. When time for bed arrives and he is told to go to bed, his rejoinder is, "I've got to do my homework. Don't you want me to do my homework?" He is right; you are wrong. He has the best of intentions; you have the worst (Otherwise how could he be suspicious?). A patient in group therapy accused another of being a "phoney" whereupon the accused recalled a bit of "phoney" behavior of the first patient. Unruffled, the first patient retorted, "You're right but at least I'm an honest phoney. I *admit* it." You must do his bidding; he is exempt from doing yours. He is clean, and the remainder of the world is dirty (6). This contrast in cleanliness is most vividly exhibited in the neurotic controller, the compulsive with a washing compulsion, whose home reeks from the absence of any attempts at housekeeping (1). And in all of this movement we observe his lack of social interest. He lives only for the greater glory of God, and guess who God is!

What are some of the influences to which the controller is especially receptive in his formative years? Among the family influences, controlling parents influence children to be controlling, either in imitation of or in reaction to the parents. Similarly the parents' exercise of control in response to the child's efforts to control them eventuates in power contests where the child wins or the parents regret that they won a Pyrrhic victory. The child trains himself as a consequence in those forms of behavior which will permit him to control the situation or to avoid the control of others—temper tantrums, dawdling, stubbornness, stomach aches before school, crying and sensitivity and other forms of what Dreikurs includes under Goal II and Goal IV behavior (10). Dependency, when seen in Adlerian movement terms, may be defined as putting others into one's service and thus can be legitimately included in this category. While some personality theorists view the controlling individual as emerging from the pressures centering about toilet training, it seems more probable that parents who exert such control in toilet training also endeavor to control the child in other ways. More parents apparently fight over eating, and over a longer period of time, than they do over toilet training.

Social and cultural influences external to the family also make their contribution. Reward and punishment form the vehicles for distinguishing between prescribed and proscribed behavior. Despite the ineffectiveness of these methods in controlling behavior (11), educators declare their bankruptcy by utilizing them because they know no better methods for influencing behavior. Reward and punishment remain effective only so long as an authoritarian structure in interpersonal relationships is agreed upon and maintained. Since teachers often find it difficult to control children, the emphasis shifts to self control, and then it is no longer the teacher's responsibility. If the pupil does not conform to the teacher's wishes, he is merely given a check in "self control" on his report card. The communications media assault the eye and ear with advice on how to control the difficult to control—eating, smoking, weight, figure, and birth.

And psychology contributes its bit. To the extent that certain psychological systems portray man as driven, as irrational, as irresponsible, these systems must create certain psychological constructs to combat or neutralize the "base instincts." Every id must have a countervailing ego to oppose it and as the patient who is unwilling to accept responsibility for himself reminds us, "Intellectually I accept the interpretation but emotionally I don't feel it." A counterpart may be found in some religious instruction where the potentially evil substructure of man, his passions, must be controlled. And here we have an opportunity to see perhaps most clearly how the controller who attempts to avoid his responsibility for himself creates the necessary conditions. He perceives life as a drama in which God and the Devil are locked in unending struggle for his soul—with neither ever winning.

REFERENCES

1. Adler, A., *The Case of Mrs. A.* Chicago, Alfred Adler Inst., 1969.
2. Adler, A., "Compulsion Neurosis" (1931), in Ansbacher, H. L. and Rowena, eds, *Superiority and Social Interest.* Evanston, Ill., Northwestern Univ. Press, 1964.

3. Adler, A., "The Death Problem in Neurosis" (1936), in Ansbacher, H. L. and Rowena, eds., *Superiority and Social Interest*. Evanston, Ill., Northwestern Univ. Press, 1964.
4. Adler, A., "The Fundamental Views of Individual Psychology." *Int. J. Indiv. Psychol.*, 1(1), (1935), pp. 5-8.
5. Adler, A., *The Individual Psychology of Alfred Adler*. New York, Basic Books, 1956, pp. 273-276.
6. Adler, A., *Problems of Neurosis*. New York, Harper Torchbooks, 1964.
7. Adler, A., "Sleeplessness" (1929), in Ansbacher, H. L. and Rowena, eds., *Superiority and Social Interest*. Evanston, Ill., Northwestern Univ. Press, 1964.
8. Adler, A., "Two Grade School Girls," in Ansbacher, H. L. and Rowena, eds., *Superiority and Social Interest*. Evanston, Ill., Northwestern Univ. Press, 1964.
9. Adler, A., "A Typology of Meeting Life Problems" (1935), in Ansbacher, H. L. and Rowena, eds., *Superiority and Social Interest*. Evanston, Ill., Northwestern Univ. Press, 1964.
10. Dreikurs, R., *The Challenge of Parenthood*. New York, Hawthorn Books, 1948.
11. Dreikurs, R., "The Cultural Implications of Reward and Punishment." *Int. J. Soc. Psychiat.*, 4(1958), pp. 171-178.
12. Leifer, R., "Avoidance and Mastery: An Interactional View of Phobias." *J. Indiv. Psychol.*, 22(1966), pp. 80-93.
13. Mosak, H. H., "The Getting Type: A Parsimonious Social Interpretation of the Oral Character." *J. Indiv. Psychol.*, 15(1959), pp 193-198.
14. Mosak, H. H., "The Interrelatedness of the Neuroses Through Central Themes." *J. Indiv. Psychol.*, 24(1968), pp. 67-70.

The Early Recollections of Adler, Freud, and Jung*

Early recollections (ERs) have a long tradition of interest and value for the clinical psychologist. Freud, in 1899, described his views on the subject in his paper on "Screen Memories" (11). While Adler began to develop his views together with his general goal-oriented theory, around 1907 to 1913, he did not present them specifically until some twenty years later as chapters in several of his more popular books (2, 3, 4). Though both, Freud and Adler, observed that patients' ERs tended to be innocuous in content, their explanations of this fact reflected basic differences in their theories. Freud believed that the banality of the memories demonstrated their "screening" function, distorting presumed original traumatic experiences which are so threatening to the adult ego that they cannot be admitted into the consciousness. Adler, in contrast, felt that the apparent unimportance of remembered childhood events reflected the role of memory in the overall life style—namely, that an individual selectively remembers only what is consistent with his present view of himself, the world, and other people (5, 15). Thus, ERs can be used as a tool for assessing the current subjective reality within which each person operates. Following Mosak (16), we have distinguished between a recollection and a report in choosing the memories reported in this paper. In order to qualify as a recollection, the memory had to be visualized by the informant, and it had to be an incident that could be described as a single occurrence.

In this paper, we apply the Adlerian methodology to the ERs of Adler, Freud, and Jung. Our purpose is to illustrate this approach with three well-known subjects, and to see how well their recollections reflect their personalities and their theories. Our analysis will therefore concentrate on what seem to us to be the most salient features and trends in the memories. In an effort to achieve balanced presentation, we have omitted

*Reprinted by permission from JOURNAL OF INDIVIDUAL PSYCHOLOGY, 1973, 29, 157-166.

memories which repeated themes found in those included in our analysis.

Freud's recollections were found in Ernest Jones' biography of Freud (13), and Freud's *Interpretation of Dreams* (9). The sources of Adler's memories are the biography by Phyllis Bottome (7) and Adler's *Practice and Theory* (1). Jung's recollections are from his *Memories, Dreams, and Reflections* (15). We should point out that while Jung and Adler give their own ERs, most of Freud's are related by Jones and may therefore not accurately convey the ERs as Freud would have reported them.

In the following we are representing the recollections of our three subjects, each recollection set off in smaller type and followed by our interpretation in regular type.

ADLER'S MEMORIES

ER 1. Age 2. I remember sitting on a bench bandaged up on account of rickets, with my healthy elder brother sitting opposite me. He could run, jump, and move about quite effortlessly, while for me, movement of any sort was a strain and an effort. Everyone went to great pains to help me and my mother and father did all that was in their power to do (7, pp. 30-31).

This recollection expresses Adler's attitude that he is deficient. He compares himself to others and finds himself wanting. The movement and actions of a person are important. There is a payoff for organ inferiority: Others become involved; others are showing social interest.

ER 2. Age 3. My parents left us two boys for a few days in the care of a governess. When they came back I met them, singing a street-song, the words of which are in my mind today, as is the melody to which I sang it. The song was about a woman who explained that she couldn't eat chicken because she was so hurt by the killing of her little hen. At this, the singer asks how she can have such a soft heart, when she thinks nothing of throwing a flowerpot at her husband's head (7, p. 32).

Actions speak louder than words; you can profess good intentions but you will be judged by your actions. We are reminded that Adler quoted Martin Luther's aphorism, "not to watch a person's mouth but his fists" (5, p. 18). There is also concern for good human relations. There is an interest in music.

ER 3. Age 4 or 5. I had pneumonia. The doctor, who had suddenly been called in, told my father that there was no point in going to the trouble of looking after me as there was no hope of my living. At once a frightful terror came over me and a few days later when I was well I decided definitely to become a doctor so that I should have a better defense against the danger of death and weapons to combat it superior to my doctor's (7, pp. 32-33).

Adler is incapacitated and this brings the concern of others. There is fear of dying. It terrifies him when people lose hope or are pessimistic. Adler resolves to compensate by learning appropriate skills. As he later stated: "The recollection of sickness or death is occasionally linked . . . with the attempt to become better equipped to meet them, possibly as a doctor or a nurse" (1, p. 354).

ER 4. Age 5 to 7. The father of one of my playmates, a lamp-maker, asked me what I was going to be in life. "A doctor," I said. He answered, "Then you should be strung up at once to the nearest lamp-post." This remark made no adverse impression upon my choice of a profession: I merely thought, "There's another who's had a bad time at the hands of a doctor. But *I* shall be a *real* doctor" (7, p. 33).

People's criticisms of him make no impact—in fact, they strengthen his resolve. A *real* doctor does not give his patients a hard time. He shows an interest in outcome, in the future.

ER 5. Age 5. Adler found that he could not quite believe in the Angel of the Passover visiting each Jewish home and being able to distinguish which was the leavened, and which the unleavened bread prepared for him. Adler therefore, one Passover night after the rest of the family had gone to bed, crept downstairs in his nightshirt and substituted leavened for unleavened bread, sitting up for the rest of the night in a cupboard with the door ajar, to discover through the crack the effect upon the Angel. "Nor was I altogether surprised," he told the writer, "when the Angel did not turn up" (7, pp. 33-34).

Adler is skeptical of the beliefs of others especially in regard to religion, and he will experiment and observe, in an effort to find the truth. It is interesting to note that Adler joined the Protestant Church in 1904, a small minority group in Austria at that time, which was considered most liberal (6, p 331; 8, pp. 583-584).

ER 6. Age 5. I remember that the path to the school led over a cemetery. I was frightened every time and was exceedingly put out at beholding the other children pass the cemetery without paying the least attention to it, while every step I took was accompanied by a feeling of fear and horror. Apart from the extreme discomfort occasioned by this fear, I was also annoyed at the idea of being less courageous than the others. One day I made up my mind to put an end to this fear of death. Again, I decided on a treatment of hardening. I stayed at some distance behind the others, placed my school-bag on the ground near the wall of the cemetery and ran across it a dozen times, until I felt that I had mastered the fear. After that, I believe, I passed along this path without any fear (1, pp. 179-180).

Adler is afraid of death. He can overcome fear by taking action. Again—he compares himself to others and comes out on the short end. Fear inhibits one's movement.

It should be noted that the cemetery recollection turned out to be a fiction. Adler wrote: "Thirty years after that I met an old schoolmate and we exchanged childhood reminiscences . . . He insisted there never had been a cemetery on the way to our school. Then I realized that the story . . . had been but a poetic dress for my longing to overcome the fear of death" (1, p. 180).

Summary. Adler's memories express the attitude: I am inferior (ERs 1, 3). I don't measure up to others, and, although others show concern because of my inadequacies, I want to overcome in a useful way these deficiencies and fears, particularly my fear of death (ERs 1, 3, 6). I am indifferent to the criticisms of others and skeptical of their beliefs, religious and otherwise (ERs 4, 5). Furthermore, I am not deterred by their pessimistic attitudes—they only strengthen my resolve (ERs 3, 4). By focusing on my actions and movements and by experimenting on my own, I will be able to overcome these obstacles and thereby discover the truth (ERs 5, 6).

Actions speak louder than words, and I judge people by their actions and not their intentions (ERs 1, 2). If you don't have and show concern for others, it doesn't matter what else you feel (ER 2).

FREUD'S MEMORIES

ER 1. Age 2. Freud would still wet his bed, and it was his father . . . who reproved him. He recollected saying on one of these occasions: "Don't worry, Papa. I will buy you a beautiful new red bed" (13, p. 7).

This recollection carries the message: Words speak louder than actions—don't look at my deeds, notice instead my good intentions. It also includes concern with a specific organic function and a father-son controversy, both of which became prominent in Freud's theory. The mention of color in a recollection is generally considered to indicate an aesthetic interest.

ER 2. Age 2½. Freud's Nannie disappeared. . . . Having reason to suspect his brother's implication in the disappearance, Freud asked him what had become of her and received the . . . answer: *"Sie ist eingekastelt."* An adult would have understood this as meaning: "She has been locked up in prison," but Freud took it more literally as "she has been put in a chest" (13, pp. 9-10).

Freud is looking for answers, and upon receiving an answer, interprets it in an unusual way, which differs from the conventional meaning.

ER 3. Age 3. On the way to Leipzig the train passed through Breslau, where Freud saw gas jets for the first time; they made him think of "souls burning in hell" (13, p. 13).

We might think of this as the forerunner of free association. There is an interest in symbolism and in religion.

ER 4. Age 6. I was expected to believe that we were all made of earth and must therefore return to earth. This did not suit me and I expressed doubts of the doctrine. My mother thereupon rubbed the palms of her hands together—just as she did in making dumplings, except that there was no dough between them—and showed me the blackish scales of *epidermis* produced by the friction as a proof that we were made of earth. My astonishment at this ocular demonstration knew no bounds and I acquiesced in the belief which I was later to hear expressed in the words: "Thou owest Nature a death" (9, p. 238).

Freud is skeptical of statements made by others, but will acquiesce when shown "evidence." He is concerned with death, particularly with its inevitability. This recollection is consonant with his later theory of Thanatos.

232

ER 5. Age 7 or 8. Freud recalls having urinated (deliberately) in his parents' bedroom, and being reprimanded by his father, who said, "That boy will never amount to anything" (13, p. 16).

Freud is deliberately provocative and evokes negative attention. Others will judge him negatively. In addition there are the organic function and the father-son controversy of ER 1.

Summary. Summarizing Freud's memories, we construct the following picture: I am a skeptic and a doubter who is looking for answers (ERs 2, 4). I see and interpret things in a non-conventional, non-obvious way (ERs 2, 3). I am deliberately provocative (ER 5). I give meanings to things which others don't share. I will alter my ideas when they are contradicted by the "evidence" (ER 4).

People should judge me by my intentions rather than by my actions (ER 1). Through my natural urges I am likely to get into trouble with the authorities (ERs 1, 5). I am awed by the inevitability of death (ER 4).

This last point reminds us of Freud's death instinct hypothesis: "If we are to take it as a truth that knows no exception that everything living dies for *internal* reasons—becomes inorganic once again—then we shall be compelled to say that the aim of all life is death" (10, p. 70). The preceding point is a reminder of Freud's concepts of the Oedipus complex and of the respression of drives.

JUNG'S MEMORIES

ER 1. Age about 4. Strangers, bustle, excitement. The maid comes running and exclaims, "The fishermen have found a corpse—came down the Falls—they want to put it in the wash house!" My father says, "Yes, yes." I want to see the dead body at once. My mother holds me back and sternly forbids me to go into the garden. When all the men had left, I quickly stole into the garden to the washhouse. But the door was locked. I went around the house; at the back there was an open drain running down the slope, and I saw blood and water trickling out. I found this extraordinarily interesting (15, p. 7).

Jung finds death interesting. Women try to prevent him from satisfying his curiosity. He doesn't give up. He is determined to have his way.

ER 2. Age 3 or 4. One hot summer day I was sitting alone, as usual, on the road in front of the house, playing in the sand. The road led past the house up a hill, then disappeared in the wood on the hilltop . . . Looking up the road, I saw a figure in a strangely broad hat and a long black garment coming down fromt he wood. It looked like a man wearing women's clothes. Slowly the figure drew nearer, and I could now see that it really was a man wearing a kind of black robe that reached to his feet. At the sight of him I was overcome with fear, which rapidly grew into deadly terror as the frightful recognition shot through my mind: "That is a Jesuit." The man coming down the road must be in disguise, I thought; that was why he wore women's clothes. Probably he had evil intentions. Terrified, I ran helter-skelter into the house, rushed up the stairs, and hid under a beam in the darkest corner of the attic. I don't know how long I remained there, but it must have been a fairly long time, because when I ventured down again to the first floor and cautiously stuck my head out of the window, far and wide there was not a trace of the black figure to be seen (15, pp. 10-11).

Jung tries to reconcile discrepant observations. He corrects his conclusions on the basis of closer observations. His statement that he is alone "as usual" suggests that being alone is characteristic for him. When he is terrified, he runs and hides. There is confusion with respect to religion and perhaps masculinity and femininity. Either Catholicism, the confusion, or both frighten him.

ER 3. Age about 6. An aunt showed me the stuffed animals in the museum. We stayed a long time, because I wanted to look at everything very carefully. At four o'clock the bell rang, a sign that the museum was about to close. My aunt nagged at me, but I could not tear myself away from the showcases. In the meantime, the room had been locked, and we had to go by another way to the staircase, through the gallery of antiquities. Suddenly I was standing before these marvelous figures! Utterly overwhelmed, I opened my eyes wide, for I had never seen anything so beautiful. I could not look at them long enough. My aunt pulled me by the hand to the exit—I trailing always a step behind her—crying out, "Disgusting boy, shut your eyes; disgusting boy, shut your eyes!" Only then did I see that the figures were naked and wore fig leaves. I hadn't noticed it at all before. Such was my first encounter with the fine arts. My aunt was simmering with indignation, as though she had been dragged through a pornographic institute (15, p. 16).

Jung is observing again. A woman is interfering with his aesthetic searches. He focuses on the artistic beauty in things, where others may only see the erotic-sexual aspects. It will be recalled in this connection that Jung "de-sexualized" libido in his theory, saying that the so-called "primal" sexual libido should be considered a universal "life-urge" (7, pp. 49-50; 14, pp. 120-121). Some people make excessive fuss regarding sexual matters.

> ER 4. Age 2 or 3. A lovely summer evening. An aunt said to me, "Now I am going to show you something." She took me out in front of the house, on the road to Dachsen. On the far horizon the chain of the Alps lay bathed in glowing sunset reds. The Alps could be seen very clearly that evening. "Now look over there"—I can hear her saying to me in Swiss dialect—"the mountains are all red." For the first time I consciously saw the Alps. Then I was told that the next day the village children would be going on a school outing to the Alps, near Zurich. I wanted so much to go, too. To my sorrow, I was informed that children as small as I could not go along; there was nothing to be done about it. From then on the Alps and Zurich became an unattainable land of dreams, near to the glowing, snow-covered mountains (15, p. 7).

Someone is opening the world to Jung. Becoming conscious of things is important. The mention of color suggests an artistic orientation again. He is little and is left out because of it; he does not get to the Promised Land.

> ER 5. Age about 4. I am restive, feverish, unable to sleep. My father carries me in his arms, paces up and down, singing his old student songs. I particularly remember one I was especially fond of and which always used to soothe me. To this day I can remember my father's voice, singing over me in the stillness of the night (15, p. 8).

Others soothe him when he's uncomfortable. He is sensitive to voice quality and music. He is interested in contrast and opposites.

> ER 6. Age about 4. Fourteen people were drowned and were carried down by the yellow flood water to the Rhine. When the water retreated, some of the corpses got stuck in the sand. When I was told about it, there was no holding me. I actually found the body of a middle-aged man, in a black frock coat; apparently he

had just come from church. He lay half covered by sand, his arm over his eyes (15, p. 15).

While death horrifies others, it interests Jung. He is not afraid to look where others are afraid. Once again, color suggests an artistic sense. Can he be saying that church-goers can come to a horrible end?

Summary. All of Jung's memories may be summarized as follows: I am a sensitive, curious observer, and I experience the world through all senses (ERs 3, 4, 5). Becoming aware and conscious of things is very important to me (ER 4). I am interested in contrasts (ERs 2, 5), try to reconcile discrepant observations, and I will modify my conclusions if they prove wrong after closer observation (ER 2).

Life is wonderful when I can be alone with nature (ER 2), but people can come between me and nature (ER 3). I am infatuated by the artistic beauty in what I see (ERs 3, 4, 6) though others are attracted only to the erotic and sexual aspects (ER 3). Others can interfere with my aesthetic search and they may also try to prevent me from satisfying my curiosity (ERs 1, 3). They can also open my eyes to new horizons, however (ER 4).

I am interested in death, although it may horrify others (ERs 1, 6).

I am small and want others to do things for me and care for me (ER 5). Smallness can also be a liability in human relations, but it is not a handicap in relation to nature (ER 4).

COMPARATIVE ANALYSIS

When we compare the portraits of these three men drawn from their memories, one similarity is that each of them emerges as a thinker and inquirer. Adler, Freud, and Jung draw conclusions from "evidence," and all three test and modify their beliefs in the light of facts. However, their style of inquiry distinguishes them from each other. Jung observes through his senses, Freud symbolizes and makes unique interpretations, and Adler observes and compares the actions and movements of people. Also, Freud and Adler display a generally skeptical stance toward traditional explanations.

Although all three show an interest in death, they differ in their approach to it. Jung is intrigued by death, Freud is awed by death's inevitability, while Adler resolves to work to overcome death. Also, Jung's interest in nature, art, and in the contrasting juxtaposition of things differs from Adler's preoccupation with people's actions and interactions, with deficiencies, and with overcoming obstacles; while Freud's main interest is in explaining things in non-conventional ways.

You will note that each man secured the involvement of other people, but in a different manner: Freud by being provocative, Adler by displaying and overcoming inadequacy, and Jung by being small and helpless, although there is the danger that being small and helpless could also result in his being left out. Though Freud anticipates that his provocative behavior may result in negative attention from others, he shrugs it off—it does not bother him. Adler also anticipates criticism from others, but he is ready to respond to it with increased effort and resolve. Jung similarly anticipates trouble from others, expecting them to interfere with his attempts to get closer to the experience of nature and to satisfy his curiosity.

Reflections of each man's theoretical position appear in their recollections. Adler's ERs allude to organ inferiority (ER 1), to movement (ERs 1, 2), to inferiority feeling (ERs 3, 6), to compensation (ERs 3, 6), and to social feeling (ER 2). Freud's ERs allude to free association (ER 3), the oedipal situation (ERs 1, 5), symbolic interpretation (ER 3), non-conventional interpretations (ER 2), and the death instinct (ER 4). Jung's desexualization of libido, the reconciliation of opposites in his typology, his interest in artistic production may all be discerned in his ERs.

Finally, the dominant life goals of each man emerge from their recollections. Adler's goal is to overcome inadequacy through effort and resolve. Freud strives to comprehend through analysis and interpretation, while Jung moves toward communion with nature through sensual awareness. Note also that feelings play a different role in the pursuit of each man's goal. For Adler, feelings facilitate and energize his movement; for Jung, feelings are another dimension of sensual experience; while Freud de-emphasizes the role of feelings, stressing intellectual understanding instead.

SUMMARY

Early childhood memories recalled by Adler, Freud, and Jung are presented, interpreted, and summarized within an Adlerian framework. Similarities between the early recollection themes and each man's theoretical position are indicated. Finally, the three sets of memories are compared and the commonalities and distinguishing characteristics that emerge are noted.

REFERENCES

1. ADLER, A. *The practice and theory of Individual Psychology* (1920). Totowa, N. J.: Littlefield, Adams, 1969.
2. ADLER, A. *Problems of neurosis* (1929). New York: Harper & Row, 1964.
3. ADLER, A. *What life should mean to you* (1931). New York: Capricorn Books, 1958.
4. ADLER, A. *Social interest: a challenge to mankind* (1933). New York: Capricorn Books, 1964.
5. ADLER, A. *The Individual Psychology of Alfred Adler.* Ed. by H. L. & Rowena R. Ansbacher. New York: Basic Books, 1956.
6. ADLER, A. *Superiority and social interest: a collection of later writings.* Ed. by H. L. & Rowena R. Ansbacher. 3rd ed. New York: Viking Compass Book, 1973.
7. BOTTOME, PHYLLIS. *Alfred Adler: a portrait from life.* New York: Vanguard Press, 1957.
8. ELLENBERGER, H. F. *The discovery of the unconscious.* New York: Basic Books, 1970.
9. FREUD, S. *Interpretation of dreams* (1900). New York: Avon Books, 1967.
10. FREUD, S. *Beyond the pleasure principle* (1928). New York: Bantam Books, 1967.
11. FREUD, S. Screen memories (1899). In *Collected papers.* Vol. 5. London: Hogarth, 1950. Pp. 47-69.
12. HARPER, R. *Psychoanalysis and psychotherapy: 36 systems.* Englewood Cliffs, N. J.: Prentice-Hall, 1959.
13. JONES, E. *The life and work of Sigmund Freud.* Vol. I. New York: Basic Books, 1953.
14. JUNG, C. G. *Modern man in search of a soul.* New York: Harcourt, Brace and World, 1963.
15. JUNG, C. G. *Memories, dreams, and reflections.* New York: Vintage Books, 1963.
16. MOSAK, H. H. Early recollections as a projective technique. *J. proj. Tech.*, 1958, 22, 302-311. Also in G. Lindzey & C. S. Hall (Eds.), *Theories of personality.* New York: Wiley, 1965. Pp. 105-113.

Purposes of Delusions and Hallucinations*

It is axiomatic from an Adlerian viewpoint that most behavior, thoughts, and feelings reflect the person's life style and are best understood in that context. His life style is his stance toward life aimed at achieving his final goal of superiority. Delusions and hallucinations are included in such behavior. Understanding their purposes should, hopefully, put us in a better position to help the person reconstruct and correct his beliefs. According to an early statement by Adler:

> Hallucinations are connected with a strong empathy into a role and represent encouraging or warning voices. They arise always when the patient wants something unconditionally, yet at the same time wants to be considered free from responsibility. Like dreams, they must be understood as a metaphor; while they need not be intelligible to the patient, they depict the tactics he wants to use toward a specific problem. The hallucination, again like certain dreams, turns out to be a device for objectifying subjective impulses, to the apparent objectivity of which the patient is absolutely committed . . . To this is added, as a fortification for the delusional system, the biased, tendentious selection of recollections (3, p. 259; translation according to 5, pp. 317-318).

Elsewhere Adler states, "We see in hallucination an expression of the psychological ability to contradict logic and the truth of social life, a trace of which can also be found in all conceptions and in memory . . . A person who hallucinates has removed himself from the realm of social interest and, circumventing logic and curtailing the sense of the truth, strives for another goal than one to which we are more accustomed" (2, p. 54; translation modified from the original).

The reader may have noted two things. (a) Adler does not use the term life style. The reason is that at this time Adler had not yet adopted the term; this came only twelve to fourteen years later. (b) Hallucinations are functionally likened to dreams and recollections. The relationship to recollections is brought out again in the following statement about the function

*Reprinted by permission from JOURNAL OF INDIVIDUAL PSYCHOLOGY, 1973, 29, 176-181.

of memory in the neurotic. "Memory images . . . which may be realized in a hallucinatory fashion must be equated with optical and acoustic hallucinations. Understandably, they will usually be closely related to the [individual's] guiding line . . . to enhance his self-esteem" (1, pp. 79-80). To this Adler added in a footnote from his later period: "This is why Individual Psychology attaches great importance to the understanding of earliest childhood recollections and has shown that they represent revealing signs from the period when the style of life was constructed" (1, p. 80n).

GENERAL

Hallucinations may be roughly defined as the perception of something in the absence of a sensory stimulus. Although it is characteristic of psychosis, neurotics also occasionally hallucinate, as might normal individuals in situations of monotony or reduced sensory input. Some hallucinations are very much like the creation of an imaginary playmate in childhood. The individual may feel that something is missing in his life and hallucinates to compensate for his experienced deficit.

Delusions also are present in almost all psychoses but not limited to these. The individual believes something, in spite of its absurdity. He may even know it is absurd and still believe it. Delusions are frequently extensions of what we do normally— holding on to ideas we cherish. Like other beliefs, they help organize the environment, make it meaningful, and to that extent may be useful (see 6, p. 170).

The distinction between hallucinations and delusions is not too clear and their functions are ordinarily identical. In fact, as we have seen, Adler spoke in the above quotations only of the former. Shulman, a contemporary Adlerian psychiatrist, lists hallucinations and delusions as tactics designed to reinforce the patient's "private logic and insuring the correctness of his position" (7, p. 50).

Hallucinations as well as delusions create pseudo-tasks as a means of avoiding the more important life tasks. The person gives the impression of dealing with his life tasks, but is in fact afraid of them. This is the "sideshow" function which is also the purpose of compulsions and obsessions, as altogether the compulsion neurosis was for Adler the prototype of all mental disturbances (4, p. 138). "The compulsion neurotic is apparently at a secondary theater of operations *(sekundärer Kriegsschauplatz),* and exhausts himself *there,* instead of . . . solving his problem of life" (4, p. 115). As long as the patient is holding a dialogue with the Devil, for instance, he cannot listen to the therapist.

Through hallucinations and delusions the individual also announces, "The things that happen to other people don't happen that way to me. I am different, I am very special." But while most people want to be seen as individuals, and in this sense as special, the psychotic wants to be special also in being exempt from the common sense and the expectations it implies, including especially responsibility. By defying any attempt at consensual validation he gains the further advantage of being able to say to the therapist: "If you do not hear or see or otherwise sense, what I am experiencing, it is because you just do not have my powers." But if you do not have his powers, how can you cure him?

DELUSIONS

The purpose of the present paper is to discuss the functional characteristics of the various delusions, particularly as these are relevant to the process of psychotherapy. We identify seven kinds of delusion: delusions of persecution, influence, reference, grandeur, sin and guilt, nihilism, and hypochondriasis. Of these the first three are statements about others, and the last four, statements about oneself. The individual "chooses" that particular delusion which gives him the best chance of accomplishing his "purpose."

Persecution

The message of the delusion of persecution is, "They are after me, want to take advantage of me, steal from me, kill me." While we all feel this way from time to time, we know it is not so. What kind of person would entertain this delusion? First, it is an announcement that the person is very important. Out of the whole world he was selected to be so persecuted. His delusion, aired to others, points out to himself and those about him that he is something special. Secondly, this delusion means that the person does not have to accept responsibility for not "making it" in life. He is saying, in effect, "It's not that I am not capable, but they won't let me. I am a victim. Look what they're doing to me." In fact, that he is able to function at all may, at least in his own eyes, make him of heroic stature. Thirdly, it implies that the world is a jungle, a dangerous place, which in turn leads to justification for venting aggression. The delusion makes it only right. "They started it. I'll finish it." This stance has the additional advantage of allowing the person to evade responsibility because his actions are justified as self-defense.

Influence

In delusions of influence the individual feels that he is being controlled by others. He is thereby saying that he is not to be blamed or to be held responsible for his actions. On the contrary, he is a victim himself. "They are making me do something I don't want to do. I am minding my own business and they won't let me alone."

The issue is one of control; he is being externally controlled. As a victim of such control he may see himself as noble; he is also entitled to help and recognition, and may demand these; and he is allowed to fight back against those depriving him of his autonomy. At the same time, since "others make" him do it, he can in fact do whatever he wants—without taking responsibility or blame.

Reference

In a delusion of reference the individual believes everything he sees or hears is related to him. It is the kind of feeling we have when we are learning to. dance—everyone is watching us to see how often we step on our partner's toes, although the dynamics here are somewhat different. This delusion is often found in the deaf, so that in these cases it is necessary to evaluate the hearing to comprehend more fully the implications of the delusion. In a cartoon, a spectator at a football game watching the team go into a huddle is commenting: "I just know they're talking about me." Again, a person is saying, "Look how important I am." In effect the whole world

242

recognizes his importance, to the point that everyone pays attention to him. It is a clear externalization of wanting to be recognized. The individual is saying, "Love me or hate me, but do not ignore me."

Grandeur

In this delusion the individual announces to the world, "Look how great I am." The person does this at least in part with the idea that once others have become aware of his exalted state, they will give him the honor and recognition which are his due. The delusion often has religious or sexual content. It is compensatory for feelings of social inferiority or spiritual unworthiness.

Sin and Guilt

The feeling of sinfulness and guilt becomes delusional when the individual is convinced that he is completely beyond redemption. Then it is not uncommon for him to proclaim himself the world's worst person or sinner, utterly beyond redeeming features, hope of forgiveness, or salvation. The listener sometimes wonders whether the "sinner" is complaining or bragging. One of the implications is that he is more special than God by being beyond God's power to redeem. God is thereby neutralized, and the individual need no longer worry about Him. He is morally even superior to God since God can forgive, but he can't—his moral standards are higher.

Adler tells the story of a very ambitious 18-year old girl who began to reproach herself for religious transgressions and sinful thoughts. "One day her spiritual adviser attempted to relieve her of her entire burden of sins . . . The next day the girl planted herself before him in the street and shouted out that he was unworthy of entering the church because he had taken such a great burden of sin upon himself" (5, p. 272).

Nihilism

Nihilist delusions are seen only rarely, usually in severe depression. The individual feels profoundly that all is lost, that not even he exists or is real. He thus proclaims that there is no need for any action since nothing will make any difference.

He is also saying, "I am not responsible, and even if I am, there is nothing that can be done anymore." At the same time the patient is telling the therapist that he is also unable to do anything since perhaps neither of them are real. This is an effective neutralization of any possible influence by the therapist as well as the ultimate "put down" of him.

Hypochondriasis

Hypochondriasis, the exaggerated concern about one's health, as a delusion in psychosis typically becomes bizarre. One may believe that one's bowels have not moved in six months or that hydrochloric acid has eaten the stomach away. The individual is proclaiming his specialness by a symptom exhibited by no one else. At the same time this obviously reflects an internal state truly experienced by him. The symptom also serves as an excuse from life's expectations, for: How could such a sick person function? It also implies: How could one hope for a cure?

SUMMARY

From the Adlerian viewpoint delusions and hallucinations are used by the individual to avoid responsibility and to proclaim his specialness. In reference to the real tasks of living of which he is afraid they are useless "sideshows," a wasting of time. But they provide excuses for failure and thus safeguard the self-esteem. Like other aspects of the individual they are in line with his style of life, and have social implications. As symptoms, they carry normal modes of wanting to be somebody special to bizarre and absurd extremes, more or less disregarding the common sense. The functional characteristics of seven kinds of delusions are discussed with particular reference to the process of psychotherapy.

REFERENCES

1. ADLER, A. Über den nervösen Charakter (1912). 4th ed. Frankfurt am Main: Fischer Taschenbuch Verlag, 1972.
2. ADLER, A. Contributions to the theory of hallucinations (1912). In Practice and theory of Individual Psychology. Totowa, N. J.: Littlefield, Adams, 1968. Pp. 51-58.
3. ADLER, A. Melancholia and paranoia (1914). In Practice and theory of Individual Psychology. Totowa, N. J.: Littlefield, Adams, 1968. Pp. 246-262.

4. ADLER, A. Compulsion neurosis (1931). In *Superiority and social interest.* Ed. by H. L. & Rowena R. Ansbacher. New York: Viking Compass Book, 1973. Pp. 112-138.
5. ADLER, A. *The Individual Psychology of Alfred Adler.* Ed. by H. L. & Rowena R. Ansbacher. New York: Basic Books, 1956.
6. KRECH, D., & CRUTCHFIELD, R. S. *Theory and problems of social psychology.* New York: McGraw-Hill, 1948.
7. SHULMAN, B. H. *Essays in schizophrenia.* Baltimore: Williams & Wilkins, 1968.

In Memory of Rudolf Dreikurs, 1897-1972*

Like Bernie [Shulman], I don't really know what to say
My usual facility in public speaking eludes me. Until Thursday
I was chairman of a committee to observe Dr. D.'s 75th birthday
at this banquet, and while I knew he could not make it here
physically, at least we had arranged for a telephone hookup so
that he could address you from Chicago. Then I thought that
with his death my committee was discharged. About ten
minutes before the banquet started this evening, I was asked to
sort of summarize his life. But I don't know how to summarize
his life; I don't even know really how to express the feelings I
have. For more than two decades I probably spent as much or
more time with him than I did with my own family. I lived with
him day by day, seeing patients with him, teaching with him,
doing child guidance with him, and having the same kinds of
experiences that Bronia [Grunwald] described for you. Perhaps
rather than summarize his life I would like to share some
reminiscences with you.

The first thing that impressed me about Dr. D. when I came
to work with him was his courage. I was probably the first
clinical psychologist in Chicago to enter full-time private practice. This was at a time when clinical psychologists didn't do
things like practice psychotherapy, but he hired me anyway. He
felt that good therapy is good therapy. He didn't care what kind
of degree you had in order to do it. The next thing I knew, I was
being charged with practicing medicine without a license. For
about seven or eight months we fought that battle through, as
we fought through a good number of other battles after that

While Dr. D. enjoyed international acclaim, he was a
prophet without honor in his own city for a large part of his
professional career. At his own medical school the Department
of Psychiatry no longer assigned him classes. But two months
ago, at the Chicago Medical School, which every year has a
brief psychotherapy conference, this year's conference was

*Reprinted by permission from JOURNAL OF INDIVIDUAL PSYCHOLOGY, 1973, 29
16-18.

dedicated to Adlerian psychology, and we spent two days there.[1]
The week before that, Dr. D. who was pretty ill, said, "I can't
make it. We'll have Shulman deliver my speech, and you will do
one of the demonstrations, and somebody else will do the other
demonstration." He asked me, in the last several months, to
serve as his "psychotherapist" because he was kind of depressed. He did not know how to be sick gracefully. And I told
him at this time, "No, we don't want your paper; we want you."
Those of you who were in Chicago for that conference saw Dr.
D. come and give some of the most brilliant performances of
family counseling and interviewing that he had ever given. The
next day he went to the hospital, but those two days, he was in
there, doing his job. It was in the introduction to this conference that the dean of the Medical School said that as a student and later as a psychiatrist he had not been interested in
the approach of Dr. Dreikurs, but that time had proved him
right in pointing in the direction in which psychiatry was
moving.[2]

For years the psychiatric community and the psychological
community did not treat him well, and yet he just went about
doing his job. When I returned to Chicago about 21 years ago to
work with Dr. Dreikurs, I met a professor from the University
of Chicago who asked me what I was doing back in Chicago. I
told him I had come to work with Dr. Dreikurs, and he said,
"That man? When is he going to learn some psychiatry?" Three
years ago we started an internship in clinical psychology in our
private practice. Our first intern came from the University of
Chicago. The director of clinical training at the University of
Chicago was this same professor. I am told that he told our intern that he would get the very best internship in this country.
So, things have really changed throughout the years, and I was
elated the night of the banquet of the Chicago Medical School
conference to see Dr. Dreikurs finally receive honor from
hundreds of people, practitioners in his own home town, who
had come to listen and to do him honor.

He was sick, and he did not take sickness very well. Some
years ago when he had his heart attack he called me and asked

---

[1]For a complete report of the proceedings of this conference see this JOURNAL, 1972,
28, 119-266.
[2]See this JOURNAL, 1972, 28, 123-124.

me whether I could take an engagement up in Minnesota. I said, "Why do you want me to go?" He said, "I had a heart attack two days ago." I said, "Oh, what have you been doing since?" He said, "Well yesterday I had an engagement in Kalamazoo, so I went up there and kept it before getting some treatment." I said, "Dr. D., You had a heart attack and you went up to Kalamazoo?" He said, "Don't worry, I didn't drive. Somebody else drove me." Subsequently in the last few months he was depressed at times, and yet he kept in there working. Just a week ago Friday I was at his bedside with Bronia. It was a day when he was alert; he wasn't heavily medicated. While we were talking, he suddenly said, "Harold, let's do some work. You know, we have been making some tapes. Let's continue." So we made tapes, and his mind was just as alert as ever. He fished in his memory for things fifty years back, and he found them every time. Some of these tapes, I imagine, will either be distributed or published in one way or another.

As much in pain, uncomfortable and sometimes depressed as he was, he did not lose his sense of humor. One Sunday I received a call to come and see him. I went over. He was depressed and behaved like every depressed patient. He knew all the patients' tricks very well. I decided that to get him out of this depression I had better do what he taught me, that is, get the patient angry. So I set out to provoke him, and I got him real angry. He flared at me. But right in the middle he stopped, smiled, shook his finger at me, and said, "Harold, I taught you too good!" I am glad he did, because he stopped being depressed.

There are thousands of things like this that happened over the years that I could share with you. But I guess we have to leave some for other times. We have come here not to mourn, but to honor the memory of Dr. Dreikurs who at once was our friend, mentor, healer, a man who tried to bring to fruition his vision that man could be a fellowman to other fellowmen. He was a *Mitmensch* himself. We shall miss him. We shall not see the likes of him again soon.

Comment: A Peak at the Future Through the Rear-View Mirror*

My friend, Paul Rom, has written a highly personal account of his introduction to Adlerian psychology as preface to his observation that Adlerian assumptions are now being incorporated "in the center of most therapeutic endeavors." While the range of direct and indirect influence of Adlerian psychology upon psychotherapy has undoubtedly expanded in the last two decades, the use of the word "most" must be considered hyperbole. The Adlerian humanistic, holistic, teleological approach still finds competition from psychologies based upon atomistic, causalistic, and mechanistic hypotheses, as Paul himself points out later in his paper.

Paul's personal preferences possess a European perspective, reflecting the views of only some of the pre-World War II Adlerians. These views are not shared by American Adlerians. The European still makes the theory of organ inferiority a cornerstone of theory. The American regards organ inferiority and compensation as observations rather than as central to theory. In the last twenty years only one American Adlerian paper on organ inferiority has been written. (13). It also should be remembered that the theory was propounded while Adler was still a member of the Freudian circle.

Some of the early Adlerians also attempted to make of Adlerian psychology an extension of Marxist theory, and Rom's biases lean in this direction. The equation of these two theories lacked universal acceptance even among European Adlerians, and American Adlerians keep their political and psychological ideologies separate and independent. I have taken issue with Paul previously on this score (11).

The eleven "ways of preventing and correcting people's asocial and antisocial attitudes" which are proposed will probably encounter little disagreement. Adlerians have been in the forefront in implementing community outreach programs

*Reprinted by permission from VOICES, 1973, 9(2), 41.

(2, 9), family guidance centers (1, 4, 8, 12), parent and teacher study groups (14), psychotherapy in prisons (3, 7), day hospitals (5), and therapeutic social clubs (6, 10). Rom sees these as the trends of the future. Other Adlerians consider these as part of a rich past, their contribution to today's psychotherapy, and look forward to devising new methods of enriching man's existence.

REFERENCES

1. Adler, A. *Erziehungsberatungsstellen.* In A. Adler and C. Furtmüller (Eds.), *Heilen und Bilden.* Munich: Bergmann, 1922. Pp. 119-121.
2. Adler, A. *Gesundheitsbuch für das Schneidergewerbe.* Berlin: C. Heymanns, 1898.
3. Adler, A. *The individual criminal and his cure: An address.* New York: National Committee on Prisons and Prison Labor, 1930.
4. Adler, A. *The problem child.* New York: Capricorn Books, 1963.
5. Bierer, J. *The day hospital, an experiment in social psychiatry and synthoanalytic psychotherapy.* London: H. K. Lewis, 1951.
6. Bierer, J. and Haldane, F. P. "A self-governed patients social club in a public mental hospital." *Journal of Mental Science,* 1941. 87, 419-426.
7. Brown, C. *Manchild in the promised land.* New York: Signet Books, 1965.
8. Dreikurs, R., Corsini, R. J., Lowe, R., and Sonstegard, M. *Adlerian family counseling.* Eugene, Ore.: University of Oregon Press, 1959.
9. La Porte, G. H. "Social interest in action: A report of one attempt to implement Adler's concept." *Individual Psychologist,* 1966, 4 (1), 22-26.
10. Mohr, Erika and Garlock, Rose. "The social club as an adjunct to therapy." In K. A. Adler and Danica Deutsch (Eds.), *Essays in Individual Psychology.* New York: Grove Press, 1959. Pp. 465-467.
11. Mosak, H. H. "What is your opinion?" *Individual Psychology Newsletter,* 1973, 22 (1), 9-10.
12. Seidler, Regine and Zilahi, L. The Vienna child guidance clinics. In A. Adler and associates, *Guiding the child.* London: Allen & Unwin, 1949. Pp. 9-27.
13. Shulman, B. H. and Klapman, H. "Organ inferiority and psychiatric disorders in childhood." In E. Harms (Ed.), *Pathogenesis of nervous and mental diseases in children.* New York: Libra, 1968. Pp. 49-62.
14. Soltz, Vicki. *Study group leader's manual.* Chicago: Alfred Adler Institute, 1967.

INDEX
TO
ON PURPOSE

COLLECTED PAPERS

of

HAROLD H. MOSAK, Ph.D.

ALFRED ADLER INSTITUTE
OF CHICAGO

Subject Index

Author Index